grace Wadsley.
1983

PIT[...]
SHORTHAN[...]

NEW ERA EDITION

PITMAN
SHORTHAND
INSTRUCTOR

A COMPLETE EXPOSITION
OF SIR ISAAC PITMAN'S
SYSTEM OF SHORTHAND

NEW ERA EDITION

Isaac Pitman

PITMAN

PITMAN PUBLISHING LIMITED
39 Parker Street, London WC2B 5PB

Associated Companies
Copp Clark Pitman, Toronto
Fearon Pitman Publishers Inc, San Francisco
Pitman Publishing New Zealand Ltd, Wellington
Pitman Publishing Pty Ltd, Melbourne

All rights reserved. Sir Isaac Pitman's system of shorthand is the
exclusive copyright of Pitman Limited. No part of this publication may be reproduced, stored in a retrieval system, or
transmitted in any form or by any means, electronic,
mechanical, photocopying, recording and/or otherwise without
the prior written permission of the publishers. This book may
not be lent, resold, hired out or otherwise disposed of by way of
trade in any form of binding other than that in which it is
published, without the prior consent of the publishers.

Text set in 9/10 pt Monotype Times New Roman,
printed by photolithography and bound in Great Britain
at The Pitman Press, Bath

U.K. Edition ISBN 0 273 00358 5
Overseas Edition ISBN 0 273 42350 9

G9—(671/625:24)

PREFACE

THE system of shorthand writing presented in the following pages was invented by Sir Isaac Pitman, who in 1837 published his first treatise on the art. In 1840 the second edition of his work appeared, under the title "Phonography, or Writing by Sound, being also a New and Natural System of Shorthand." In the numerous editions of Phonography published in succeeding years, many improvements were introduced. These were the fruit of long and varied stenographic experiments, and of the valuable criticism and experience of large numbers of expert writers of the system who had applied it to work of every description. No other system of shorthand designed for the English language has been subjected to tests so prolonged, so diverse, and so severe as those which Pitman Shorthand—as the system is now generally styled—has undergone since its introduction, with the result that it has been most successfully adapted to the practical requirements of all classes of shorthand writers.

Although students, as a rule, experience no difficulty in understanding the method here set forth of "writing by sound," it is desirable that they should have, at the beginning of their study, an intelligent grasp of all that is conveyed by that term. Therefore, before the mastery of the first chapter is attempted, the Introduction which follows this Preface should be read with care.

The advantage of practical ability in the art of shorthand writing is so universally acknowledged in the present day that it is unnecessary to emphasize it. It is obvious, however, that the value of shorthand, whether as a vehicle for private communication or for use in various ways in business or professional life, would be largely diminished if the same system—and that the best—were not employed. This important fact is now generally recognized; and statistics, the testimony of public men, and general observation, concur in demonstrating that the system which Sir Isaac Pitman invented is taught and used as the shorthand *par excellence* for all who speak the English language. Further and very significant evidence to the merits of his system is the fact that it has been adapted to no fewer than twenty foreign languages.

The Publishers take this opportunity of tendering their sincere thanks to the large number of expert writers and teachers of Phonography who have offered valuable suggestions for the improvement of the present edition.

INTRODUCTION

PHONOGRAPHY, the name originally given to Pitman Shorthand, has been briefly but accurately defined as "the art of representing spoken sounds by character; a system of shorthand." The first question that will occur to the student will be, what is the fundamental difference between the shorthand characters and the letters in ordinary writing and printing? To answer this question it is necessary to consider the alphabet of the language. It is obvious that the usual or Romanic alphabet of twenty-six letters cannot represent by distinct characters the thirty-six typical sounds of the English language. As a consequence, many of the letters of that alphabet are of necessity used to represent different sounds. It is manifest, therefore, that any system of shorthand founded on the common alphabet would prove a very imperfect and cumbrous instrument for recording spoken utterances with certainty and speed—the chief object of shorthand. With such an alphabet either a single sign standing for one of the letters would be required to do duty for several sounds, or more than one character would have to be used to represent a single sound, as is done in ordinary spelling. On the other hand, the three consonants C, Q and X are unnecessary, inasmuch as they represent sounds provided for by other consonants. Two simple illustrations will demonstrate the difference between the ordinary spelling and the phonetic method, which is the distinctive feature of Pitman Shorthand.

The first illustration deals with consonants, and is concerned with the ordinary spelling of the words *gaol* and *gale*, in which the *sounds* of the first consonant are different, although represented in longhand by the same letter. If the common spelling were followed in shorthand, we should have the same shorthand symbols for both words. But the initial sounds in these words are different; in the first the sound is *jay*, in the second *gay*. For these dissimilar sounds the Pitman system provides dissimilar shorthand signs. The second illustration deals with vowels, as, for example, in the words *tub* and *tube*. If the shorthand symbols were the equivalents of the letters of the common alphabet (the final *e* of *tube* being omitted because it is not sounded), the stenographer would be obliged to write both words by precisely the same characters, namely, *t-u-b*. Pitman Shorthand, however, provides for the representation of the different sounds *ŭ* and *ū* heard in the respective words, and these are indicated by different symbols.

The phonetic notation of the system of shorthand developed in the present work has been found, after widely extended use, to possess important practical advantages. By the employment of the phonetic alphabet, which has been termed the "alphabet of nature," spoken language can be recorded with one-sixth of the trouble and time that longhand requires, by those who use Pitman Shorthand simply as a substitute for the ordinary longhand writing. With the adoption of the systematized methods of abbreviation developed in the more advanced stages, this method of shorthand can be written legibly with the speed of the most rapid distinct articulation, and it may be read with the certainty and ease of ordinary longhand writing.

An explanation on one point, however, is desirable. In the study and use of Pitman Shorthand it should be borne in mind that although the system is phonetic it is not designed to represent or record minute shades of pronunciation. The Pitmanic alphabet, in the words of Max-Müller, "comprehends the thirty-six broad typical sounds of the English language and assigns to each a definite sign." It does not seek to mark, for example, the thirty or more variations of sound which have been found to exist in the utterance of the twelve simple vowels. The pronunciation of the vowels, as Max-Müller has shown, varies greatly in different localities and in the various countries of the world in which the English language is spoken, and in which Pitman Shorthand is practised. The standard of pronunciation, as exhibited in printed shorthand, cannot, therefore, be expected to coincide minutely with the pronunciation of English in all parts. Experience has abundantly proved that the representation of the broad typical sounds of English as provided for in Pitman Shorthand is ample for all stenographic purposes.

The presence of *r* has a modifying effect upon a preceding vowel. The student's attention is, therefore, directed to the following observations with regard to the consonant *r*, to certain vowels when preceding *r* and to a class of vowels which may be described as more or less obscure.

(*a*) With the exception of *worsted* (the woollen material) and a few proper names, as *Worcester*, wherever the consonant *r* occurs in a word, in Pitman Shorthand it must be *represented as a consonant*.

(*b*) In such words as *bar, far, mar, tar, jar*, the vowel-sign for *ah* is to be used; but in such words as *barrow, Farrow, marry, carry*, and *Jarrow*, the first vowel-sound is to be represented by the vowel-sign for *ă*.

(*c*) In such words as *four, fore, roar, lore, wore, shore, door, pour, core, gore, tore, sore*, the vowel-sign for *ō* is to be used.

(*d*) In such words as *torch, morn, fork*, the vowel-sign for *ŏ* is to be used.

(*e*) In such words as *air, fair, lair, bare*, the vowel-sign for *ā* is to be used.

(*f*) In such pairs of words as *fir, fur; earth, worth; per, purr; Percy, pursy;* the vowel-sound in the first word of the pairs is to be represented by the vowel-sign for *ĕ;* the vowel-sound in the second word of the pairs is to be represented by the vowel-sign for *ŭ*.

(*g*) In words like *custody*, *custom*, *baron*, *felony*, *colour*, *factory*, the second vowel-sound is represented by the vowel-sign for ŭ.

(*h*) In words like *village*, *cottage*, *breakage*, the second vowel-sound is represented by the vowel-sign for ĕ.

(*i*) In words like *suppose*, the second vowel-sound is represented by the vowel-sign for ō; but in words like *supposition*, *disposition*, the second vowel-sound is represented by the vowel-sign for ŭ.

With the accurate employment of the phonographic signs, there need be no uncertainty as to what those employed for a particular word are intended to represent, and, as Max-Müller has testified, "English can be written rationally and read easily" with the Pitmanic alphabet. To use Pitman Shorthand successfully, the rules of the system must be thoroughly mastered. By the employment of the various abbreviating devices, the most important benefit to be derived from shorthand will be attained, namely, the maximum of speed combined with legibility.

DIRECTIONS TO THE STUDENT

The system of shorthand set forth in the following pages received the name of Phonography (a term derived from two Greek words meaning "sound writing") because it affords the means of recording the sounds of spoken language. From the outset, therefore, the student should remember that he is learning to write by SOUND, i.e., to write words as they are pronounced; that each simple character represents one definite sound and no other; and that the ordinary spelling—with its many irregularities and inconsistencies—as exhibited in printing and in longhand writing, is not to be followed or imitated.

When the student has mastered the value of the phonographic signs, he should use those which represent the equivalent sounds in forming the characters for the words he desires to write. For example, if he wishes to write in Phonography the word *knee* (spelt with four letters, though made up of only two sounds), he uses but two phonographic signs, namely, that for the consonant *n* and that for the vowel *ē*. To spell in this fashion, a mental analysis of the sounds of words must be made, but the ability to do this is very easily acquired, and is soon exercised without conscious effort.

For working the exercises and for ordinary phonographic writing, a pen and ruled paper should be used. Speaking generally, it is not so easy to acquire a neat style of writing by the use of a pencil as it is by the use of a pen. No doubt, the pencil is frequently employed; in some cases, indeed, it may be found impossible to use a pen for note-taking. The student would do well, therefore, to accustom himself to write either with a pen or a pencil in the more advanced stages of his progress, though for writing the exercises given in this book the pen only should be used.

The pen should be held lightly, and in such a manner as to permit of the shorthand characters being easily written. The wrist must not be allowed to rest upon the notebook or desk. In order to secure the greatest freedom of movement, the middle of the forearm should rest on the edge of the desk. The writer should sit in front of his work, and should have the paper or notebook parallel with the edge of the desk or table. For shorthand writing, the nib employed should not be too stiff, but should have a sufficiently fine and flexible point to enable the thick and thin characters of the system to be written so as clearly to distinguish the one from the other. Paper with a fairly smooth surface is absolutely essential.

The student should thoroughly master the explanations and rules which precede the respective exercises, and write out several times the illustrative words appearing in the text, afterwards working the exercises. As the secret of success in shorthand is PRACTICE, it is advisable that the various exercises should be written and re-written until they can be done with perfect freedom and accuracy. The perusal of progressive reading lessons in printed shorthand will also be found helpful to the student in forming a correct style of writing; and the practice of writing the characters, at first with careful accuracy, afterwards with gradually accelerated speed, will materially assist him in forming a neat style of shorthand writing.

The system is fully explained in the following pages, and can be acquired from the instruction books alone by anyone who is prepared to devote ordinary perseverance and application to the study. With the assistance of a teacher, however, more rapid and satisfactory advance will be made in the mastery of the art. Should any difficulty be experienced in finding a teacher, the publishers will be pleased to furnish any student with the names and addresses of the nearest teachers of Pitman Shorthand. It should be pointed out that satisfactory progress in acquiring the art of shorthand will only be made if a certain portion of time is regularly devoted to the study EVERY DAY; or, in the case of school or class instruction, by a thorough and punctual performance of the allotted portions of work forming the course. Study at irregular intervals of time is of little value; but an hour, or a longer period, devoted daily to the task will give the student a knowledge of the system in a comparatively short time, and constant and careful practice will bring speed and dexterity.

CONTENTS

CHAPTER I

THE CONSONANTS

"Consonants are the result of audible friction or stopping of the breath in some part of the mouth or throat." (*Prof. Sweet.*)

Forms of Consonants. 1. For the representation of all the consonant sounds, (except *w*, *y*, and the aspirate *h*), the simplest geometrical forms are used, namely, the straight line and the shallow curve, as shown in the following diagrams—

Arrangement of Groups. 2. The order of the arrangement of each group of consonants, as exhibited in the Table on a following page, follows the order of the oral movements from the lips inwards in the utterance of their respective sounds. The first pair of consonants, *p*, *b*, are pronounced between the lips, and the next seven pairs at the several barriers further back in the mouth, in the succession indicated in the phonographic alphabet.

Classes of Consonants. 3. The first eight consonants, represented by straight strokes, are called "explodents," because, in pronouncing them, the outgoing breath is forced in a sudden gust through barriers previously closed.

4. The next eight, represented by upright or sloping curves, are called "continuants," because in uttering these the outgoing breath, instead of being expelled

suddenly, is allowed to escape in a continuous stream through similar barriers partially open.

5. The "nasals," represented by a horizontal curve, are produced by closing the successive barriers in the mouth against the outgoing air-stream, so that it has to escape through the nose.

6. The "liquids" flow into union with other consonants, and thus make double consonants, as in the words *cl*iff, *dr*y, where the *l* or *r* blends with the preceding consonant.

7. The "coalescents" precede vowels and coalesce or unite with them.

8. The "aspirate" is a breathing upon a following vowel. Thus by a breathing upon the vowel *ă* in the word *at*, the word is changed into *hat*.

Pairs of Consonants. 9. The first sixteen consonants form pairs; thus, *p* and *b*; *t* and *d*; *ch* and *j*; *k* and *g*; *f* and *v*; *th* and th; *s* and *z*; *sh* and *zh*. The articulations in these pairs are the same, but the sound is light in the first consonant of each pair and heavy in the second. The consonants of each pair are represented by the same stroke, but for the second consonant this is written *thick* instead of *thin*; as ＼ *p*, ＼ *b*, ⌐ *t*, ⌐ *d*, ⌣ *f*, ⌣ *v*, etc. We have, therefore, a *light sign* for the *light sound*, and a *heavy sign* for the *heavy sound*. In this, as in the fact that each pair of consonants is represented by kindred signs, a natural relation is preserved between the *spoken* sound and the *written* sign. Throughout this book whatever relates to the light strokes applies also to the corresponding heavy strokes unless the contrary is stated.

Size of Strokes. 10. The consonants should be written about one-sixth of an inch long, as in these pages. It is of the utmost importance that from the

outset the student should learn to form the whole of
the strokes uniformly as to length. Whatever size be
adopted, all the strokes should be made equal in length.
Later there will be introduced a principle for writing
strokes half the normal length, and later still another
for the making of strokes double the normal length.
It is thus imperative that the student should obtain a
fixed and strictly uniform length from the start. Care
should be taken to form the curved thick letters, when
standing alone, thus ＼ *v*,) *z*. If made heavy throughout they look clumsy: they should be thick in the
middle only, and should taper off at each end, except
when a joining such as ＼ *v g* or ＼ *b ng* is made.
Thick strokes are never written upward. As an aid to
remembering the strokes for *th* and *s*, the student should
note that) *s* is the curve on the right side of ℰ) . The
consonants *l* and *r* form the *l*eft and *r*ight sides of an
arch ⌂. The consonant *l* is most commonly written
upwards; but it may be written downward in certain
cases in accordance with rules which will be explained
later.

Names of Consonants. 11. Until the student is
perfectly familiar with the names of the consonants and
the characters representing them, he should, in writing
out the exercises, name aloud each shorthand stroke as
he writes it. The strokes must always be called by their
phonetic names: thus, "ch" is to be named *chay;* "g"
gay; "ng" *ing*. The reason for this is that each phonetic
character has a fixed value and, therefore, requires to
be called by a name which indicates the sound that it
invariably represents.

Divisions	Character	Name	Letter	As sounded in	
Explodents	\	pee	P	post	rope
	\	bee	B	boast	robe
	|	tee	T	tip	fate
	|	dee	D	dip	fade
	/	chay	CH	chest	etch
	/	jay	J	jest	edge
	—	kay	K	cane	leek
	—	gay	G	gain	league
Continuants	(	ef	F	fat	safe
	(	vee	V	vat	save
	(	ith	TH	thigh	wreath
	(	thee	*TH*	thy	wreathe
	)	ess	S	seal	base
	)	zee	Z	zeal	baize
	)	ish	SH	she	dash
	)	zhee	ZH	treasure	vision
Nasals	⌢	em	M	met	seem
	⌣	en	N	net	seen
	⌣	ing	NG	kingly	long
Coalescents Liquids	(up	el	L	light	tile
	/ up down	ar, ray	R	tire	right
	/ up	way	W	wet	away
	/ up	yay	Y	yet	ayah
Aspirate	down ⌀ up	hay	H	high	adhere

Exercise 1

*(To be written by the student. The arrow →→ shows the
direction in which the stroke is to be written. The
curves* m, n *and* ng *and the straight strokes* k *and* g
are written on the line.)

P, B

T, D

CH, J
(chay)

K, G
(gay)

F, V

TH, *TH*
(ith) (thee)

S, Z
(zee)

SH, ZH
(ish) (zhee)

M

N

NG
(ing)

L

R

R
(ray)

W
(way)

Y
(yay)

H
(hay)

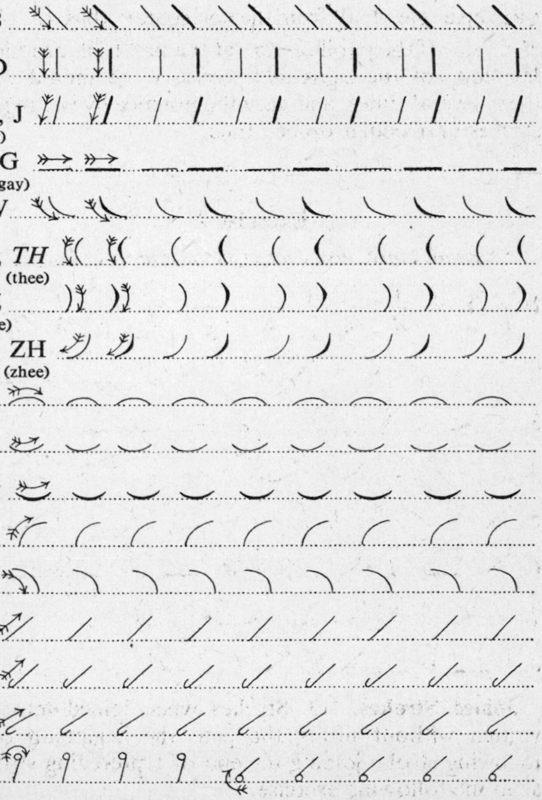

Chay and Ray. 12. These strokes are somewhat similar. They differ, however, in slope and in the direction in which they are written. It is scarcely possible, moreover, to mistake one for the other, inasmuch as *chay* is always written DOWN at an angle of 30° from the perpendicular, and *ray* is always written UP at an angle of 30° from the horizontal; thus ⟍ *chay*, ⟋ *ray*. If the pupil cannot, at the first trial, produce a fair copy of the signs in Exercise 1, he should write them several times, and vary the practice by writing the strokes in irregular order; thus,

Exercise 2

Read, copy, and transcribe as shown in line 1

1. ⟍ | | /   /   ⎯   ⎯   ⟋   ⟍   ⸜   ⟍   ⟋
    p   b   t   d   ch   j   k   g   w   y   h   h   r

2.

3.

4.

5.

6.

7.

8.

Joined Strokes. 13. Strokes when joined must be written without lifting the pen, the beginning of a following stroke joining the end of a preceding stroke, as in the following exercise.

Exercise 3

Read and copy

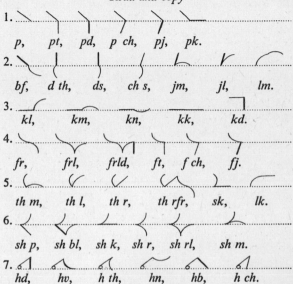

1.   p,   pt,   pd,   p ch,   pj,   pk.

2.   bf,   d th,   ds,   ch s,   jm,   jl,   lm.

3.   kl,   km,   kn,   kk,   kd.

4.   fr,   frl,   frld,   ft,   f ch,   fj.

5.   th m,   th l,   th r,   th rfr,   sk,   lk.

6.   sh p,   sh bl,   sh k,   sh r,   sh rl,   sh m.

7.   hd,   hv,   h th,   hn,   hb,   h ch.

Exercise 4

Read, copy, and transcribe

1.

2.

3.

4.

5.

6.

The student will see the correct angles for the upright and sloping characters if he will copy and practise the following forms in combination—

Summary

1. Pitman Shorthand is phonetic, words being written according to their sound.
2. The strokes are twenty-six in number, and each stroke has a distinct name and value.
3. To represent the consonants there are mainly two elements, a straight stroke and a shallow curve.
4. The strokes (straight and curved) are thin and thick for the representation of pairs of similar sounds.
5. Thin strokes are written sometimes upward, sometimes downward; thick strokes are never written upward.
6. Strokes must be of a uniform length, about one-sixth of an inch.
7. Strokes are written by one impression, and the thick curves taper at each end.
8. The stroke representing *chay* is written downward; the stroke representing *ray* is written upward.
9. Strokes when joined must be written without lifting the pen.

CHAPTER II

THE VOWELS

"If the mouth-passage is left so open as not to cause audible friction, and voiced breath is sent through it, we have a vowel." (*Prof. Sweet.*)

Vowel-sounds. 14. There are six simple long vowel-sounds in the English language, namely—

$$ah, \quad \bar{a}, \quad \bar{e}; \quad aw, \quad \bar{o}, \quad \overline{oo};$$

as heard in the words

b*ah*! *ā*le, *ēa*ch; *ā*ll, *ōa*k, *oo*ze.

15. There are six corresponding short vowel-sounds in the language, namely—

$$\breve{a}, \quad \breve{e}, \quad \breve{i}; \quad \breve{o}, \quad \breve{u}, \quad \breve{oo}$$

as heard in the words

*ă*t, *ĕ*tch, *ĭ*t; *ŏ*dd, t*ŭ*b, b*oŏ*k.

The long vowels may be remembered by repeating the sentence "*Pa may we all go too?*" The short vowels may be remembered by repeating the sentence "*That pen is not much good.*"

Vowel-signs. 16. The long vowels are represented by a heavy dot and a heavy dash. The short vowels are represented by a light dot and a light dash.

Vowel-places. 17. There are three points on a stroke close to which a vowel-sign may be placed, namely, at the beginning, the middle, and the end. The vowels are accordingly called first-place, second-place, and third-place vowels respectively.

The places of the vowels are counted from the point where the stroke begins. In the case of downstrokes, therefore, the vowel-places are counted from the top downward. In the case of upstrokes, the vowel-places are counted from the bottom upward. In the case of horizontals, the vowel-places are counted from left to right; thus,

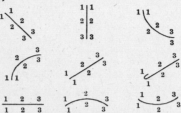

Value of Vowel-signs. 18. The vowel-signs are put in the places which correspond with their numbers. A heavy dot in the first-place represents the long vowel *ah;* in the second-place it represents the long vowel *ā;* in the third-place it represents the long vowel *ē.* A heavy dash in the first place represents the long vowel *aw;* in the second place it represents the long vowel *ō;* in the third place it represents the long vowel *ōo.*

19. The light vowel-signs for the short vowels are put in the same places as the heavy vowel-signs for the long vowels; thus,

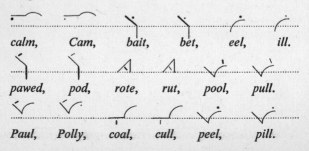

calm,   Cam,   bait,   bet,   eel,   ill.

pawed,   pod,   rote,   rut,   pool,   pull.

Paul,   Polly,   coal,   cull,   peel,   pill.

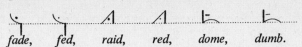

fade,   fed,   raid,   red,   dome,   dumb.

Vowels preceding and following Strokes. 20. When a vowel-sign is placed on the left-hand side of an upstroke or downstroke, it is read *before* the stroke, as *ale,* /\ *earth,* \ *ape,* '/ *age,* ⌋ *eat.*

When a vowel-sign is placed on the right-hand side of an upstroke or downstroke, it is read *after* the stroke, as ⌐ *lay,* / *ray,* \ *pay,* |· *jay,* ⌐) *shoe.*

When a vowel-sign is placed above a horizontal stroke it is read *before* the stroke, as ‥ *ache,* ‥ *eke.*

When a vowel-sign is placed below a horizontal stroke it is read *after* the stroke, as ⎯ *Kay,* ⎯ *key,* ⎯ *no.*

PRECEDING VOWELS

1.

ebb,   aid,   etch,   edge,   off,   oath.

2.

ache,   egg,   aim,   inn,   ore.

FOLLOWING VOWELS

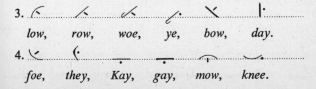

3.

low,   row,   woe,   ye,   bow,   day.

4.

foe,   they,   Kay,   gay,   mow,   knee.

Preceding and Following Vowels

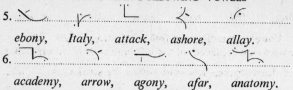

5.

ebony,   Italy,   attack,   ashore,   allay.

6.

academy,   arrow,   agony,   afar,   anatomy.

Exercise 5

Read, copy, and transcribe

Write the outline of the word first; then put in the vowel-sign.

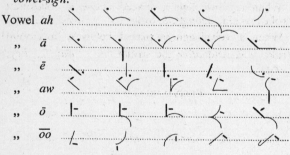

Vowel *ah*

,,   *ā*

,,   *ē*

,,   *aw*

,,   *ō*

,,   *ōo*

Exercise 6

Read, copy, and transcribe

Vowel *ă*

,,   *ĕ*

,,   *ĭ*

,,   *ŏ*

,,   *ŭ*

,,   *ŏo*

Exercise 7

Write in shorthand

1. Pay, paid, bay, bait, Tay, tame.
2. Say, essay, Esk, escape, low, load.
3. Show, showed, foe, foam, may, make.
4. Weigh, weighed, eight, Etna, nay, name.

Summary

1. There are six long vowels, represented by a heavy dot and dash, and six corresponding short vowels, represented by a light dot and dash.
2. The vowels are called first-place, second-place, and third-place vowels, respectively.
3. The vowel-places are called first-, second-, and third-places respectively, and vowel-signs are put in the places which correspond with their numbers.
4. Vowel-places are counted from the point at which the stroke begins.
5. The order of reading vowel-signs with their strokes is: with downstrokes and upstrokes, from left to right; with horizontal strokes, from top to bottom. Thus:

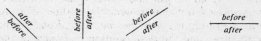

6. In writing a word, the word-form is written first and then the vowel-sign.

CHAPTER III

INTERVENING VOWELS AND POSITION

Intervening Vowels. 21. FIRST- and SECOND-PLACE vowel-signs when occurring between two strokes are written *after the first stroke;* thus, ⌐ *talk,* ⌐ *gate.* THIRD-PLACE vowel-signs are written *before the second stroke* at the end, because the vowel-sign is more conveniently written in that place; thus, ⌐ *deem,* ⌐ *dim,* ⌐ *read,* ⌐ *rid,* ⌐ *pool,* ⌐ *pull.* The vowel-sign is still in the third place, as indicated in the following diagram—

INTERVENING VOWEL-PLACES

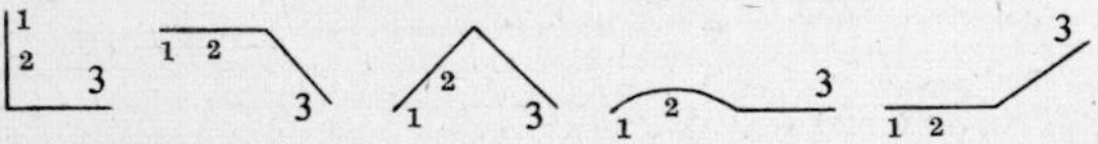

Compound Words. 22. In compound words the vowel-sign is generally placed to the separate words; as, ⌐ *ear-ache.*

Position of Outlines. 23. Just as there are three places in which to put the vowel-signs, so there are three positions in which to write the outlines of words. The *first* position is *above the line;* the *second* position is *on the line;* and the *third* position is *through the line.* The *first sounded vowel* in the word determines the position of the outline.

When the *first sounded vowel* in a word is a *first-place* vowel, the outline is written in the *first position;* as, ⌐ *palm,* ⌐ *talk,* ⌐ *got,* ⌐ *rod,* ⌐ *wrought.*

When the *first sounded vowel* in a word is a *second-place* vowel, the outline is written in the *second position;* as, ⌐ *bake,* ⌐ *share,* ⌐ *load,* ⌐ *road,* ⌐ *code.*

When the *first sounded vowel* in a word is a *third-place* vowel, the outline is written in the *third position;* as, ⌐ deem, ⌐ dim, ⌐ lead, ⌐ lid, ⌐ keyed, ⌐ kill.

24. The first upstroke or downstroke in the outline indicates the position, as shown in the foregoing examples.

It is not practicable to write a horizontal stroke through the line; therefore, when an outline consists entirely of horizontal strokes, it is written in the *first* position if the first sounded vowel is a first-place vowel, and in the *second* position if the first sounded vowel is either a second- or a third-place vowel; as, ⌐ mocking, ⌐ making, ⌐ meek, ⌐ cook.

Exercise 8

Read and copy

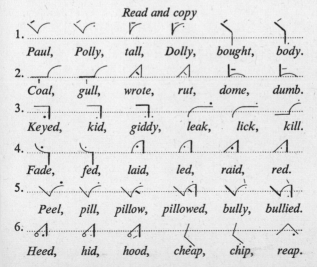

1. Paul, Polly, tall, Dolly, bought, body.

2. Coal, gull, wrote, rut, dome, dumb.

3. Keyed, kid, giddy, leak, lick, kill.

4. Fade, fed, laid, led, raid, red.

5. Peel, pill, pillow, pillowed, bully, bullied.

6. Heed, hid, hood, cheap, chip, reap.

Exercise 9

Read, copy, and transcribe

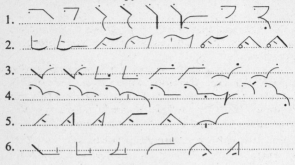

Exercise 10

Write in shorthand

1. Patch, batch, Fanny, shop, shoddy, jolly.
2. Paid, page, bake, beck, jail, jelly.
3. Leap, lip, leave, live, lead, lid.
4. Nave, navy, enough, bale, bell, below.
5. May, make, name, namely, comb, money.
6. Feed, food, sheep, ship, loom, limb.

Grammalogues. 25. Frequently-occurring words are represented in shorthand by a single sign, as ＼ for *be*. These words are called *grammalogues* or letter-words, and the shorthand characters that represent them are called *logograms*, or word-letters. At the head of the following Exercises some logograms are given, which must be committed to memory. These characters are written *above*, *on*, or *through* the line, as, ˌ | ˌ ┃ ˌ ┼ .

Punctuation. 26. The period, or full stop, is represented by a small cross; thus, × ; the dash thus, ⌐ ;

the note of interrogation and the note of exclamation
⸮ and ⸘ respectively. Other punctuation marks are
written as usual. Two short lines underneath an outline
indicate an initial capital.

GRAMMALOGUES

⸫ *a, an,* ⸬ *the;* ＼ *all,* ↘ *two, too;* ＼ *of,* ↘ *to;*
| *on,* | *but;* ′ (down) *awe, ought, aught,*
／ (down) *who;* ＼ (up) *and,* ／ (up) *should.*

Exercise 11

Read, copy, and transcribe

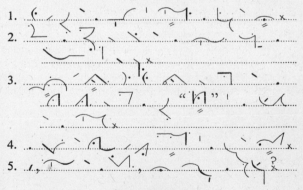

Exercise 12

Write in shorthand

(THE WORDS PRINTED IN ITALIC TYPE ARE
GRAMMALOGUES)

1. They *should* ask *the* Head *of the* Academy *to* change
   the date.
2. *Who* took *the* padlock off *the* gate *of the* paddock?

3. Up *to the* date *of the* party she looked both rich *and* happy.
4. *The* head *of the* bank may leave *on* Monday.
5. They *ought to* change *the* date *on the* cheque *to the* fourth *of the* month.

Summary

1. FIRST-PLACE and SECOND-PLACE vowel-signs when occurring between two strokes are written after the first stroke; THIRD-PLACE vowel-signs are written before the second stroke.
2. The position of an outline is governed by the first sounded vowel in the word.
3. A *grammalogue* is a frequently-occurring *word* represented by a single sign. The *sign* for a grammalogue is called a *logogram*.
4. The full stop is indicated by a small cross, × ; the dash by ⌐; mark of interrogation and mark of exclamation by ⌣̇ and ⌣̇ respectively.
5. Two short lines underneath an outline indicate an initial capital.

CHAPTER IV
ALTERNATIVE SIGNS FOR *R* AND *H*

Consonant R. 27. The consonant *r* is provided with two different forms in order to facilitate the joining of strokes together, and also for the purpose of indicating an initial or a final vowel-sound.

28. Initial *r* is written downward when preceded by a vowel-sound; as, ⌐ *oar*, ⌐ *array*, ⟍ *Arab*. In other cases, the general rule is to write initial or final *r* upward when it is followed by a vowel-sound, and downward when it is not followed by a vowel-sound; as, ⟋ *ray* but ⌐ *air*; ⌣ *parry* but ⟍ *par*; ⟋ *tarry* but ⌐ *tar*; ⟋ *sherry* but ⌐ *share*.

29. Downward *r* is always written initially before *m* because of the easier joining.

Consonant H. 30. The upward form of *h* is most commonly used; but the downward form is written when the letter stands alone or is immediately followed by ___ *k* or ___ *g*; as, ⟍ *hay*, ⟍ *hake*, ⟍ *Haig*.

Exercise 13
Read, copy, and transcribe

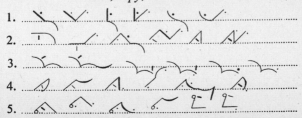

Exercise 14

Write in shorthand

1. Arm, aroma, Orkney, arcade, arrow, ear.
2. Rob, rod, Rodney, Ruth, rage, roach.
3. Perry, Derry, Murray, furrow, morrow, ferry.
4. Deer, jeer, gear, fear, veer, leer.
5. Racy, writ, retail, revere, reverie, wreck.
6. Hook, hog, heath, hatch, hedge, hood.

GRAMMALOGUES

put;   be,   to be;   it;   had,   do,
difference, different;   much,   which.

Exercise 15

Read, copy, and transcribe

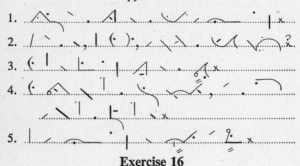

Exercise 16

Write in shorthand

1. They hope *to* reach Orkney *on the* fourth *of* May.
2. *The* red colour *on the* door *and the* yellow *on the*
   window *had a* poor effect.
3. He *ought to be* fair, *and* pay *the difference to* Reid
   and Hannah.

4. If they get *the* money *it should* make *much difference to the* firm.
5. They *had a* heavy mail *on* Monday.
6. Tom saw *the* head *of the* firm leave at four or so.

Summary

1. The consonant *r* initially is written downward if a vowel precedes, and upward if a vowel does not precede.
2. The consonant *r* finally is written upward if a vowel follows, and downward if no vowel follows.
3. Downward *r* is written before *m*.
4. The consonant *h* standing alone, or followed by *k* or *g*, is written downward; in other cases the upward form is written.

CHAPTER V

DIPHTHONGS

"A diphthong is a union of two vowel-sounds in one syllable." (*Prof. Skeat.*)

Diphthongs. 31. There are four common diphthongs, namely, *ī*, *ow*, *oi*, and *ū*, as heard in the sentence *I now enjoy music*.

They are represented as follows—

$$\bar{I} \quad ^{\vee}| \qquad OW \quad {}_{\wedge}| \qquad OI \quad ^{7}| \qquad \bar{U} \quad {}_{\cap}|$$

32. The signs for *ī* and *oi* are written in the first place; the signs for *ow* and *ū* are written in the third place; thus, `⌐ᵛ` *tie*, `⌐ᵛ` *time;* `⌐ᴾ` *toy,* `⌐ᴾ` *toil;* `___ᴧ` *cow,* `⌐⌐ᴧ` *cowed;* `⌐` *duty,* `___` *mule.*

Joined Diphthongs. 33. The diphthong-signs may be joined to the consonant in many words; thus, `⌐` *item,* `⌐` *idle,* `⌐` *ivy,* `⌐` *ice,* `⌐` *eyes,* `⌐` *ire,* `⌐` *isle,* `⌐` *I am,* `⌐` *nigh,* `⌐` *now,* `⌐` *bow,* `⌐` *avow,* `⌐` *dew,* `⌐` *Matthew,* `⌐` *issue,* `⌐` *owl.*

34. The semicircle representing *ū* may be written `⌐` for convenience in joining; thus, `___` *cue,* `___` *argue,* `___` *mew,* `___` *new,* `___` *value.* The sign for *ī* is abbreviated when prefixed to *l* and *m*, and the sign for *ow* is abbreviated when affixed to *n*, as shown in the examples in paragraph 33.

Triphones. 35. A small tick attached to a diphthong-sign represents any vowel immediately following the diphthong; thus, ⟋⟍ *diary,* ⟋ *loyal,* ⟋ *towel,* ⟋

attenuate, ⟍ *fewer,* ⟍ *annuity,* ⟍ *riot,* ⟍ *ingenuous.*

These signs are called *triphones* because they represent three vowels in one sign.

Abbreviated W. **36.** The initial sound of *w*, before *k, g, m, r* is represented by a right semicircle; thus, ⟋ *wake,* ⟋ *wig,* ⟋ *womanish,* ⟋ *wear,* ⟋ *wary.*

37. When *w* is preceded by a vowel, the stroke ⟋ must be written; as, ⟋ *awake,* ⟋ *awoke,* ⟋ *aware.*

Exercise 17

Read, copy, and transcribe

1.
2.
3.
4.
5.
6.
7.

Exercise 18

Write in shorthand

1. Bite, tile, time, timely, ripe, ride, fire, fiery.
2. Coil, coiling, toyed, joy, enjoy, coinage, Doyle.
3. Rout, rowdy, cowed, pouch, vouch, loud.

4. View, review, dupe, tunic, fury, mule.
5. Item, eyes, nigh, deny, voyage, argue, arguing, genuine.
6. Wear, wary, weary, woke, awoke, war, warm.

GRAMMALOGUES

.⋏. *how,* ⌐ *why;* ⌒ *beyond,* ⌒ *you;* / *large;* — *can,* _____ *come;* — *go,* — *give-n;* ＼ *for;* ＼ *have.*

Exercise 19

Read, copy, and transcribe

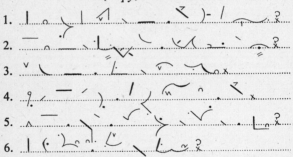

Exercise 20

Write in shorthand

1. *How can you* attach *the* wire *to the* high chimney?
2. They were due *to* arrive at five, *but* were delayed *a* long time at Wick.
3. *You should* verify each item *on the* bill.
4. *Do you* like *the* new tyre *you have had put on the* car?
5. Few *of the* party knew *why you had to go to* Newquay *on the* tenth *of* July.
6. *A* week ago I saw Doyle, *but* he *had* no time *to give to* my work; he *had to* hurry *for the* boat.

Summary

1. The four diphthongs are *ī, ow, oi, ū*.
2. The diphthongs *ī* and *oi* are put in the first vowel-place; and *ow* and *ū* in the *third* vowel-place.
3. A diphthong may be joined to a stroke where convenient.
4. A small tick attached to a diphthong-sign indicates the addition of a vowel to the diphthong.
5. Initial *w* before *k, g, m, r*, is represented by a right semicircle.

CHAPTER VI

PHRASEOGRAPHY

Phrasing. 38. Phraseography is the writing of two or more words together without lifting the pen, the resulting outline being called a *phraseogram*. The best phraseograms are those which combine the qualities of *facility*, *lineality*, and *legibility*. A phraseogram should be easy to write; it should not ascend too far above, nor descend too far below, the line; and it must be legible when written. Subject to the observance of these conditions, the practice of phrase writing will greatly increase the writer's fluency and speed.

(*a*) The first word-form of a phraseogram must occupy the position in which it would be written if it stood alone. Thus, the phrase *how can they* would be represented by the outline ⌒⁊, commencing *on* the line, because *how*, if it stood alone, would be written on the line. Similarly, ⌇ *I have* commences *above* the line, because *I*, standing alone, would be written above the line.

(*b*) A first-position word-form may be slightly raised or lowered, however, to permit of a following stroke being written *above*, *on* or *through* the line, as, ⌇ *I thank you* (and using the logogram ͨ *with*), ⌇ *with much*, ⌇ *with which*, ⌇ *with each*.

26

(*c*) When joined to *k, m, l* (up), the sign ⌄ may be shortened; thus, ⌐ *I can,* ⌐ *I am,* ⌐ *I will.*

(*d*) With rare exceptions it is unnecessary to vocalize phraseograms. The word *he* standing alone, or at the beginning of a phrase, is written ⌐ ; but in the middle of a phrase the word is represented by the logogram ⌐ ; thus, ⌐ *he may,* ⌐ *if he may,* ⌐ *he should know,* ⌐ *if he should know.* For the sake of an easier joining the word *much* is sometimes written in full in phrases; as, ⌐ *so much,* ⌐ *how much;* and *were* is written either ⌐ or ⌐ ; thus, ⌐ *they were,* ⌐ *you were,* ⌐ *if they were,* ⌐ *if he were.* In phrases, the word *him* should have the dot vowel inserted; thus, ⌐ *of him,* ⌐ *to him.*

Tick *the.* **39.** The word *the* may be expressed by a light slanting *tick*, joined to a preceding character and written either downward (from right to left) or upward (from left to right).

(*a*) DOWNWARD: > *of the,* ⌐ *and the,* ⌐ *should the,* ⌐ *with the,* ⌐ *by the,* ⌐ *if the,* ⌐ *have the.*

(*b*) UPWARD: ⌐ *beyond the,* ⌐ *what the,* ⌐ *how the,* ⌐ *at the,* ⌐ *which the,* ⌐ *was the.*
This tick for *the* must never be used initially.

NOTE— ⌐ *on the* and ⌐ *but the* should slope a little to secure a better angle.

PHRASES

I thank you		why have you
I think you should be		with you
I have the		so much
I have had		with much
I saw the		with which
I see		with each
I am		when they
I may be		what do you
I will		what was
I will be		what can be
you should		it would be
you should be		it should be
you can		it will be
you will		it was
you will be		which was
you may be		which were
you were		he should be
if you were		he will be
they were		if he
how can they		if he were
why do you		too much

GRAMMALOGUES

(*thank-ed,* (*think;* (*though,* (*them;*) *was,*

) *whose;* / *shall,*) *wish;* ⊂ *with,* ⊂ *when;*

⊃ *what,* ⊃ *would;* ' *O, oh, owe,* ı *he.*

Exercise 21

Read, copy, and transcribe

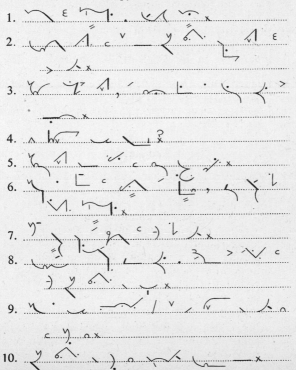

1.

2.

3.

4.

5.

6.

7.

8.

9.

10.

Exercise 22

Write in shorthand

(Phraseograms in the following letterpress exercises are
indicated by the hyphen.)

1. *Why-do-you think* he-*was* aware *of-the* likely failure
   of-the firm?
2. I-*thank-you for-the* tube *of* colour, *which* I-*think*
   should-be all-right.
3. They deny they-were at-*the* Tower at-*the* time *of-the*
   fire.
4. I-*think-you* owe the Head *an* apology *for-the* way
   you hurried away *on*-Monday.
5. If-*he*-were aware *of-the* date, he-*would*, I-*think*,
   have come with us.
6. Kenneth Doyle, *whose* view *all of* us share, wrote *to*
   say he-*would* arrive at five.
7. I-*think too*-much time *was-given to-the* topic. *What-
   do-you think*?

Summary

1. *Phraseography* is the name given to the principle of
   joining word-forms together. The outline thus
   obtained is called a *phraseogram*.
2. The following must be carefully noted—
   (*a*) Awkward joinings must be avoided.
   (*b*) The first word-form in a phraseogram must
   occupy its own position. A first-position word-
   form may, however, be raised or lowered to
   permit of a following stroke being written above,
   on or through the line.
3. The word *the* may be expressed by a light slanting
   tick joined to a preceding character and written
   either downward or upward. The tick for *the* is
   never used initially.

CHAPTER VII

CIRCLE *S* AND *Z*

Circle S and Z. 40. The consonants *S* and *Z* are represented not only by the strokes)͟ and)͟ but also by a small circle o.. Initially the circle represents the light sound of *s* only; medially and finally it represents the sound of *s* or *z*. The sound of *z* initially must be represented by the stroke)͟ as, ⌒ *zeal*, ⌒ *zero*, ⌒ *zenith*.

Left and Right Motion. 41. In this chapter, and in the following pages, the term *Left Motion* means the motion of the hand in writing the longhand letter 𝒪 ⊃ , the opposite motion being termed the *Right Motion* ⊋ . The circle *s*, when standing alone, is written with the *left* motion.

42. The circle *s* is written (*a*) *inside* curves, (*b*) *outside* angles formed by two straight strokes, and (*c*) with the *left* motion when joined to straight strokes not forming an angle; thus,

(*a*) ⌒ *safes*, ⌒ *soothes*, ⌒ *essays*, ⌒ *sashes*, ⌒ *seems*, ⌒ *sense*, ⌒ *sings*, ⌒ *slays*, ⌒ *source*, ⌒ *fossil*, ⌒ *thistle*, ⌒ *Cecil*, ⌒ *muscle*, ⌒ *nestles*, ⌒ *designs*, ⌒ *lisps*.

(*b*) ⌒ *gasp*, ⌒ *rasp*, ⌒ *risk*, ⌒ *task*, ⌒ *Biscay*, ⌒ *justice*, ⌒ *hasp*.

(*c*) ⌒ *space*, ⌒ *seeds*, ⌒ *sages*, ⌒ *soaks*, ⌒ *sorrows*, ⌒ *Busby*, ⌒ *tacit*, ⌒ *cask*, ⌒ *razor*, ⌒ *wiser*.

43. Initial circle *s* is always read *first;* final circle *s* is always read *last;* and vowel-signs are placed and read in relation to the stroke consonant, and not to the circle, as in the foregoing examples.

44. The circle *s* may be added to a stroke logogram, as, _____ *come,* ___o *comes,* ＼___ *put,* ＼o *puts.*

Stroke L and Circle. 45. When the stroke *l* immediately precedes or follows a circle which is attached to a curve, it is written in the same direction as the circle; thus, 6... *lesson,* ___ *cancel,* ⤵ *vessel,* ⌒ *loser.*

46. A lightly-sounded vowel may be omitted, as in ⤵ *poison,* ⤴ *refusal,* ___ *answer,* ⤵ *desire.*

Exercise 23

Read, copy, and transcribe

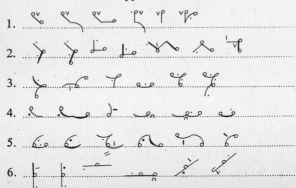

Exercise 24

Write in shorthand

1. Lays, slays, oars, soars, face, facing.
2. Poison, poisonous, pacifies, voicing, rising, toilsome.
3. Dusky, excites, customs, justice, rusty, suffice.
4. Less, Leslie, shame, shameless, shamelessly, slums.
5. Excusing, refusing, spacing, basin, dozen, resigns.
6. Hope, hopeless, hopelessly, consul, pencil, fossils.

GRAMMALOGUES

⟍ usual-ly; ∘ as, has, ⊙ is, his; ⌐ because;

⌐ itself; ⌡ those, thyself, ⌡ this, ⌡ thus.

Exercise 25

Read, copy, and transcribe

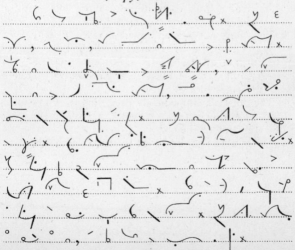

Exercise 26

Write in shorthand

If Miss Nelson *wishes to* see-*the* works, she *can come to-this* office *on* Tuesday or Wednesday *of-this* week, *and*-I-*shall-be* happy *to* show *all-the* details she may desire *to* see. I-*think-it-is* but fair *to* say *this is-the* busy season *with* us, *and* I-*shall-have* but *a* few minutes *to* spare *to* Miss Nelson. My deputy *can* take charge *of-the* lady. I-will *thank-you* if-*you*-will *put-the* facts *to-the* lady *as* nicely *as* you-can, *because* she may *think* I-am *an* idle fellow *with-much* time at-my disposal. I-know *you*-will excuse *this* appeal, *and*-I hope *you*-will-*do what* I ask, *as* I *should-be* sorry *to* upset Miss Nelson, or *to* appear *to be* rude *when* she *comes*.

Summary

1. A small circle used initially represents *s* only; medially and finally it represents *s* or *z*.
2. The circle *s* is written outside angles, inside curves, and with the left motion to straight strokes not forming an angle.
3. An *initial* circle is always read *first*; a *final* circle is always read *last*.
4. The stroke *l*, immediately preceding or following a circle attached to a curve, is written in the same direction as the circle.
5. The circle *s* may be added to stroke logograms.

CHAPTER VIII

STROKE *S* AND *Z*

Stroke S and Z. 47. Wherever there is an initial or a final *vowel-sound*, there must be a stroke consonant, to provide a place for the *vowel-sign*. Therefore, the stroke *s* must be written when a vowel precedes initial *s*, or when a vowel follows final *s* or *z;* thus, ⟩ *ace,* ⟩ *say;* ⟩ *ooze,* ⟩ *zoo;* ⟨ *asp,* but ⟨ *sap;* ⟨ *ask,* but ⟨ *sack;* ⟨ *racy,* but ⟨ *race;* ⟨ *busy,* but ⟨ *bees.*

48. Where the stroke *s* is written initially in the root word, it is retained in compounds and in derivatives formed by means of a prefix; thus, ⟨ *saw,* ⟨ *saw-bench,* ⟨ *assailed,* ⟨ *unassailed,* ⟩ *ease,* ⟨ *disease.*

The stroke is also written—

(*a*) In words like ⟨ *science,* ⟨ *sewer,* where a triphone immediately follows initial *s.*

(*b*) In words like ⟨ *cease,* ⟨ *saucer,* where initial *s* is immediately followed by a vowel and another *s* or *z.*

(*c*) In words like ⟨ *sinuous,* ⟨ *tortuous,* ⟨ *joyous,* where the final syllable *-ous* is immediately preceded by a diphthong.

Exercise 27

Read, copy, and transcribe

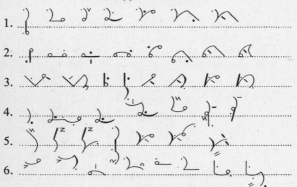

Exercise 28

Write in shorthand

1. Asp, aside, assess, Assam, assailing, asylum, assayed.
2. Base, basso, juice, juicy, legs, legacy, coals, colza.
3. Spouse, espouse, seek, Essex, score, Oscar, Isaac.
4. Essays, essence, escapes, Eskimo, say, aces.
5. Siamese, sciatica, sighing, easy, uneasy, uneasily, uneasiness.
6. Sinuous, tortuous, vacuous, tenuous, ingenuous.

GRAMMALOGUES

me, him; myself, himself; special-ly,

speak; subject-ed; several.

Exercise 29

Read, copy, and transcribe

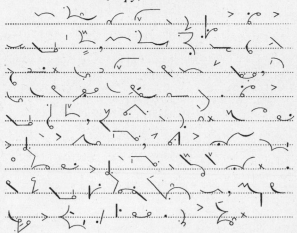

Exercise 30

Write in shorthand

For several special reasons I *should* like *you to-come to* see *me on* Wednesday *as* early *as you-can*. I *specially* desire *you to*-write out-*the* names *of all-the* firms *with-which-you have-had* business dealings since *you* came *to* us. I-*shall* discuss a new policy *with-you*, *and-the* names *for-which* I ask may-*be of* use. I-*am* a bit upset at-*the* refusal *of* Askew *and* Benson *to*-take *those* Eskimo rugs, *and*-I *should* like *to* know-*the* reasons *for-the* refusal. I-*have several subjects* besides these *of-which* I-*wish* to *speak to-you* when I-see-*you on* Wednesday. Ask *to* see *me as* soon *as you* arrive.

Summary

The stroke *s* or *z* must be written:

1. When a vowel precedes initial *s* or follows final *s* or *z*.
2. When initial *s* is immediately followed by a vowel and another *s* or *z*.
3. When initial *s* is immediately followed by a triphone.
4. When the final syllable *-ous* is preceded by a diphthong.
5. When the word is a compound like *sea-mew*, *saw-bench*.
6. When the word is a derivative like *unceasing*, *unassailed*, where the stroke would be written in the root word.

CHAPTER IX
LARGE CIRCLES *SW* AND *SS* OR *SZ*

SW Circle. 49. A large INITIAL circle, written with the same motion as the circle *s*, represents the double consonant *sw*, thus, ⨍ *seat*, ⨍ *sweet*, ⌒ *sum*, ⌒ *swum*. As a vowel cannot be written to a circle, the stroke *w* must be written in words like ⤴ *sway*, ⤴ *suasive*. The *sw* circle is used initially only.

SS Circle. 50. A large MEDIAL or FINAL circle, written with the same motion as circle *s*, represents *s-s*, having a light or heavy sound, with the intervening vowel ĕ; thus, ⨍ (*ses*) *necessity;* ⤵ (*sez*) *passes;* ⤵ (*zes*) *possessive;* ⨍ (*zez*) *causes.* When a vowel other than ĕ intervenes, it is indicated by placing the vowel-sign within the circle; thus, ⨍ *exist*, ⨍ *exhaust*, ⨍ *exercised.* Final *s* is added thus, ⨍ *exercises.* The large circle is also used to express the sounds of two *s's* in consecutive syllables, as in ⤳ *mis-spell.*

Plurals and Possessives. 51. As ⤵ *Lucy,* ⤵ *policy,* ⤵ *jealousy,* etc., are written with the stroke *s*, the stroke *s* is retained in the derived words ⤵ *Lucy's,* ⤵ *policies,* ⤵ *jealousies.* (See also pars. 47 and 48.)

52. A few words ending in *s-s* are written with the circle and stroke, or the stroke and circle, in order to distinguish them from other words containing similar consonants, and in which the large circle is employed;

thus, ⟍ *possess*, but ⟍ *pauses*; ⟍ *access*, but
⟍ *axis*; ⟍ *recess*, but ⟍ *races*.

Large Circles in Phraseography. 53. The *sw* circle
is used for the words *as we* in phrases like ⟍ *as we have*,
⟍ *as we can*, and for *as w-* in ⟍ *as well as;* and the *ss*
circle for the two *s's* in phrases like ⟍ *in this city*,
⟍ *this is*, ⟍ *as is*, or *as has*, ⟍ *is as* or *is his*.

Exercise 31

Read, copy, and transcribe

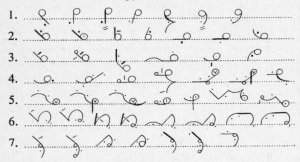

Exercise 32

Write in shorthand

1. Sweetly, sweetness, swig, swain, swing, swimmer.
2. Entices, reduces, revises, ounces, minces, laces.
3. Roses, peruses, terraces, essences, fences, romances.
4. Dazes, decisive, races, resist, misses, Mississippi.
5. Fallacy, fallacies, Morrissey, Morrissey's, curacy,
   curacies.
6. Thesis, emphasis, paralysis, Genesis, Nemesis, axis.

GRAMMALOGUES

⁓ *in, any,* ⌇ *own;* ⌒ *your,* ⌐ *year;* ⁄ *are,*
⁄ *our, hour;* ∮ *ourselves,* ⌡ *themselves.*

Exercise 33

Read, copy, and transcribe

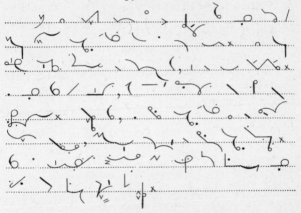

Exercise 34

Write in shorthand

The invoices *and* bills *of* lading *for-the* valances *and* laces *are* ready *for* dispatch, *and-the* cases *themselves are to*-leave *by-the* "Swiss Valley," sailing *on* Wednesday. *The* advices *should-be with our* customers *by-the* tenth *of*-March, *and-they-will-do all-they can to*-make *a* success *of-the* deal. They know-*the* business thoroughly, *and you*-may safely leave *it to-them. It-is* scarcely necessary *to* emphasize *what* they *themselves* know *al*ready.

Summary

1. A large initial circle represents *sw*.
2. A large medial or final circle represents the light or heavy sound of *s-s* with an intervening vowel.
3. Where a root word ends with stroke *s*, the plural, possessive, or third person singular is formed by the addition of the circle *s*.
4. Where a root word ends with a circle *s*, the plural, possessive, or the third person singular is formed by the use of the large circle *ses*.
5. A few words ending in *s-s* are written with the circle and stroke, or with the stroke and circle, to distinguish them from words in which the large circle is employed.
6. The *sw* circle is used in phrases like *as well as, as we know;* and the *ss* circle in phrases like *it is said, in this city.*

CHAPTER X

LOOP *ST* AND *STR*

Loop ST. 54. The combination *st*, as in *st*eam, mi*st*, pa*ssed* (pa*st*) is represented by a loop made half the length of the stroke to which it is attached; thus,

꠹. *seem*, ꠹. *steam*, ꠹. *sown*, ꠹. *stone*, ꠹. *sake*, ꠹. *stake*, ꠹. *miss*, ꠹. *mist*, ꠹. *lace*, ꠹. *laced*, ꠹. *pass*, ꠹. *past*.

Like the circle *s*, the *st* loop is written with the Left motion to straight strokes and inside curves, as shown above. Like the circle *s*, too, the *st* loop is always read first at the beginning of the stroke and last at the end.

55. Since a final *vowel-sound* requires a final *stroke*, in order to provide a place for the vowel-sign (par. 47), it follows that the *st* loop cannot be employed finally when a vowel follows *t*; thus, ꠹. *best*, but ꠹. *bestow*; ꠹. *rust*, but ꠹. *rusty*; ꠹. *honest*, but ꠹. *honesty*.

56. The *st* loop may also be employed finally for the heavy sound of *zd*, as in the words ꠹. *fused*, ꠹. *refused*, ꠹. *opposed*, ꠹. *disposed*. The word *caused* is written ꠹. to distinguish it from ꠹. *cost*.

Loop STR. 57. A large loop, extending two-thirds of the length of the stroke to which it is attached, represents *str*. This *str* (ster) loop *is never written at the beginning of an outline.* Like the circle *s* and the *st* loop, the *str* loop is written with the Left motion to

straight strokes, and inside curves; thus, ⟍ _pass_,
⟍ _past_, ⟍ _pastor_, ⟍ _fast_, ⟍ _faster_.

58. The _st_ and _str_ loops may be used medially
where a good joining results; thus, ⟋ _justify_,
⟋ _elastic_, ⟋ _masterpiece_.

59. The _st_ loop cannot be employed when a vowel
occurs between _s_ and _t_, nor can the _str_ loop be written
when a strongly sounded vowel occurs between _st_ and
_r_, because where there is a vowel-sound there must be a
stroke consonant to provide a place for the vowel-sign
(par. 47). Compare ⟍ _best_ and ⟍ _beset_, ⟋ _rest_
and ⟋ _receipt_, ⟍ _pastor_, ⟋ _pasture_, ⟍ _poster_,
⟋ _posture_.

60. The circle _s_ is added to a final loop as follows—
⟍ _taste_, ⟍ _tastes_; ⟋ _lustre_, ⟋ _lustres_.

Exercise 35

Read, copy, and transcribe

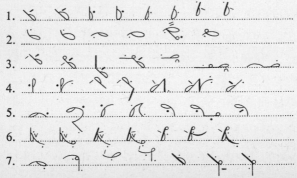

Exercise 36

Write in shorthand

1. Stout, stoutly, stock, stockade, style, stylish.
2. Rust, rusts, nest, nests, waste, wastes.
3. Box, boxed, lapse, lapsed, refuse, refused.
4. Coaster, coasters, boaster, boasters, muster.
5. Stone, stole, stave, stem, stung, star.
6. Gassed, gazette, vest, visit, rust, russet.
7. Bolsters, barrister, waster, lustre, sinister, minister.

GRAMMALOGUES

first, influence, influenced, next, most, language, owing, thing, young, Lord, we.

Exercise 37

Read, copy, and transcribe

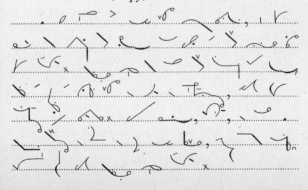

Exercise 38

Write in shorthand

The language of-the young barrister in-the case was
most stately, and it-must have influenced both judge
and jury. It almost looked as-if-the case was lost at-the
first, because of-the calm way in-which-the opposing
counsel set out to state-the facts for-his side. But-the
young barrister faced the test fairly, and-his language
and style, though different, showed him to be a master
of-law and logic. We-shall watch his career at-the bar,
and-we-think he-must succeed because of-his abilities.

Revisionary Exercise (A)

Write in shorthand

If-you-can put me up for a week in August, I-shall-be
ready to-go and stay with-you. You-can-have as much
walking as you-like. I-shall-be at-your disposal at
almost any hour, and-as I-am a rare walker myself,
I-think I-can say you-will-have all-the exercise you wish.
You ought-to be a different fellow when I-leave, if-you-
will-be influenced by-me. I-think I-can give-you a mile
in six and beat you. I-have-had some talk with young
Lord Robson several-times in-the past week, and he
says you-can-do five miles an hour. Those-who saw you
last autumn and-know what you-can-do, all say-the
same thing. This-is all I-know as to-your form. But-
we-shall-see for ourselves. I-think-you-will own I-am
far beyond you in speed. It-will-be a case of-each for-
himself and-the race to-the faster of-the two. Oh,
I-know I-shall beat you, unless you-are faster this year.
Those-who think poorly of-themselves only induce those-
who know them to-think-the same. I speak for-myself,

because I-know *myself. * I-*can* say *a* deal *on-this subject,* *and*-I *usually do*-so. *You* ask *why* I-*have* stayed away so-long. *The* answer *is* business keeps *me* away. *When would-you* like *me to-come*? *The* best *of* luck *to-you and to-the* rest *of-the* family! *It*-will-*be* nice *to* see *them all, though* I-saw *most of-them a* month or-*two* ago.   (283 words)

Summary

1. A small loop represents *st;* a large loop represents *str*.
2. The *st* loop may be used initially, medially or finally.
3. The *st* loop may be employed finally to represent the sound of *zd*.
4. The *str* loop may be used medially or finally, but not initially.
5. The *st* loop cannot be employed when a vowel occurs between *s* and *t*, nor can the loop be written immediately before a final vowel.
6. The *str* loop cannot be written when a strongly sounded vowel occurs between *st* and *r*.

CHAPTER XI

INITIAL HOOKS TO STRAIGHT STROKES AND CURVES

Double Consonants. 61. The liquids *r* and *l* frequently blend with other consonants so as to form a double consonant, as in the words *pr*ay, *bl*ow, *dr*ink, *gl*are, *fr*y, *fl*y, or are separated from a preceding consonant by an obscure vowel only, as in pa*per*, ma*ker*, ta*ble*, ba*bel*. These consonant combinations are represented by prefixing a hook to the simple shorthand characters to indicate their union with *r* and *l*.

R Hook to Straight Strokes. 62. A small initial hook, written with the Right motion, adds *R* to straight strokes; thus,

p,   pr,   br,   tr,   dr,   chr,   jr,   kr,   gr.

L Hook to Straight Strokes. 63. A small initial hook, written with the Left motion, adds *L* to straight strokes; thus,

p,   pl,   bl,   tl,   dl,   chl,   jl,   kl,   gl.

R Hook to Curved Strokes. 64. A *small* initial hook, written inside the curve, adds *r* to a curved stroke; thus,

f,   fr,   vr,   thr,   THr,   shr,   zhr,   mr,   nr.

L Hook to Curved Strokes. 65. A *large* initial hook, written inside the curve, adds *l* to a curved stroke; thus,

f,   fl,   vl,   thl,   shl,   ml,   nl.

66. The stroke ⟋ *r* is not hooked initially, because the characters ⟋ and ⟍ are employed for *w* and *y*.

SHR and SHL. 67. The double consonant ⟋ *shr* is always written *downward*, and the double consonant ⟍ *shl* is always written *upward*.

Small Hook to NG. 68. The hooked form ⟋ represents *ng-kr* or *ng-gr*, as heard in the words ba*nker*, fi*nger*.

69. The hooked forms should be called by their syllabic names; as, ⟍ *per*, ⟍ *pel*, ⟍ *fer*, ⟍ *fel*, etc.

Vowels and Double Consonants. 70. Vowels are placed and read to the hooked forms as they are placed and read to the simple forms; thus, ⟋ *pie*, ⟋ *ply*, ⟋ *apply*; ⟋ *lead*, ⟋ *leader*, ⟋ *leaderless*; ⟋ *pity*, ⟍ *pretty*; ⟍ *Peter*, ⟍ *Peterloo*; | *tie*, | *try*, ⟍ *trifle*, ⟍ *trifler*.

Extended Use of L Hook. 71. In order to obtain easier forms the *l* hook is sometimes used in words in which the *l* properly belongs to the following syllable, and not to the stroke to which it is attached; thus,

| *deeply*, ⟍ *briefly*, ⟍ *briefless*, ⟍ thinly, ⟍ *enlivener*, ⟍ *peevishly*.

Exercise 39

Read, copy, and transcribe

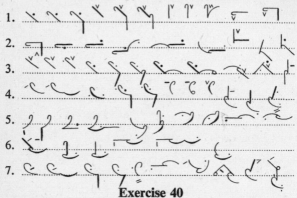

Exercise 40

Write in shorthand

1. Pry, pride, preach, preacher, bray, break, breaker.
2. Crow, croak, cricket, grew, group, grape, bigger.
3. Ply, plied, played, plum, place, replace, replaces.
4. Problem, enclose, enclosure, blow, blows, bluster.
5. Double, pedal, fiddle, model, fickle, glow, gloat.
6. Fred, afraid, tougher, other, otherwise, every, usher, pressure, inner.
7. Honour, honourable, flavour, flower, Fletcher, faithful, privilege, Marshall, specialize.

GRAMMALOGUES

principle, principal-ly;   liberty,   member, remember-ed,   number-ed;   truth;   Dr., doctor,   dear,   during;   chair,   cheer;   larger;   care.

Exercise 41

Read, copy, and transcribe

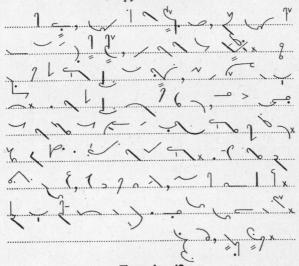

Exercise 42

Write in shorthand

Dear-Sir,

Thank-you for-yours *of-the* first *of* April, *and-for* mailing *me your* price-lists *and* samples *of* blue *and* black inks *and* glue *in-the several* sizes *of* bottles. I-*think-the* labels *are* better *and* brighter now. I-*shall give-the* samples *a* fair trial *during-the next* few weeks, *and*, if suitable, I-may-*be* able *to* stock *a large number of-the* smaller sizes. *As* I-*think-you* know, my *principal* business *is with* legal offices, *and*, *as you*-will agree, *it-is* essential *to* offer *them* only *first*-class inks.

Yours-truly,

Summary

1. A small initial hook written with the Right motion adds *r* to simple straight strokes except ⟋.
2. A small initial hook written with the Left motion adds *l* to simple straight strokes except ⟋.
3. The hooked signs should be called by their syllabic names.
4. A small initial hook to curves adds *r;* a large initial hook to curves adds *l.*
5. *Shr* is always written downward, and *shl* is always written upward.
6. *Ng* with a small initial hook represents the sounds of *ng-kr, ng-gr.*
7. Hooked forms may be considered as representing syllables.

CHAPTER XII

ALTERNATIVE FORMS

Additional Signs for FR, VR, etc. 72. The strokes
⌐ *r*, ⌐ *s*, are not hooked for the addition of *r* or *l*.
They are, however, hooked to provide alternative forms
for *fr, vr, fl, vl, thr,* THr; thus,

⌐	⌐	⌐	⌐	⌐	⌐
fr,	*vr,*	*thr,*	THr,	*fl,*	*vl.*

The first form of each pair is called a *left* curve,
because it is made with the Left motion; the second
form of each pair is called a *right* curve, because it is
made with the Right motion. There is only one form
for *thl* ⌐, namely, the left curve.

73. (*a*) When standing alone, the *left* curves for
fr, vr, thr, are used if a vowel precedes, and the *right*
curves if a vowel does not precede; thus, ⌐ *affray*,
⌐ *fray,* ⌐ *ether,* ⌐ *three*.

(*b*) When joined to another stroke, the form is used
which gives the easier joining, preference being given
to the right forms; thus, ⌐ *Friday,* ⌐ *virtue,* ⌐
frame, ⌐ *verbal,* ⌐ *thermal,* ⌐ *leather,* ⌐
coffer, ⌐ *lover.* Generally, it will be found that the
left curves join better with strokes written towards the
left, and the *right* curves with strokes written towards
the *right*.

FL and VL. 74. The right curves ⌐ *fl,* ⌐ *vl* are
used only after *straight upstrokes* and the *horizontals*
⌐ *k,* ⌐ *g,* ⌐ *n;* thus, ⌐ *cavil,* ⌐ *naval,*

53

~~~~ *rifle*, ~~~~ *weevil*. In all other cases the left curves

~~~~ *fl*, ~~~~ *vl* are used; thus, ~~~~ *flow*, ~~~~ *aflow*,

~~~~ *flake*, ~~~~ *flicker*, ~~~~ *joyful*, ~~~~ *arrival*.

Intervening Vowels. 75. (*a*) In order to obtain a briefer or an easier outline, an initially hooked form may be used even when a vowel separates *l* or *r* from the stroke consonant. Where necessary, an intervening dot vowel between a stroke and an initial hook may be indicated by writing a small circle, instead of a dot, either after or before the stroke; thus, ~~~~ *barley*, ~~~~ *challenge*, ~~~~ *narrate*, ~~~~ *sharply;* and an intervening dash vowel or diphthong may be indicated by striking the sign through the stroke consonant; thus, ~~~~ *Burma*, ~~~~ *coarsely*, ~~~~ *nullify*, ~~~~ *lecture*.

(*b*) If the vowel-sign cannot easily be written through the stroke, it may be placed at the beginning or the end for a first-place or a third-place vowel respectively; thus, ~~~~ *corner*, ~~~~ *tolerable*, ~~~~ *captures*.

(*c*) In words like ~~~~ *perceive*, ~~~~ *telegraphy*, ~~~~ *mercury*, ~~~~ *nervously*, the hooked form sufficiently represents the first syllable of the word. With the exception of ~~~~ *nurse*, ~~~~ *Turk*, ~~~~ *dark*, and a few other words, the initially hooked strokes are not used in monosyllables where the consonants are separated by a vowel. Such words as ~~~~ *pair*, ~~~~ *pale*, ~~~~ *tare*, ~~~~ *tore* are written with the separate strokes, so as to indicate the intervening vowel.

Exercise 43

Read, copy, and transcribe

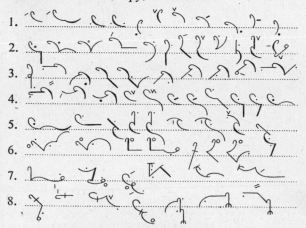

Exercise 44

Write in shorthand

1. Fray, three, Friday, frank, differ, endeavour.
2. Free, freely, thrifty, recover, waver, Waverley.
3. Flood, flask, flock, playful, grateful, effectively.
4. Baffle, trifle, shovel, removal, inflame.
5. Rival, roughly, hovel, cavalry, gravel.
6. Charming, courage, encourage, furnace, Norwich.

GRAMMALOGUES

people;   belief, believe-d;   tell,   till;

deliver-ed-y;   largely;   call,   equal-ly;

over,   however;   valuation.

Exercise 45

Read, copy, and transcribe

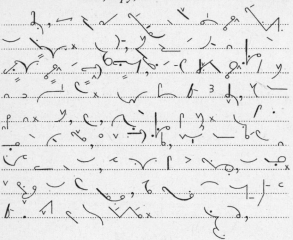

Exercise 46

Write in shorthand

Have-you ever noticed *what* useful lessons *you*-may-receive through *a* shrewd look at-*the* faces *of the people you come* across *in* travelling? *You*-will-see *in-them* humour *and* gloom; generosity *and* miserable stinginess; pluck *and* nervous fear; wisdom *and* simplicity. *You*-will-notice *the* drinker *and-the* abstainer; *the* hopeful *and-the* fearful; *the* clever talker *and-the* bore; *the* flighty *and-the* modest; *the* pilferer *and-the* honest fellow; *the* loafer *and-the* worker. Five minutes *in a* tramway car may offer us many lessons if-*we care to*-take *them*.

Summary

1. (a) When standing alone, the left curves ⌣ *fr*, ⌣ *vr*, (*thr*, (THr are used if a vowel precedes, and the right curves ⌐ *fr*, ⌐ *vr*,) *thr*,) THr, if a vowel does not precede.

   (b) When joined to another stroke either curve is used in order to secure an easier joining.

2. The right curves ⌐ *fl*, ⌐ *vl* are used after straight upstrokes, and after the horizontals ‾‾ *k*, ‾‾ *g*, and ⌣ *n;* in all other cases the left curves ⌣ *fl*, ⌣ *vl* are used.

3. (a) An intervening dot vowel between a stroke and an initial hook is shown by writing a small circle for the dot vowel, either after or before the stroke.

   (b) An intervening dash vowel, or a diphthong, is shown by intersecting the sign for the vowel or diphthong.

CHAPTER XIII

CIRCLE OR LOOP PRECEDING INITIAL HOOK

S before Straight Strokes Hooked for R. 76. Initial *s*, or *sw*, or *st*, preceding a straight stroke hooked for *r*, is expressed by writing the circle or loop on the same side as the *r* hook, that is, with the Right motion; thus, ⌐ *pry*, ⌐ *spry;* ⌐ *tray*, ⌐ *stray;* ⌐ *crew,* ⌐ *screw;* ⌐ *eater*, ⌐ *sweeter;* ⌐ *utter*, ⌐ *stutter;* ⌐ *ochre*, ⌐ *stoker.*

S before other Hooked Strokes. 77. In other cases *s* is written inside the initial hook, so that both circle and hook are clearly shown; thus, ⌐ *offer*, ⌐ *suffer,* ⌐ *sever*, ⌐ *deceiver*, ⌐ *soother*, ⌐ *sinner,* ⌐ *prisoner*, ⌐ *plies*, ⌐ *supplies*, ⌐ *possible,* ⌐ *pedestal*, ⌐ *settle*, ⌐ *satchel*, ⌐ *sickle*, ⌐ *bicycle,* ⌐ *exclaim*, ⌐ *evil*, ⌐ *civil*, ⌐ *prosper,* *offspring*, ⌐ *destroy*, ⌐ *extra*, ⌐ *mystery,* *nostrum*, ⌐ *lisper*, ⌐ *reciter*, ⌐ *wiseacre.*

(*a*) Where *l* hook cannot be clearly shown in the middle of a word, the stroke *l* is written; thus, ⌐ *forcible*, ⌐ *unsaddle*, ⌐ *musical.*

(*b*) When *skr* or *sgr* follows *t* or *d*, the circle is written with the Left motion; thus, ⌐ *tacker*, ⌐ *Tasker;* ⌐ *degree*, ⌐ *disagree;* ⌐ *digress,*

⌐⌐ *disgrace*. When *skr* occurs after *p* or *b*, the hook *r*
may be omitted; thus, ⟍⟋ *prescribe*, ⟍⟋ *subscriber*.

Exercise 47

Read, copy, and transcribe

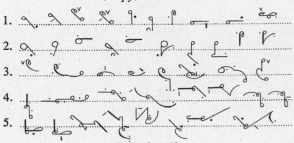

Exercise 48

Write in shorthand

1. Set, setter, settle, stab, stabber, sable, sweet, sweeter,
   sweetly, seek, seeker, sickle.
2. Supreme, sublime, cider, sidle, sacred, seclude.
3. Traceable, disclosure, plausible, classical, distressed,
   extremity, Tasker, task.
4. Suffers, simmers, sinners, peacefully, explosive,
   expels, risible, rasper.
5. Disgraces, discloses, prescribes, crossways.

GRAMMALOGUES

⟍⟍ *from;* ⟍ *very;*) *there, their;* ⌒ *more,*
remark-ed, ⌒ *mere, Mr.;* ⌣ *nor,* ⌣ *near;*
⟋ *surprise,* ⟍ *surprised;* ⟋ *sure;*) *pleasure.*

PHRASE

) *they are.*

Exercise 49

Read, copy, and transcribe

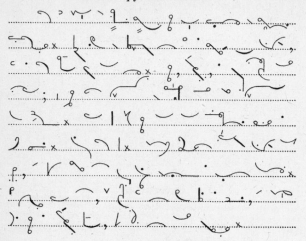

Exercise 50

Write in shorthand

We-are surprised to know *from-your* favour *of-the* sixth *of* August *of-the* extremely long delay *in-the delivery of-the* Surrey *and* Gloucestershire books. So far *as-we-can* discover, *there-is-*no *very* clear reason *for-the* delay. *We-have* looked *into-the* case, *as you-may-be-sure, and it-is* still *a* mystery. *Mr.* Strong, *our* dispatch clerk, expressly disclaims *any* blame, *but,* if-possible, he-will take *more care with-the* books still *to-come.* He-will personally supervise *the* addressing *of-the* parcels. *By-the* way, *we* hope *to-have-the* new Uxbridge book ready *very* soon. *It-will-be in-the* same style *as our* classical library.

Summary

1. The circles *s* and *sw* and the loop *st* are prefixed to the straight strokes hooked for *r* by writing the circle or loop with the Right motion.

2. The circle *s* is prefixed to all other initially hooked strokes by writing the circle inside the hook, so that both the circle and hook are clearly shown.

3. The circle in words like *tusker* and *disgrace* is written with the Left motion; but when *skr* follows *p* or *b*, the *r* is omitted.

CHAPTER XIV

N AND *F* HOOKS

N Hook. 78. A small final hook, struck by the Right motion ‿ adds *n* to all straight strokes; thus, 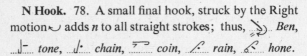 *Ben,* tone, chain, coin, rain, hone.

79. The hook which represents *r* at the beginning of a straight stroke, and that which represents *n* at the end, are both struck by the Right motion; thus, ☇ *brain,* train, crane.

80. A small final hook, written inside the curve, adds *n* to all curved strokes; thus, *fain, thin, assign, shine, moon, lean.*

F-V Hook. 81. A small final hook, struck by the Left motion ‿, adds *f* or *v* to all straight strokes; thus, *buff, tough, chafe, cave, rave, hive.*

82. The hook which represents *l* at the beginning of a straight stroke, and that which represents *f* or *v* at the end, are both struck by the Left motion; thus, *bluff, cliff, glove.*

83. There is no *f* or *v* hook to curves; therefore the stroke *f* or *v* must always be employed if *f* or *v* follows a curved stroke. The following pairs of words illustrate this: *fine, five; line, live; nine, knife; moon, move.*

84. A final hook cannot be employed when the word ends with a vowel sound, because a final vowel requires

a final stroke (par. 47). Compare ⟍ *pen* and ⟍⸴ *penny;* ⟍ *puff* and ⟍⸴ *puffy;* ⟍ *fun* and ⟍⸴ *funny;* ⟋⸴ *men* and ⟋⸴ *many.*

LN and SH N. 85. The hooked forms *ln* and *sh n* when joined to another stroke may be written upward or downward; thus, ⟋ *gallon,* ⟋ *melon;* ⟍ *fallen,* ⟍ *aniline;* ⸍ *situation,* ⟍⸴ *extenuation.*

Hooks used Medially. 86. The *n* and *f* hooks may be employed medially when they join easily and clearly with the following stroke; thus, ⟍ *plenty,* ⸍ *agent,* ⸍ *suddenness,* ⟍ *punish,* ⸍ *painful,* ⟍ *defence,* ⸍ *divide,* ⸍ *refer,* ⟋ *graphic.* If these outlines are compared with the following, it will be observed that a stroke is often used medially in preference to a hook in order to secure more facile outlines, or for purposes of distinction: ⟍ *brandy,* ⸍ *agency,* ⟍ *suddenly,* ⟍ *pronounce,* ⟍ *painless,* ⟋ *reviewer,* ⟍ *gravity.*

Syllable -NER. 87. The hook *n* and downward *r* are used for the representation of the final syllable *-ner* when following a straight upstroke; in all other cases, the syllable is represented by the sign ⟍ ; thus, ⟍ *opener,* ⟋ *joiner,* ⟍ *keener,* ⟍ *liner;* but ⟍ *runner,* ⟍ *winner,* ⟍ *yawner.*

N and F Hooks in Phraseography. 88. The *n* hook is sometimes used in phraseography for the words *been, than, on,* and *own,* and the *f-v* hook for the words *have* and *of;* thus, ⟋ *I have been,* ⟋ *I had been,* ⟋ *better than,* ⟋ *carried on,* ⟋ *their own,* ⟋ *our own,* ⟋ *which have,* ⟋ *out of.*

Exercise 51

Read, copy, and transcribe

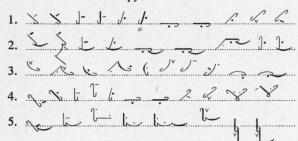

Exercise 52

Write in shorthand

1. Open, opening, tune, tuning, dine, dining, strain.
2. Begin, beginning, run, runner, win, winner, join.
3. Fan, fancy, fin, finish, vain, vanish, mean, meanness, noun, renown.
4. Pave, paving, prove, provide, provoke, chaff, chaffinch, refer, referring, preserve.
5. Pen, penny, deaf, defy, fun, funny, men, many.

GRAMMALOGUES

⟍ *been;* ⟋ *general-ly;* ⟨ *within;* ⟨ *southern;* ⟋ *northern;* ⟍ *behalf;* ⟨ *advantage,* ⟋ *difficult.*

Exercise 53

Read, copy, and transcribe

Exercise 54

Write in shorthand

Local authorities, *as* borough *and* urban councils, *generally* derive *their* main revenue *from-the* rates they levy. They-may, *of-*course, receive profits *from any* business carried-*on* by-*them within-the* borough. *Over and* above *all-this* they receive allowances *from-the* state. Either men or women may appeal *to-the* authorities, *and-*they *very* often *do*, if-they *think* they-*have-been* unfairly assessed. *But it-*will-*be difficult for-them to* obtain relief unless they-*are* able *to-*prove *their* case, *and* satisfy-*the* authorities *as to a* supposed *over*charge.

Summary

1. A small final hook struck by the Right motion adds *n* to straight strokes.
2. A small final hook struck by the Left motion adds *f* or *v* to straight strokes.
3. A small final hook adds *n* to curves.
4. There is no *f* or *v* hook to curves.
5. When a word ends with a vowel a final stroke must be used.
6. When joined to other strokes, *ln* and *sh n* may be written either upward or downward.
7. Hooks *n, f* or *v* may be used medially where an easy and legible joining is secured.
8. The final syllable *-ner* is represented by ╲⌣╱ when following any stroke except the straight upstrokes.
9. In phraseography, the *n* hook is sometimes used to represent the words *been, than, on,* and *own,* and the *f-v* hook for the words *have* and *of.*

CHAPTER XV

CIRCLES AND LOOPS TO FINAL HOOKS

Straight Strokes followed by NS, etc. 89. The sound of *s* or *ses*, *st* or *str* is added to the hook *n* attached to a straight stroke by writing the circle or loop on the same side as the hook, that is, with the Right motion, as

⨍ *Dan*, ⨍ *dance*, ⨍ *dances*, ⨍ *danced*, ⨍ *Dunster;*

⟍ *pen*, ⟍ *pens*, ⟍ *expense*, ⟍ *expenses;*

⟍ *spin*, ⟍ *spins*, ⟍ *spinster*, ⟍ *spinsters;*

⟋ *glen*, ⟋ *glens*, ⟋ *glances*, ⟋ *glanced;*

⫫ *dispense*, ⫫ *dispenses*, ⫫ *dispensed.*

Curves followed by NS, etc. 90. (*a*) The small circle (representing the sound of *z*) is added to the hook *n* attached to curves by writing the circle inside the hook; thus, ⟍ *fine*, ⟍ *fines;* ⟍ *vines*, ⟍ *frowns*, ⟍ *thrones*, ⟍ *shines*, ⟍ *balloons*, ⟍ *earns*, ⟍ *zones*, ⟍ *mines*, ⟍ *nines*, ⟍ *lawns*. The effect of the preceding rule is that the hook *n* and the small circle attached to a curve represent in all cases the *heavy* sound of *nz*, as in the words *fens* (nz), *vans* (nz), *Athens* (nz), *zones* (nz), *shines* (nz), *shrines* (nz), *moans* (nz), *nouns* (nz), *loans* (nz), *earns* (nz).

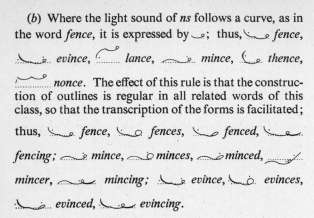

(b) Where the light sound of *ns* follows a curve, as in the word *fence*, it is expressed by ⌣; thus, ⌣ *fence*, ⌣ *evince*, ⌣ *lance*, ⌣ *mince*, ⌣ *thence*, ⌣ *nonce*. The effect of this rule is that the construction of outlines is regular in all related words of this class, so that the transcription of the forms is facilitated; thus, ⌣ *fence*, ⌣ *fences*, ⌣ *fenced*, ⌣ *fencing*; ⌣ *mince*, ⌣ *minces*, ⌣ *minced*, ⌣ *mincer*, ⌣ *mincing*; ⌣ *evince*, ⌣ *evinces*, ⌣ *evinced*, ⌣ *evincing*.

Circle S added to F-V Hooks. 91. The circle *s* is added to the hook *f* or *v* by writing the circle inside the hook; thus, ⌣ *puff*, ⌣ *puffs*, ⌣ *caves*, ⌣ *waves*, ⌣ *heaves*, ⌣ *operatives*, ⌣ *observes*, ⌣ *archives*, ⌣ *sheriffs*.

Medial NS or NZ. 92. When *ns* or *nz* occur medially both letters must be shown, as in the words ⌣ *pensive*, ⌣ *density*, ⌣ *chancel*, ⌣ *Johnson*, ⌣ *cancer*, ⌣ *cleanser*, ⌣ *fencer*, ⌣ *immensity*, ⌣ *rancid*, ⌣ *ransack*, ⌣ *wincer*, ⌣ *lonesome*, ⌣ *ransom*, ⌣ *winsome*, ⌣ *hansom*.

Exercise 55

Read, copy, and transcribe

1.
2.
3.
4.
5.
6.

Exercise 56

Write in shorthand

1. Pence, expense, sixpence, sixpences, dispense, dispenses, dispensed.
2. Button, buttons, train, trains, entrance, entrances, entranced, disappearance, disappearances.
3. Shun, shuns, ocean, oceans, mean, means, linen, linens, saloon, saloons.
4. Reprieve, reprieves, native, natives, chief, chiefs, observe, observes.
5. Fence, offence, offences, immense, immensity, allowance, allowances, prominence.

GRAMMALOGUES

balance;   circumstance;   deliverance;

signify-ied-icant;   significance;   opinion.

Exercise 57

Read, copy, and transcribe

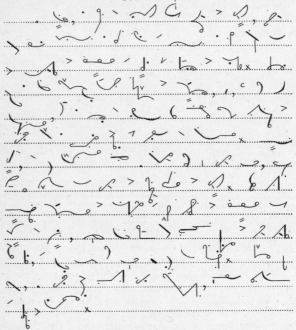

Exercise 58

Write in shorthand

If I annoy *you in-the deliverance of*-my *opinion*, *as-the* chances *are* I-may, *put it* down *to a* reading man's reverence *for* books, *and-his* diligence *in-the* pursuit *of a* course *which* lightens many *an hour for-him*. *Think of*-these *significant* facts, *and your* frowns may vanish. If-*you have a* love *of* books, *you*-will feel no

loneliness if *and when* men forget *you*.   *You-can* dispense
with-them in-the circumstances; for you-will-*have within
your*self,   through-*the*   brains   *of-your*   authors,   many
better men *to*-replace *them.   The balance of advantage
in-the* change *is* likely *to be in-your* favour.   *You*-will
grasp-*the significance of-this remark*, I-am-*sure; for-the*
man *who* derives *pleasure from* reading books makes
for-himself reserves *of* strength *to-call*-upon against *the*
time *of*-trouble or stress.

Summary

1. The sound of *s* or *ses*, *st* or *str* is added to hook *n*
   attached to straight strokes by writing the circle
   or loop on the same side as the hook.
2. Circle *s* is added to straight strokes hooked for
   f or *v*, and to curves hooked for *n*, by writing the
   circle inside the hook.
3. The light sound of *ns* after a curve is expressed by
   the sign ⸗ *ns*.
4. The heavy sound of *nz* after a curve is expressed by
   the circle *s* written inside the hook *n*.
5. When *ns* or *nz* occur medially both letters must be
   shown.

CHAPTER XVI

THE *SHUN* HOOK

The Termination -SHUN. 93. The termination *shun* or *zhun*, variously spelt *-tion*, *-sion*, *-cian*, *-tian*, *-sian*, etc., is represented by a large hook, to which circle *s* may be added as required, as, ⤴ *notion*, ⤴ *notions*, ⤴ *caution*, ⤴ *cautions*.

94. The *shun* hook is written inside curves; thus, ⤴ *fashion*, ⤴ *fashions*, ⤴ *motion*, ⤴ *nation*, ⤴ *nations*.

95. (*a*) When added to a straight stroke with an initial attachment (circle, loop, or hook) the hook is written on the side *opposite* to the initial attachment, in order to preserve the straightness of the stroke; thus, ⤴ *citation*, ⤴ *sections*, ⤴ *oppression*, ⤴ *Grecian*.

(*b*) The *shun* hook is written with the Right motion after the form ⤵, light or heavy, and with the Left motion after the forms ⤴ ⤴, in order that the *k* or *g* may be kept straight; thus, ⤴ *affection*, ⤴ *vacation*, ⤴ *selection*, ⤴ *selections;* and

96. (*a*) On the side opposite to the last vowel when following a straight stroke *without* an initial attachment, in order to indicate where the last vowel occurs; thus, ⤴ *passion*, ⤴ *option*, ⤴ *action*, ⤴ *cautions*, ⤴ *occasion;* but

(b) On the right side of ⎸ *t*, ⎸ *d*, ╱ *j*, because it is known that the last vowel always occurs after these letters, and there is no need to indicate the fact, and also because the writing of the hook on the right-hand side of these letters carries the hand forward in readiness for the next word; thus, ⟋ *rotation*, ⟍ *notation*, ⟍ *gradation*, ⟋ *logicians*.

Exercise 59

Read, copy, and transcribe

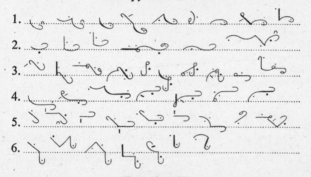

Exercise 60

Write in shorthand

1. Erasion, invasions, division, elevation, mansion.
2. Solution, desolation, relations, stipulations.
3. Exception, impression, celebration, recitation, discussion, exclusion.
4. Specification, infection, navigation, relegation.
5. Occupation, Russian, occasion, education, obligation, lubrication.
6. Deputation, adaptation, imitation, presentation.

Shun following Circles S and NS. 97. When *shun* follows the circle *s* or circle *ns*, it is expressed by a small hook written on the opposite side to the circle and with the same motion; thus ⟨shorthand⟩ *decision*, ⟨shorthand⟩ *dispensation*.

(*a*) A third-place vowel between the circle and the *shun* hook is expressed by the vowel-sign being written outside the hook; thus, ⟨shorthand⟩ *position*, ⟨shorthand⟩ *physician*, ⟨shorthand⟩ *transition*. The circle *s* may be added thus, ⟨shorthand⟩ *positions*, ⟨shorthand⟩ *transitions*.

(*b*) When a second-place vowel is to be read between the circle and *shun* it need not be indicated; thus, ⟨shorthand⟩ *possession*, ⟨shorthand⟩ *accession*, ⟨shorthand⟩ *sensation*. First-place vowels do not occur between the circle and *shun*.

Shun Hook Medially. 98. The *shun* hook may be used medially; thus, ⟨shorthand⟩ *additional*, ⟨shorthand⟩ *actionable*, ⟨shorthand⟩ *devotional*, ⟨shorthand⟩ *positional*, ⟨shorthand⟩ *transitional*.

Words ending in -uation and -uition. 99. When a diphthong and a vowel occur immediately before *shun*, the stroke *sh* and the hook *n* must be written thus, ⟨shorthand⟩ *extenuation*, but ⟨shorthand⟩ *extension;* ⟨shorthand⟩ *intuition*, but ⟨shorthand⟩ *notation*. This does not apply to such words as ⟨shorthand⟩ *accentuation*, ⟨shorthand⟩ *perpetuation*, where, in order to avoid a lengthy outline, the large hook is used.

Exercise 61

Read, copy, and transcribe

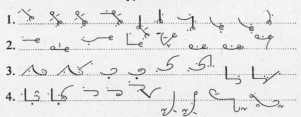

Exercise 62

Write in shorthand

1. Proposition, propositions, precision, procession, processions.
2. Disposition, indisposition, accusation, accusations, vexation.
3. Mission, missions, missionary, commission, commissions, commissionaire, exception, exceptional.
4. Discretion, discretionary, affection, affectionate.

GRAMMALOGUES

ꕷ *subjective,* ꕷ *subjection;* ꕴ *signification;*
ꕴ *information;* ꕷ *satisfaction,* ꕷ *justification,*
ꕷ *generalization.*

Exercise 63

Read, copy, and transcribe

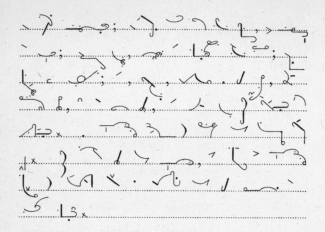

Exercise 64

Write in shorthand

Lord Macaulay *was* blessed *with-the* possession *of* rare powers *of*-memory. *His* accumulation *of* facts *was* immense. He-*was almost in a* state *of subjection to-his* memory, *and a subjective* examination *of-the information in-his* possession at *any*-time *would have-been a* revelation even *to-himself*. *The* retention *and* repetition *of* figures, *the* manipulation *of* facts *in* discussion, *the* selection *and* citation *of* authorities caused *him* no hesitation. He-*was to-have-been a* barrister, *but-the* legal profession *had* no fascination *for-him*. Macaulay took *a* share *in-the* promotion *of* education, *but-his* reputation rests mainly *on-his* famous essays. *His* criticisms brought *him in*to opposition *with several* fashionable authors, *and-his* expositions occasionally produced bitterness *in* opposite factions.

Summary

The hook -*shun* is written—

To curves	Inside the curve.
To straight strokes with initial attachment	On the side opposite to the initial attachment.
To *k* and *g* following the curves ‿ ⌒ ‿ (up)	With the Left or Right motion as required to keep the *k* or *g* straight.
To straight strokes other than *t*, *d* or *j* without initial attachment	On the side opposite to the last vowel.
To *t*, *d* and *j* without initial attachment	On the right side.
Following the circles *s* or *ns*	On the side opposite to the circle.
Finally	In *punctuation* and a few similarly long words.
Medially	Like the other hooks.

CHAPTER XVII

THE ASPIRATE

Upward H. 100. The upward form of *h* is employed in the great majority of cases, because it joins more readily with other strokes and abbreviations; as,

⟋⟍ hope, ⟋⟋ head, ⟋⟍ hatch, ⟋⟋ hedge, ⟋⟍ hush,
⟋⟍ honey, ⟋⟍ hung, ⟋ hero, ⟋⟍ hearth, ⟋⟍ hose,
⟋⟍ husk, ⟋ hisses, ⟋ haste, ⟋⟍ hove, ⟋⟍ hen,
⟋⟍ Henry, ⟋⟍ hackle, ⟋⟍ hawker, ⟋⟍ hammer,
⟋⟍ upheave, ⟍⟋ behead, ⟍⟋ adhesive, ⟋⟍ Jehovah,
⟋⟍ overhaul, ⟋⟍ enhance, ⟋⟍ rehearse.

Downward H. 101. The downward form of *h* is used

(*a*) When standing alone, as in ⟋ hay, ⟋ high, and in compounds and derivatives like ⟋ haystack, ⟋ higher, ⟋ highly;

(*b*) When *h* is followed by ⸻ *k* or ⸻ *g; as,* ⟋ hawk, ⟋ hog;

(*c*) When *h* follows upward *l* or a horizontal stroke; as, ⟋ Lahore, ⟋ coherence, ⟋ mahogany, ⟋ unhook.

Following S, etc. 102. (*a*) In a few words like ⟋ Soho and ⟋ Sheehy, the circle of *h* is written inside the curve; and in such words as ⟋ Fitzhugh, and ⟋ racehorse, where *s* and *h* occur medially, the circle is enlarged for the representation of *s*.

(b) When *h* follows another stroke, it must be written so that it cannot be misread for *s ch* or *sr;* thus, ⁀⁀ *cohere*, but ⁀⁀ *exchequer;* ⁀⁀ *abhor*, but ⁀⁀ *observer*.

Tick H. 103 (a) When preceding strokes ⁀⁀ *m*, ⁀⁀ *l*, ⁀⁀ *r*, initial *h* is represented by a short tick, written in the direction of downward *h;* thus, ⁀⁀ *home*, ⁀⁀ *healthy*, ⁀⁀ *harm*.

(b) The tick *h* may be employed medially in phrasing, but not in words; thus, ⁀⁀ *for whom*, ⁀⁀ *of her*, ⁀⁀ *to her;* but ⁀⁀ *inhuman*, ⁀⁀ *overhaul*.

Dot H. 104. Where a stroke form of *h* is not convenient in the middle of a word, *h* is represented by placing a light dot before the vowel which is to be aspirated; thus, ⁀⁀ *apprehensive*, ⁀⁀ *perhaps*, ⁀⁀ *vehicle*, ⁀⁀ *hogshead*, ⁀⁀ *uphill*, ⁀⁀ *downhill*, ⁀⁀ *manhood*.

Exercise 65

Read, copy, and transcribe

1.
2.
3.
4.
5.

Exercise 66

Write in shorthand

1. Head, hitch, huge, hyphen, hurry, hurries.
2. Host, hone, heave, hovel, haggle, hence, hover, boyhood, prohibition, cohesive.
3. Hack, hackney, hawk, Hawkins, hoax, cohere, high, higher.
4. Home, hall, hallow, hire, neighbourhood, freehold.

PHRASES

Dear Sir, *yours truly,* *every circumstance,*
all circumstances, *you will remember,*
I believe, *I will tell you,* *I am surprised.*

Exercise 67

Read, copy, and transcribe

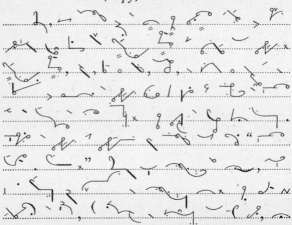

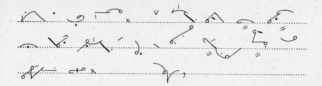

Exercise 68

Write in shorthand

Dear-Sir,—*The* heavy mahogany table *for-your* new home, "Hillside," Woodhouse Lane, *is* ready *for delivery* at *any*-time *when-we* hear *from-you*. *We* hope *to-have-the* hangings fixed *tomorrow*, *and-the* curtains hung by Wednesday *next*. *The* new hammocks *and* hassocks *are almost* ready, *and*-they-will-*be delivered next* week. *Our* van may-*be in-your* neighbourhood *on*-Monday, *in-which-case you shall-have-the* hall *chairs and-the* whole *of-the* small household *things* then. *But for a* mishap at *our* Harley Works, *you would-have had-the* hair cushions *for-the* settee before *this*. *We* hope, *however*, *to*-receive *them on*-Friday, *and to-deliver them with-the* other *things on*-Monday. *Yours*-truly,

Summary

1. The upward form of *h* is most commonly used.
2. The downward form is written when *h* is the only stroke in the word and in compounds and derivatives like *hayrick, high-flown;* also before *k* or *g*.
3. The tick *h* is written initially to ⌒⌒. The word HoMeLieR forms a useful mnemonic.
4. The dot *h* is used as an alternative to the stroke in the middle of a word.

CHAPTER XVIII

UPWARD AND DOWNWARD *R*

In order to present a complete statement of the rules for the writing of the alternative forms of *r*, the directions given to the student in par. 27 are repeated here.

Vowel preceding R. 105. When initial *r* is preceded by a vowel, the downward form is used; thus, ⌐ *air*, ⌐ *airy*, ⌐ *erase*, ⌐ *ire*, ⌐ *Irish*, ⌐ *orb*.

Vowel following R. 106. In other cases, the general rule is to write initial or final *r* upward when it is followed by a vowel, and downward when it is not followed by a vowel; thus, ⌐ *rob*, ⌐ *borrow*; ⌐ *rainy*, ⌐ *narrow*; ⌐ *carry*, ⌐ *car*; ⌐ *furrow*, ⌐ *fur*; ⌐ *sorry*, ⌐ *soar*; ⌐ *story*, ⌐ *store*; ⌐ *wary*, ⌐ *ware*; ⌐ *siren*, ⌐ *stern*.

107. Initial *r* followed by *m* is always written downward, because of the easier outline thus obtained; as, ⌐ *roam*, ⌐ *ram*.

108. Facility of outline is of the utmost importance, however, and accordingly either form of *r* is written, and vowel indication ignored, in order to secure a facile form. The upward form is written, therefore, in ⌐ *irate*, ⌐ *arch*, ⌐ *urge*, ⌐ *earth*, ⌐ *oracle*, and similar words where *r* is immediately followed by ⌐ *t*, ⌐ *d*, ⌐ *ch*, ⌐ *j*, ⌐ *th* or ⌐ *kl*, ⌐ *gl*, ⌐ *w*.

109. Generally, the upward form is preferable after two downstrokes; as, ⌐ *prepare*, ⌐ *trampler*,

Shakespeare, because the hand is thereby carried back to the line of writing. But the downward form is better in *pinafore*, *shuffler*, *persevere*, etc., because of the easier joining with the preceding *f* or *v*.

110. After a single straight upstroke, the upward form is easier, because it avoids an angle; thus, *roar*, *aware*, *yore;* but the suffix *-er* must be written with downward *r* in *roarer*, *rarer*, because a treble-length straight upstroke would not be easily readable.

111. The upward form is obviously better in *officer*, *nicer*, *closer*, *razor*, where *r* immediately follows a curve and circle like or , or a straight horizontal or upstroke circled for *s*.

R Finally Hooked. 112. When *r* follows another stroke and is hooked finally, it is generally written upward; thus, *spurn*, *fern*, *portion*.

Medial R. 113. Medial *r* is generally written upward; as in *park*, *parsnip*, *terrify*, *mark*, *roared;* but the downward form is retained in some derivative words, as, *powerful*, *barely*, *disarrange;* and the use of the alternative forms provides a distinction in pairs of words such as *clerk*, *cleric*.

Exercise 69

Read, copy, and transcribe

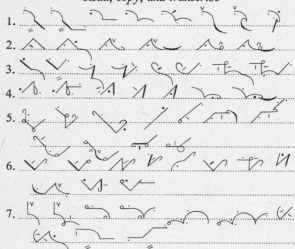

Exercise 70

Write in shorthand

1. Ear, era, erase, argue, oral, Eric, early.
2. Retire, retrace, review, reviewing, rose, roses, rank.
3. Paris, diary, gallery, victory, assurance, memory.
4. Answer, censor, cruiser, origin, turn, Lucerne.
5. Perth, veracity, parade, terrible, forty, firm.

PHRASES AND CONTRACTIONS

by all,   by all means;   at all,   at all costs;   in our,   in our opinion;   everything,   something;   anything,   nothing.

Exercise 71

Read, copy, and transcribe

Exercise 72

Write in shorthand

The food eaten by man bears *something* like-*the* same
relation *to-his* power *of* working *as-the* coal thrown
into-the furnace bears *to-the* engine *which* drives *the*
rotary press, or draws *the* train. *The* power *in-our* arms
or *in-our* brains *is* rightly said *to be* produced *in-our*
stomach, *and it-is from-the* same organ *we* derive *the*

force necessary *to*-rouse us *to* severe exertion *in-the* earning *of-the* wage or salary *we* receive *for our* services. *Something of-the* value *of-our* work rests upon-*the* strength producing value *of-our* food. At-*all*-costs, *and* by-*all*-means, *we should* take measures *to* ensure-*the* food value *of everything we* eat.

Summary

Initial *r*	Written downward when preceded by a vowel, and initially before *m;* as ..... erase, ... room.
Initial or Final *r*	Written upward when followed by a vowel, and downward when not followed by a vowel, as ..... race, ... parry, ... air, ... par.
Medial *r*	Generally written upward; but downward in some derivatives.
When hooked and following another stroke	Generally written upward; as, ... burn, ... mourn.
For an easier outline	Written either upward or downward irrespective of vowels; as, ... earth, ... answer, ... deplore, ... debar.

CHAPTER XIX

UPWARD AND DOWNWARD *L* AND *SH*

Upward L. 114. The stroke *l*, whether initial or final, is most commonly written upward; as in ⌢ *lapse*, ⌣ *spell*, ⌐ *load*, ⌐ *delay*, ⌐ *allege*, ⌐ *jelly*, ⌐ *lake*, ⌐ *coal*, ⌐ *loaf*, ⌐ *fellow*, ⌐ *loathe*, ⌐ *Othello*, ⌐ *Lacey*, ⌐ *assail*, ⌐ *sale*, ⌐ *stale*, ⌐ *leisure*, ⌐ *shallow*.

L preceding or following Curve and Circle. 115. When *l* immediately precedes or follows a circle which is attached to a curve, it is written in the same direction as the circle; thus, ⌐ *lesson*, ⌐ *nasal*, ⌐ *elusive*, ⌐ *vessel*, ⌐ *losing*, ⌐ *Kingsley*, ⌐ *lissom*.

L after N and NG. 116. After the strokes ⌐ *n* and ⌐ *ng*, final *l* is written downward so as to avoid a change of motion; as in ⌐ *only*, ⌐ *wrongly*, ⌐ *manly;* and the downward form is retained in derivatives; as, ⌐ *manliness*, ⌐ *enlisting*.

L and Vowel Indication. 117. For the purpose of vowel indication, initial *l* is written downward when preceded by a vowel and followed immediately by a horizontal, not hooked or circled initially; thus, ⌐ *alike* but ⌐ *like;* ⌐ *alone* but ⌐ *loan;* ⌐ *along* but ⌐ *long;* ⌐ *elm* but ⌐ *lame*.

118. Also for the purpose of vowel indication, final
l is written downward after ⌣ *f*, ⌣ *v*, ⌒ *sk*, or a
straight upstroke when no vowel follows, and upward
when followed by a vowel; thus, ⌐ *fall* but ⌣⌐
follow; ⌐ *vale* but ⌣ *valley;* ⌐ *scale* but
⌒ *scaly;* ⌐ *rule* but ⌐ *ruly.*

Medial L. 119. Medial *l* is generally written upward; but either form is used for an easier joining;
thus, ⌐ *unload* but ⌐ *unlock;* ⌐ *vulgar* but
⌐ *overlook;* ⌐ *facility* but ⌐ *film.*

Upward and Downward Sh. 120. (*a*) The curve
⌐ *sh*, joined to another curve, generally follows the
motion of that curve; thus, ⌣ *fish,* ⌐ *smash,*
⌐ *lash;* but it is written *downward* after the curve
⌐ *n;* thus, ⌐ *gnash.* When joined to a straight
stroke, *sh* is generally written downward; thus, ⌐
push, ⌐ *cherish,* ⌐ *shake,* ⌐ *sherry;* but it is
written *upward* after the heavy stroke ⌐ *d*, as in
⌐ *dash.*
(*b*) After a straight downstroke with an initial
attachment, *sh* is generally written on the opposite
side to such attachment; thus, ⌐ *spacious,* ⌐ *blush,*
⌐ *brush.* In other cases the form is used which
gives the easier joining; as in ⌐ *sugar,* ⌐ *shackle,*
⌐ *chauffeur,* ⌐ *shovel.*

Exercise 73

Read, copy, and transcribe

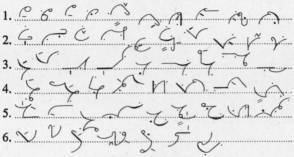

Exercise 74

Write in shorthand

1. Lie, lies, sly, slice, slices, steel, stolen, swallow.
2. Alps, Alaska, loth, loafer, lore, locker, latch.
3. Alack, lack, allocation, location, license, Allison.
4. Bale, billow, towel, Filey, veal, villa, dwell.
5. Canals, denial, frowningly, vessel, profusely.
6. Unlucky, lucky, pulling, spelling, sculling.
7. Plush, splash, crush, atrocious, waspish.

PHRASES

as is; is as; this is; last year; at first; just now.

Exercise 75

Read, copy, and transcribe

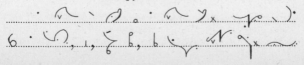

Exercise 76

Write in shorthand

Dear-Sir,

  The volumes *of-the* French Revolution *for-which-you* ask *in-your* favour *of-the first* July *shall-be delivered to-you* early tomorrow. *We-are* just-now out-*of* stock *of-the* "Life *of Lord* Lumley," last-*year's* best seller, *and we-are* unable *to* say *when-we-shall* receive copies. *We-have a* daily *delivery from-the* wholesalers, *however, and you*-may-rely upon *our* mailing-*the* volume *to-you* as-soon-*as* it reaches us. *We-are* taking-*the liberty of* enclosing *for-your* approval "Naval Lessons *of-the* War," by Philip Bailey. Please return *this with-the next* parcel if-*it* makes no appeal *to-you. Yours*-truly,

Summary

1. The upward form of *l* is most commonly written.
2. When immediately preceding or following a circle which is attached to a curve, *l* follows the direction of the circle.
3. Final *l* is written downward after *n* and *ng*, and derivatives of words similar to *manly*.
4. When preceded by a vowel and followed immediately by a horizontal, initial *l* is written downward.
5. After ⌣ *f*, ⌣ *v*, ⌣ *sk*, or a straight upstroke, final *l* is written upward when followed by a vowel, and downward when not followed by a vowel.
6. Medial *l* is generally written upward.
7. Stroke *sh*, following a straight downstroke having an initial attachment, is written opposite to the initial attachment. In other cases the form is used which gives the better joining.

CHAPTER XX

COMPOUND CONSONANTS

Initial W. 121. A *large* initial hook adds *w* to ‿‿ *k* and ‿‿ *g;* thus, ‿‿ *keen,* ‿‿ *queen,* ‿‿ *Gwynn.*

Initial W and WH. 122. A *small* initial hook to *l* represents *w*, and a *large* initial hook to *l* represents *wh;* thus, ‿‿ *ell,* ‿‿ *well,* ‿‿ *whale.*

Strokes L and R Thickened. 123. Downward *l* is thickened for the addition of *r* preceded by any lightly sounded vowel, and downward *r* is thickened for the addition of *-er* only; thus, ‿‿ *vale,* ‿‿ *valour;* ‿‿ *hire,* ‿‿ *hirer.*

Addition of P or B to M. 124. The curve ‿‿ *m* is thickened for the addition of *p* or *b;* thus, ‿‿ *hem,* ‿‿ *hemp,* ‿‿ *moss,* ‿‿ *emboss.*

Aspirated W. 125. The aspirate is added to ‿‿ *w* by enlarging the hook; thus, ‿‿ *weasel,* ‿‿ *whistle,* ‿‿ *aware,* ‿‿ *where.*

Vowel preceding W. 126. The initial hooks in *wl* and *whl* are read *first.* Therefore, if a vowel precedes *w*, the stroke form of *w* or *wh* must be written, and not the hook; thus, ‿‿ *while,* ‿‿ *awhile.*

Stroke L after KW. 127. After ‿‿ *kw*, *l* is written upward when followed by a vowel, and downward when not followed by a vowel; thus, ‿‿ *squally,* ‿‿ *squall.*

Use of LR and RR Signs. 128. The form of *l* or *r* which is used in the root word is retained in the derivative; thus, ⌣ *boil*, ⌣⌣ *boiler*, ⌿ *mill*, ⌿⌿ *miller*; ⌣ *full*, ⌣ *fuller*; ⌣ *snare*, ⌣ *snarer*. The use of ⌣ *rer* is strictly confined to derivatives of words written with downward *r*.

Vowel after Final R. 129. The thickened forms ⌒ *lr*, ⌒ *rr* must not be written finally if a vowel follows *r*; compare ⌣ *fuller* with ⌿ *foolery*; ⌡ *valour* with ⌣⌣ *valorous*.

Hooked Form of MP. 130. An initial or final hook may be attached to the sign ⌒; as in ⌒ *scamper*, ⌒ *hempen*, ⌒ *ambition*. The sign ⌒ is not used when *pr*, *br*, *pl* or *bl* immediately follows *m*. Compare ⌒ *empress* with ⌒ *emperor*; ⌒ *embrace* with ⌒ *embower*; ⌒ *imply* with ⌿ *impel*; ⌒ *emblem* with ⌒ *embolden*.

Exercise 77

Read, copy, and transcribe

1.
2.
3.
4.
5.

Exercise 78

Write in shorthand

1. Quake, earthquake, square, liquid, liquidation, require, Maguire.
2. Wall, wallflower, welfare, will, willing, unwilling, while, awhile, jump, romp.
3. Fairer, scorer, scaler, nowhere, whisper, whimper.
4. Imprison, umbrella, taller, similar, failure.

GRAMMALOGUES

⌐ whether; ⌒ impossible; ⌒ important-ance,

⌒ improve-d-ment.

Exercise 79

Read, copy, and transcribe

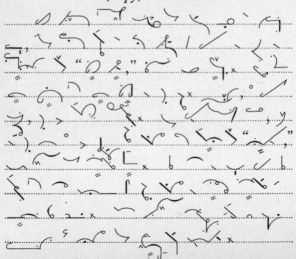

Exercise 80

Write in shorthand

I-*have*-no *wish to* impose my views upon-*the* ambassador, or *to* embarrass *him* by asking *for impossible improvements; but it-is important* I *should* impress upon *him the* chancellor's *opinion in-the* case *of-those* lumber vessels. *You*-will-see *how* imperative *it-is* I *should* see-*the* ambassador, if-*we-are to-have any improvement in-our* relations just-now. I-desire *to* discover *whether-the* whaler's story *is* true, or-*the* idle tale *of a* wilful impostor. I-*shall* occupy only *a* quarter *of an hour, and*-I-am-*sure the* ambassador will agree *the importance of-the* case *is* well worth-*the* time.

Summary

1. Table of compound consonants—

Character	Name	Letters	As in
⌒	kwā	QU	quick, request
⌒	gwā	GU	guava, lingual
⌒ (up)	wel	WL	wail, unwell
⌒ (up)	hwel	WHL	whale, meanwhile
⌒ (down)	ler	LR	feeler, scholarly
⌒ (down)	rer	RR	poorer, sharer
⌒	(emp) (emb)	MP, MB	camp, embalm
⌒	hwā	WH	where, everywhere

2. After ⌒ *kw* stroke *l* is written upward when
   followed by a vowel, and downward when not
   followed by a vowel.
3. The initial hooks to *l* are always read first.
4. When the downward forms of *l* or *r* are written in
   root words, the thickened forms ⌒ *lr*, ⌒ *rr* are
   written in the derived words.
5. The thickened forms ⌒ *lr*, ⌒ *rr* must not be used
   when a vowel follows *r*.
6. The sign ⌒ is not used when *m* is immediately
   followed by *pr*, *br*, *pl* or *bl*.

CHAPTER XXI

VOWEL INDICATION

Vowels Implied. 131. A careful reading of the rules governing the use of the circles, loops, and hooks will have led the student to realize (*a*) that when a word begins or ends with a consonant, that consonant is to be written with the briefest form; as, ⟨shorthand⟩ *soup*, ⟨shorthand⟩ *place*, ⟨shorthand⟩ *spinsters*, ⟨shorthand⟩ *dances*, ⟨shorthand⟩ *craves*, unless there is a rule to the contrary, as in the words ⟨shorthand⟩ *Siam* and ⟨shorthand⟩ *joyous;* and (*b*) that when a word begins or ends with a vowel sound, the first or last consonant, as the case may be, must be represented by a stroke in order to accommodate the vowel-sign.

It will be seen from the foregoing that in very many words an initial or a final vowel may be *implied* by the outline of the word, without the use of the vowel-sign. The following illustrations will serve as additional examples of the implication of initial or final vowels.

INITIAL VOWEL IMPLIED

asleep,	*assume,*	*arising,*	*arrives,*	*along.*
alike,	*aware,*	*awake,*	*awhile,*	*awoke.*

INITIAL CONSONANT IMPLIED

sleep,	*sum,*	*rising,*	*raves,*	*long.*
like,	*wear,*	*wake,*	*while,*	*woke.*

FINAL VOWEL IMPLIED

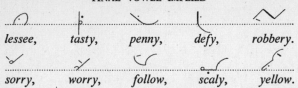

lessee,   tasty,   penny,   defy,   robbery.

sorry,   worry,   follow,   scaly,   yellow.

FINAL CONSONANT IMPLIED

less,   taste,   pen,   deaf,   repair.

sore,   wore,   fall,   scale,   yell.

In many of the words given in the following exercises an initial or a final vowel is suggested by the outline employed.

Exercise 81

Read, copy, and transcribe

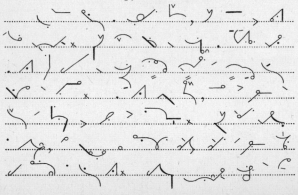

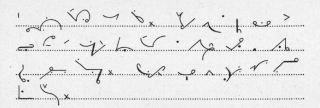

Exercise 82

Write in shorthand

The judge *in-his* charge *to-the* jury said: *This* poor
boy's injury *is very* severe, *and-*if *what-he* states *is* right,
it-was due *to-the* absence *of a* hooter *on-the* car *which*
Robinson drove along-*the* arcade at *a very* fast rate,
his speed, if-*we-can* take-*the* story *of-the* police *as*
correct, *being* at-least forty miles *an* hour, far *too* fast
in so busy *a* thoroughfare. *The* boy says *the* car came
on with *a* rush, no alarm *was given*, he-*was* struck *and-*
thrown *with* a force so terrific *as to-*break *his* right leg.
If-*you think his* story *is* right, *you*-will *give him* damages.
If-*you* assume *his* story *is* wrong, *and-*if *it* appears *to-*
you the injury *was* caused by *his own* lack *of* vigilance,
you-will refuse *him the* damages *for-which* he asks. *You*-
must *care*fully weigh both-*the* boy's case *and-the* case *as*
set out by Robinson *and* decide *on-the* facts *as-*they
appear *to-you*.

Revisionary Exercise (B)

Dear Dr. Fry,

By-*all*-means, apply *to-*my *people to-tell-you of-*my
travels *during-the* past three *years*. I-*believe* it-will-*be*
difficult *for-you to-believe all-*they-will-*tell-you*, *because-*
it-is almost beyond belief. They-will-*tell-you* a *very*
attractive story, *all-the more* striking *because of-its*

truth. If-*you*-leave *your call till next* month, *there*-may-*be more to-tell-you, and-the* news items may-*be equal to anything you have* read. Every-day brings before-*me circumstances* unknown *to-me* before, *and* every-*circumstance is* singular *in itself. It-is very difficult for-me to be surprised* at *anything* now. I-am-*surprised* at *nothing* at-*all, nor do* I-*think there-is anything to surprise me, because* my-life *during-the* past few *years has* brought *me* so-many *surprises from all* quarters. I-*have-been delivered from* troubles *when deliverance would* appear *to-have-been impossible, and when an improvement of-circumstances* looked *too difficult to be* possible. *You*-will-see-*the significance of-this when-you* know *something of what* I-*have-been* through, *though-the* tale *can-be* no-*more*-than *a mere generalization* or *general* review. Still, *it*-will-*be as near-the* facts *as* possible *in-the* circumstances. I-will-*tell-you* and Mr. Oliver *more* when I-see-*you, and it*-will-*be an advantage and an* immense *satisfaction to-me to-tell-you* both. *You*-will-then *be* at *liberty to* ask *for any number of* details, *and, as*-far-*as* I-am-*able to-remember them,* I-will *give them to-you.* I-*can* see *myself in-your* easy-*chair in-the larger of-your two* rooms at home, *with* my journal *on*-my knee *and-the cheer*ful listeners facing *me* while I-talk *of-the* days *of*-my *subjection and-of-the* dreary *subjective* examinations I gave *myself in justification of*-my actions. *In*-my *opinion, you*-will say-*the tale is significant, and, in signification of-the* happenings *in-the northern and southern* climes, far *beyond anything you* know. I-must leave-*the balance of the* tale, *however, till* I-*can go over it with-you.* I-*have* some *information, largely* personal *to-you, which* I-must *tell-you* at-*all*-costs before long. I-trust *the information* will *give-you as*-much-*pleasure as* I-*think-it-*will. *Anyway it*-will enable *you to*-set *a* right *valuation* upon-*the* rest *of*-my story. Please *remember me to-the* children at home, *and to-the* older *and larger* children also. I-*shall-be* home again *within* six months. I-*shall* hope *to* see-*the principal members of-the* local literary club *within a* few days *of-*my return. Ever *yours,* Arthur Clyde.

(468 words)

Summary

1. An initial vowel requires the use of an initial stroke, in order to give a place for the vowel-sign: a final vowel requires the use of a final stroke, for the same reason.
2. An initial or a final vowel may frequently be indicated by the form written for the initial or final consonant.
3. Words beginning with the sound of a consonant have that consonant represented in the briefest form unless there is a rule to the contrary, as in the case of the word *Siam.*
4. Similarly, words ending with the sound of a consonant, or group of consonants, have the consonant or group represented in the briefest form.

CHAPTER XXII

THE HALVING PRINCIPLE (Section 1)

General Rule. 132. Halving a stroke in length
indicates the addition of *t* or *d*. In words of one
syllable, however, unless the stroke is finally hooked,
or has a joined diphthong, a light stroke is halved for
t only, and a heavy stroke for *d* only.

Halving for either T or D. 133. (*a*) In words of more
than one syllable, a stroke may be halved for either *t*
or *d;* thus, ⌒‿ *rabbit,* ⌒‿ *rapid;* ⌐‿ *credit,* ⌊‿
debit; ‿ *honoured,* ‿ *applied.*

(*b*) A stroke having a final hook or a joined diphthong may be halved for either *t* or *d;* thus, ‿ *pave,*
‿ *paved;* ‿ *ten,* ‿ *tent* or *tend;* ‿ *men,* ‿ *meant*
or *mend;* ‿ *few,* ‿ *feud;* ‿ *prow,* ‿ *proud.*

Halving for T only, or for D only. 134 (*a*) In words
of one syllable, light strokes, without a final hook or a
joined diphthong, are halved for *t* only; thus, ‿ *play,*
‿ *plate,* but ‿ *played;* ⌒ *thaw,* ⌒ *thought,* but
⌒ *thawed.*

(*b*) In words of one syllable, heavy strokes, without
a final hook or a joined diphthong, are halved for
d only; thus, ‿ *bray,* ‿ *brayed,* but ‿ *bright;*
‿ *gray,* ‿ *grade,* but ‿ *greet.*

Vocalizing Half-length Forms. 135. Vowel-signs
to half-length forms are read next to the primary
strokes; thus, ‿ *fie,* ‿ *fight;* ‿ *off,* ‿ *oft;*
‿ *seek,* ‿ *sect;* ‿ *seeker,* ‿ *secret.*

Circle S following Half-length Forms. 136. Circle *s* at the end of a half-length form is read after the *t* or *d* indicated by the halving; thus, ⎽⊤⎽ *coat*, ⎽ρ⎽ *coats;* ⟋ *mount*, ⟋ *mounts;* ⟍ *rent*, ⟍ *rents;* ⟋ *rift*, ⟋ *rifts.*

Half-length H. 137. Half-length *h*, when not joined to another stroke, is always written upward; as, ⟋ *height*, ⟋ *heights;* ⟍ *hunt*, ⟍ *hunts;* ⟍ *haft*, ⟍ *hafts.*

Halving Principle not Employed. 138. The halving principle is not employed—

(*a*) In words of more than one syllable when a vowel follows final *t* or *d*, because a final vowel requires a final stroke; as, ⟍ *pit*, but ⟍ *pity;* ⟋ *greed*, but ⟋ *greedy;*

(*b*) When a triphone immediately precedes *t* or *d;* as, ⟍ *fight*, but ⟍ *fiat;* ⎸ *died*, but ⎸ *diadem;*

(*c*) Where a more distinctive outline is obtained by the use of the stroke *t* or *d;* as, ⟋ *secret*, but ⟍ *sacred;* ⟍ *unavoidable*, but ⟍ *inevitable;* ⟍ *hotly,* but ⟍ *hotel;*

(*d*) Where the half-length *r* [⟋] would stand alone, or with final circle *s* only [⟋] added; therefore, in such words as ⟍ *right*, ⟍ *rights*, the stroke *t* must be written. The reason for this is to prevent clashing between *rt* and the sign for *and* or *should*, and between *rts* and the sign for *and-is*. Such words as ⟍ *rents*, ⟋ *rifts*, are safely written with a half-length form.

Position of Half-length Forms. 139. Upward or downward half-length characters must not be written through the line for the indication of vowels. Where the first upstroke or the first downstroke in an outline is a half-length, the outline is written so that the half-length stroke appears over the line for the indication of a first-place vowel, and on the line for the indication

of a second or a third-place vowel; thus, ⌒⌐ *optical*, ⌒ *vertical*, ⌒ *lightly*, ⌒ *lately*, ⌒ *witness*, ⌒ *military*, ⌐ *netted*, ⌐ *artificial*, ⌐ *tint*.

Exercise 83

Read, copy, and transcribe

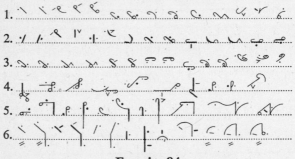

Exercise 84

Write in shorthand

1. Tie, tight, trite, Coe, coat, coats, Kate, skate.
2. Weigh, weight, weighty, fry, fright, frights.
3. Gray, grade, grades, graded, met, metal.
4. Label, labelled, open, opened, land, lands, lent.
5. Tight, tied, tidy, wit, witty, pat, patty.
6. Heat, heats, hunt, hunts, raid, raids.

GRAMMALOGUES

_quite, _ could; ⌐ accord-ing, ⌐ cared; ⌐ guard,
⌐ great; ⌐ called, ⌐ equalled, cold; ⌐ gold; ⌐ that,
⟨ without, ⌐ wished.

Exercise 85

Read, copy, and transcribe

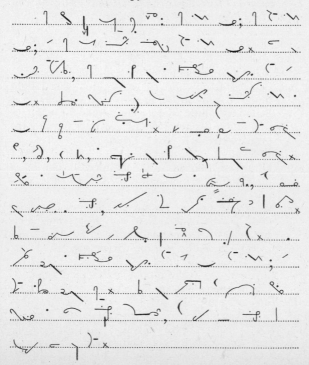

Exercise 86

Write in shorthand

It-has-been maintained *that* certainty does-not admit *of* degrees *of any* kind; *that-there-can-be* no shade *of* difference in-the intensity of-our certainty. *But* let us see. *A* man may-*be* certain *that-he* settled *his* debt *with-his* tailor *on-the* 10th *of* October, *and-in* cash, or *that-he* paid *his* local rates *on* demand. *But is-this* certainty *equalled* by-*the* certainty *with-which* he knows *that* three *and* four make seven, or *that* heat will melt butter? *Is there* not *a great difference?*

Summary

1. Halving a stroke indicates the addition of *t* or *d*.
2. Unless it is finally hooked, or has an attached diphthong, a light stroke in words of one syllable is halved for *t* only, and a heavy stroke for *d* only.
3. Vowel-signs to halved forms are read next to the primary stroke.
4. Half-length *h*, when not joined to another stroke, is always written upward; half-length upward *r* must not be written alone, or with a final circle *s* only added.
5. The halving principle is not applied when a word ends with a vowel, when *t* or *d* is immediately preceded by a triphone, and in a few other cases where the fuller form is necessary to secure distinction of outline.
6. Half-length forms should not be written through the line for vowel indication.

CHAPTER XXIII

THE HALVING PRINCIPLE (Section 2)

Strokes M, N, L, R. 140. (*a*) The four strokes ͡ ͡ ͡ ͡ which are halved to express the addition of *t*, are also halved and thickened to indicate the addition of *d;* thus, ⌒ *md*, ⌣ *nd*, ⌐ *ld* (down), ⌐ *rd*, as in the words ⌒ *mate*, ⌒ *made;* ⌒ *aimed*, ⌐ *timid;* ⌣ *neat*, ⌣ *need*, ⌣ *end;* ⌐ *old*, ⌐ *aired.*

(*b*) The half-length form ⌐ *ld*, standing alone, is used only for words beginning with a vowel; as, ⌐ *ailed*, ⌐ *old;* so that words like ⌐ *sold*, ⌐ *styled*, ⌐ *holed*, must be written with the full strokes.

(*c*) When a vowel occurs between *l-d* or between *r-d*, both consonants must be written in full. Compare ⌐ *pallid* with ⌐ *paled;* ⌐ *married* with ⌐ *marred;* ⌐ *sorrowed* with ⌐ *sword;* ⌐ *hurried* with ⌐ *hoard.*

(*d*) The signs ͡ ͡ cannot be halved to represent the syllables -*lerd*, -*rerd* respectively, because the forms ͡ ͡ are used for representing *ld*, *rd*, as explained above.

(*e*) The strokes ⌒ *mp*, *mb*, ⌣ *ng* cannot be halved for the addition of either *t* or *d*, unless they are hooked initially or finally; thus, ⌐ *impute*, ⌐ *imbued*, ⌐ *belonged;* but ⌐ *hampered*, ⌐ *rampart*, ⌐ *lingered*, ⌐ *impugned.*

RT and LT. 141. (*a*) The signs for *rt* and *lt* are generally written upward; thus, ╲ *part,* ╲╌ *pelt,* ╲╌ *fort,* ╌╌ *fault;* but ╭ *lt* is written downward after ╲╌ *n* and ╌╌ *ng,* as in ╌╮ *inlet,* ╱╌ *ringlet;* and it is written downward after ╱╌ *w* if no vowel follows *l;* thus, ╿ *dwelt,* but ╰ *twilight.*

(*b*) The light sign ╱ may be used for *rd* when it is not convenient to write ╲.; thus, ╌╌ *lard,* ╌╌ *coloured,* ╌╱ *cordage,* ╲╌ *preferred.*

(*c*) After the *shun* hook, ⟩. *st* may be written downward or upward; thus, ╲╌ *protectionist,* ╌╲╌ *progressionist.*

Joining of Strokes of Unequal Length. 142. (*a*) The halving principle may be applied to words like ╲╌ *afford,* ╌╌ *named,* where the difference of thickness shows the inequality of length; but in other cases two strokes of unequal length must not be joined unless there is an angle at the point of junction. Words like ╌╌╮ *cooked,* ╌╌╮ *looked,* ╲╌ *propped,* ╌╌╮ *minute,* ╌╌╮ *fact,* must, therefore, be written with full-length strokes.

(*b*) Half-sized *t* or *d* is always disjoined when immediately following the strokes *t* or *d;* thus, ╿ *attitude,* ╿ *treated,* ╿ *dreaded,* ╌╌╿ *credited.* The half-sized stroke is also disjoined in some other cases, as ╌╌ *aptness,* ╌╌ *tightness,* ╌╌ *hesitatingly.*

Past Tenses. 143. In past tenses *-ted* or *-ded* is always indicated by half-length *t* or *d* respectively; thus, ╌╌ *parted,* ╲╌ *braided,* ╌╌ *coated,* ╌╌ *graded.*

The Halving Principle in Phraseography. 144. The halving principle is employed in phraseography as follows—

(*a*) For the word *it*, as in ⌣ *if it*, ⌣ *if it is;* (*b*) *not*, as in ⌣ *I am not*, ⌣ *you may not*, ⌣ *I will not;* (*c*) *word* and *would* by ⌣ as in ⌣ *this word*, ⌣ *we would be;* and (*d*) in phrases like ⌣ *at all times*, ⌣ *able to make.*

Exercise 87

Read, copy, and transcribe

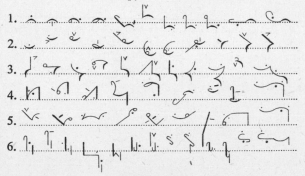

Exercise 88

Write in shorthand

1. Amid, signed, doled, dazzled, sailed, heard.
2. Collide, colt, borrowed, bored, thronged.
3. Impede, dreamed, scampered, conquered.
4. Quilt, quilled, sunlight, answered, glared.
5. Chatted, treated, pathetic, flared, deadness.
6. Liken, likened, exported, shunted, trended.

GRAMMALOGUES

⁒ *cannot;* ♪ *gentleman,* ⌐ *gentlemen;* ⌐ *particular,*
⌐ *opportunity;* ∫ *child;* ↖ *build-ing;* ∫ *told;*
⌐ *tried,* ⌐ *trade, toward,* ↳ *towards;* ⌐ *hand,* ⌐ *under.*

Exercise 89

Read, copy, and transcribe

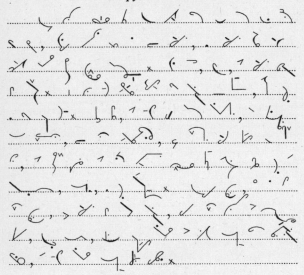

Exercise 90

Write in shorthand

Quite early *in* man's attempt *to* penetrate *into-the*
great secrets *of-the* earth, *when-he tried to-*find *its*
hidden treasures *of gold and* diamonds *for-the* purposes
of-trade, he learned one *important* fact, namely, *that-it*

grows hotter *as you* descend. *This-is* evident, also, *from-the* hot springs found *in different* parts *of-the* world, *and* still *more* evident *from-the* volcanoes *which*, *when* violently active, pour out molten rock until *it* covers *the* country around *to a* thickness *of-*many feet. *A great* authority *on-the subject has* asserted *that-there-are* slight earth tremors every quarter *of an hour. The* hand *of-*man seems weak indeed *when-we-think of-the* wondrous power *of-*these mighty forces.

Summary

1. The four strokes ⌒⌒⌒ are halved and thickened for the addition of *d*.
2. The thickened forms ⌒⌒ are not used if a vowel comes between *l-d, r-d.*
3. *Ler* and *rer* are never halved; *mp* and *ng* may be halved when initially or finally hooked.
4. *Rt* is generally written upward; *lt* is written upward, except after *n, ng;* after *w, lt* is written downward if no vowel follows *l*.
5. The upward form ⟋ may be used medially and finally for *rd*.
6. The half-length ⟩ *st* may be written downward or upward after *shun*.
7. Two strokes of unequal length must not be joined unless there is an angle at the point of junction, or unless, in the case of curves, the difference of thickness clearly shows the inequality of length.
8. Half-sized *t* or *d* is always disjoined when immediately following the strokes *t* or *d*.
9. In past tenses *-ted* or *-ded* is always indicated by half-length *t* or *d* respectively.
10. The halving principle is used in phraseography to represent *it, not, word, would.*

CHAPTER XXIV

THE DOUBLING PRINCIPLE

The General Rule. 145. With the few exceptions named below, the addition of the syllable *-tr* or *-dr*, or *-THr*, or, in common words *-ture*, is indicated by doubling the length of the preceding stroke; thus,

.... *fie,* .... *fighter;* .... *ten,* .... *tender;* .... *nigh,* ....

neither; .... *track,* .... *tractor;* .... *seek,* .... *sector;*

.... *Dow,* .... *doubter;* .... *won,* .... *wonder;* .... *grave,*

.... *grafter;* .... *impugn,* .... *impounder;*

.... *centre,* .... *central;* .... *enter,* .... *enteric;*

.... *pick,* .... *picture;* .... *few,* .... *future;*

.... *nay,* .... *nature;* .... *natural.*

Doubling of Straight Strokes. 146. The doubling principle must not be applied to a straight stroke unless it follows a circle or stroke consonant, or has a final hook, or an attached final diphthong. Compare

.... *skater* with .... *cater;* .... *captor* with ....

potter; .... *wonder* with .... *wader;* .... *doubter* with

.... *daughter;* .... *tutor* with .... *tether.*

Strokes MP and NG. 147. The character .... *mp-mb,* when not initially or finally hooked, is doubled for the addition of *-er*, and the character .... *ng* for the addition

of *-kr, -gr;* thus, ... *bump,* .... *bumper;* .... *vamp,*

.... *vamper;* .... *inker,* .... *linger,* .... *Ingersoll.*

Alternatives for MPR, MBR. 148. There are therefore alternative forms for *mpr*, *mbr*, the double-length form ⌣ and the hooked form ⌣. The hooked form is used when *mpr*, *mbr* immediately follows an upstroke or ___ *k;* in all other cases the double-length form is used; thus, ___ *umber,* but ___ *slumber;* ___ *tamper,* but ___ *hamper;* ___ *chamber,* but ___ *cumber.*

Alternatives for NG-KR, NG-GR. 149. There are alternative forms for *ng-kr*, *ng-gr*, the double-length ⌣ and the hooked form ⌣. The double-length form is used initially and when following a circle or an upstroke. In all other cases, the hooked form is written; thus, ___ *anchorage,* but ___ *bunkering;* ___ *sinker,* but ___ *drinker;* ___ *hunger,* but ___ *pinker;* ___ *rancour,* but ___ *canker.*

Stroke L. 150. The stroke *l*, standing alone, or with only a final circle attached, is doubled for *-tr* only; thus, ___ *letter,* ___ *letters;* ___ *alter,* ___ *alters;* but ___ *leader,* ___ *leather.*

Circle S and Double-length Strokes. 151. Circle *s* at the end of a double-length form is read after the syllable indicated by doubling; thus, ___ *voters,* ___ *renders,* ___ *rafters,* ___ *rectors,* ___ *pictures.*

Past Tenses. 152. When the present tense of a verb of more than one syllable is written with either a double-length character or a hooked form, the past tense is written with the halving principle; thus, ...⟍... *ponder*, ...⟍... *pondered;* ⟍⟍⟍ *canter,* ⟍ *cantered;* ...⟋... *winter,* ....⟋... *wintered;* ⟍⟍ *matter,* ...⟍... *mattered;* ⟍⟍⟍ *malinger,* ...⟍... *malingered;* ⟍⟍⟍ *conquer,* ...⟍... *conquered.*

Doubling Principle not employed. 153. The doubling principle is not employed—

(*a*) When a vowel follows final *-tr, -dr,* etc., because a final vowel requires a final stroke for the vowel sign; as, ⟍... *flatter,* but ⟍⟍... *flattery;* ...⟋... *winter,* but ...⟋... *wintry;* ⟍... *feather,* but ...⟍... *feathery;* .... *anger,* but ...⟍... *angry.*

(*b*) In words like ...⟍... *panther,* ...⟍... *Arthur,* where the *thr* is a light sound.

Position of Double-length Strokes. 154. (*a*) All double-length downstrokes are written through the line; as, ...⟍... *painter,* ...⟍... *fetter,* ⟍ *tender.*

(*b*) Double-length horizontals are written either above the line or on the line, according to the first vowel heard in the word; thus, ... *matter,* ...⟍... *mother,* ...⟍... *enter,* .... *neither.*

(*c*) Double-length upstrokes are written *above*, or *on*, or *through* the line, according to the first vowel heard in the word; thus, ⟋... *loiter,* ...⟋... *render,* ...⟋... *hinder.*

The Doubling Principle in Phraseography. 155. The doubling principle is employed in phraseography for the indication of the words *their, there;* thus, ⌣ *in,* ⌣ *in their;* ⌝ *I know,* ⌝ *I know there is;* ⌐ *take,* ⌐ *take their way;* ⬎ *I can be,* ⬎ *I can be there;* ∿ *has to be,* ∿ *has to be there;* ⟍ *upon,* ⟍ *upon their.*

Exercise 91

Read, copy, and transcribe

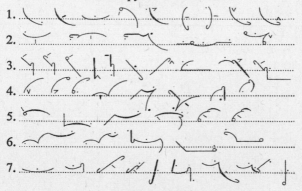

Exercise 92

Write in shorthand

1. Flatter, thither, aster, voters, enters, neuter.
2. Fender, lavender, shedder, feeders, godfathers.
3. Central, centralization, dysenteric, eccentric.
4. Bidder, spider, plotter, sector, painter, winter.

5. Louder, Lowther, builder, cylinder, chambermaid, sinker, hunger, hungered, whimper, conquer.

6. Mutter, muttered, wander, wandered, temper, tempered, alter, altered, shatter, shattered.

7. Pander, pantry, seconder, secondary, voter, votary, cinder, cindery, enter, entry.

GRAMMALOGUES

chaired, *cheered;* *sent;* *third;* *short;* *spirit;* *yard,* *word;* *rather, writer;* *wonderful-ly;* *therefore;* *school,* *schooled.*

Exercise 93

Read, copy, and transcribe

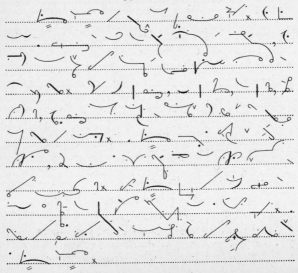

Exercise 94

Write in shorthand

*We-have to hand to*day, *under* last Wednesday's date, another copy *of-the wonderful* catalogue issued by Crowder *and* Sanderson. *Their* motor cycle department *rather* appeals *to-the* boys *in-this school, and-we-have, therefore, sent word that-we should* like *several* extra copies *of-the* catalogue. *The* new leather belt, just *over a yard in* length, *for* use *with a* waterproof coat, seems *wonderfully* cheap. *There-is*, also, *a rather* attractive lamp, *with* silvered reflector, suitable *for any* holder, *and-this should* take well *with-the* boys. These *people are* enterprising. *They-are* inventors *as*-well-*as* dealers, *and-therefore we should-be*-able-*to* rely upon-*their* motor fittings *being* absolutely up *to* date.

Summary

-tr, *-dr* or *-*THr, or, in common words, *-ture* is added	by doubling the length of the preceding stroke.
-er is added to the curve ⌢, and *-kr* or *-gr* is added to the curve ⌣.	by doubling the length of the curve.
there or *their* in a phrase is expressed	by doubling the length of the preceding stroke.

Past tenses of verbs of more than one syllable	are written with the halving principle.
The Doubling Principle is not applied	when a final vowel immediately follows -*tr*, -*dr*, etc.
The double-length form ⌢⌢⌢ -*mpr* or -*mbr*	is written (*a*) initially; (*b*) after a circle or loop; (*c*) after a down-stroke.
The hooked form ⌢ -*mpr* or -*mbr*	is written in all other cases.
The double-length form ⌢ *ng-kr* or *ng-gr*	is written initially and when following a circle or an upstroke.
The hooked form ⌢ *ng-kr* or *ng-gr*	is written in all other cases.

CHAPTER XXV

DIPHONIC OR TWO-VOWEL SIGNS

In many words two vowels occur consecutively, each being separately pronounced. To represent these, special signs have been provided, called *diphones* (from the Greek *di* = double, and *phōnē* = a sound).

Use of Diphones. 156. In most instances, the first of the two consecutive vowels is the more important, and therefore the diphonic sign is written in the vowel-place which the first vowel would take if this occurred alone. The method of using the *diphones* is explained in the following rules.

157. The *diphone* ⌄ is written as follows—

(*a*) In the first vowel-place to represent the vowel *ah* or *ă* and any vowel immediately following; thus, ⌄ *sahib*.

(*b*) In the second vowel-place to represent *ā* or *ĕ*, and any vowel immediately following; thus, ⌒ *layer*, ⌒ *laity*, ⌒ *betrayal*, ⌒ *surveyor*.

(*c*) In the third vowel-place to represent *ē* or *ĭ*, and any vowel immediately following; thus, ⌄ *real*, ⌄ *reality*, ⌄ *re-enter*, ⌄ *amiable*, ⌄ *meander*, ⌄ *geography*, ⌄ *geographical*, ⌄ *champion*, ⌄ *heaviest*, ⌄ *burying*, ⌄ *glorious*, ⌄ *creator*, ⌄ *creation*, ⌄ *serial*, ⌄ *serious*. Note ⌄ *healthier*, ⌄ *junior*.

119

158. The *diphone* ⌄ is written as follows—

(*a*) In the first vowel-place to represent *aw* and any vowel immediately following; thus, ⌣ fla*wy*, ⌐ dra*wer*, ⌣ dra*wings*, ⌐ ca*wing*.

(*b*) In the second vowel-place to represent *ō* and any vowel immediately following; thus, ⌐ sho*wy*, ⌣ besto*wal*, ⌣ p*oet*, ⌣ p*oetical*, ⌐ c*oercion*, ⌐ c*oincide*, ⌐ c*oincident*, ⌐ her*oic*.

(*c*) In the third vowel-place to represent *ōō* and any vowel immediately following; thus, ⌐ br*uin*, ⌐ br*ewery*, ⌐ L*ouisa*, ⌐ L*ewis*, ⌐ tr*uant*, ⌐ Dr*uid*, ⌐ Dr*uidical*, ⌐ sh*oeing*, ⌐ hall*ooing*.

Extended Use of Angular Sign. 159. The angular sign ⌐ is also used to represent the consecutive vowels in the small class of words like ⌐ *Spaniard*, ⌐ *million*, ⌐ *bullion*, ⌐ *question*.

Exercise 95

Read, copy, and transcribe

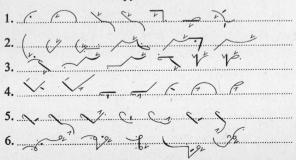

1.
2.
3.
4.
5.
6.

Exercise 96

Write in shorthand

1. Slay, slayer, bay, bayonet, air, aerometer.
2. Pay, payable, betray, betrayer, obey, abeyance.
3. Re, real, really, reinforce, readdress, readmission.
4. Billow, billowy, blow, blower, co, coincide.
5. Hero, heroic, snow, snowy, slow, slowest.
6. Cruel, brewing, jewel, ruinous, ruination.

Exercise 97

Read, copy, and transcribe

Exercise 98

Write in shorthand

Dear Mr. Brewer,

It-is to be regretted *that-the* arrangement *with-the* band *of-the* Cleopatra *has* fallen through, *but* I-*shall-be*-able-*to* re-arrange-*the* programme *and* it-will-not affect-*the* gaiety *of-the members of-the* Lyceum *on*-Monday. *We-have-had to*-reappoint *the* late manager *of-the* local theatre *as* Master *of* Ceremonies, *because-he* knows *the* ceremonial *to be* observed, *and-we-shall-have* to reassemble-*the members of-the* chorus, *and* readmit *those-who* retired last June. I-am worrying-*the* decorators, *and d*oing my ut*most to*-make these slowest *of* slow *people* finish *their* work.

Very-truly-*yours,*

Summary

Place	Value of the Diphone *ᴋ.*	Place	Value of the Diphone *ᴀ.*
1	ah or ă + any vowel	1	aw + any vowel
2	ā or ĕ ditto	2	ō ditto
3	ē or ĭ ditto	3	o͞o ditto

The angular sign *ᴋ.* is also used to represent the consecutive vowels in such words as mill*io*n.

CHAPTER XXVI

MEDIAL SEMICIRCLE

As explained in a previous chapter, a right semi-circle is used initially as an abbreviation for *w* before the strokes *k*, *g*, *m* (and *mp*) and the two forms of *r*. The medial use of a semicircle is explained in the present chapter.

Left and Right Semicircles. 160. (*a*) A *left* semi-circle is written in the middle of a word to represent the sounds *wah*, *wā*, *wē*, or their corresponding short sounds.

(*b*) A *right* semicircle is written in the middle of a word to represent the sounds *waw*, *wō*, *wōo*, or their corresponding short sounds.

161. The following diagram shows the places of the semicircles, and the sounds they represent.

Place	Left Semicircle ᴄ.	Place	Right Semicircle ᴐ.
1	represents *w* + *ah* or *ă*	1	represents *w* + *aw* or *ŏ*
2	„ „ + *ā* „ *ĕ*	2	„ „ + *ō* „ *ŭ*
3	„ „ + *ē* „ *ĭ*	3	„ „ + *ōo* „ *ŏŏ*

162. The medial semicircle is, therefore, simply an abbreviation for *w* followed by a vowel. The sign is usefully written in words like ⟍⟍ *boudoir*, ⟍ᶜ *assuage*, ₂⟍ *sea-weed*; ⟍ *seaward*, ⟍⟍ *Words-worth*, ⟍ᶜ *lamb's-wool*.

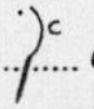

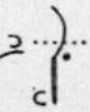

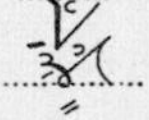

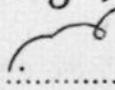

Note: ⟍ᶜ *quality*, ⟍ᵛ *qualify*.

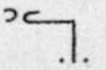

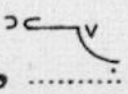

123

Exercise 99

Read, copy, and transcribe

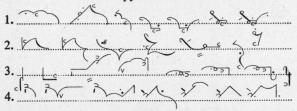

Exercise 100

Write in shorthand

1. Sealing-wax, twenty, twentieth, Cromwell, Bothwell.
2. Dwindle, dwindled, wherewith, *there*with, bewilder, bewildered.
3. Breakwater, blameworthy, seaworthy, Wandsworth, Cornwallis.
4. Wick, wicked, wickedly, weaken, weakness.

Exercise 101

Read, copy, and transcribe

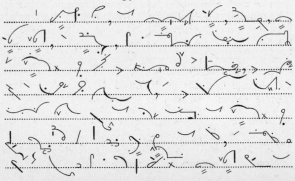

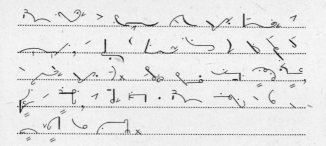

Exercise 102

Write in shorthand

Dear-Sirs,

We-thank-you for-your-letter *of*-last week *and we-are*
asking Messrs. Cromwell *and* Warbeck, *of* Wentworth,
to-look *into-the* matter forthwith. *We* hope *that-
the* flow *of*-water *into-the* workings may dwindle away
with-the advent *of-the* dry weather, *and-that-the* trouble
may cease *of-itself*. *In-any*-case, *you*-may-rely upon-us
to-do all-that-we-can to stop-*the* nuisance *in*-question.
*We-have al*ready *told our* engineer, *Mr.* Walter Welson,
to-make close enquiry *into-the* matter, *and-we-thank-
you* again *for-the* kindly way *in-which-you have* warned
us *of-the* possible loss both *to-ourselves and to-you*.

Yours-truly,

Summary

1. A semicircle is employed medially as an alternative
   to the stroke *w*.
2. A medial *left* semicircle represents *wah, wā, wē*, or
   the corresponding short sounds.
3. A medial *right* semicircle represents *waw, wō, wōō*,
   or the corresponding short sounds.

CHAPTER XXVII

PREFIXES

Initial Com- or Con-. 163. Initial *com-* (or *comm-*) or *con-* (or *conn-*) is expressed by a light dot written at the beginning of the following stroke; thus, ⟍⟍ *combine*, ⟍⟋ *commence*, ⟋ *congratulate*, ⟍⟍ *connection*. In a few words clearer outlines are obtained by writing the prefixes fully; thus, ⟋ *commotion*, ⟋ *commission*, ⟍ *commiserate*, ⟋ *consul*, ⟍ *connote*.

In words beginning with the prefix *com-* or *con-*, represented by a dot, the position of the outline is governed by the first vowel after the prefix.

Medial Com-, etc. 164. Medial *com-*, *con-*, *cum-*, or *cog-*, either in a word or in a phrase, is indicated by disjoining the form immediately following the *com-*, etc.; thus, ⟍ *becomingly*, ⟋ *welcoming*, ⟍ *incompetent*, ⟋ *uncontrolled*, ⟋ *circumference*, ⟋ *recognize*, ⟍ *in compliance*, ⟍ *by consent*, ⟍ *I am compelled*. This method may be used after a dash logogram when this is written upward, but not when it is written downward; compare ⟍ *on the committee*, ⟍ *of the committee;* ⟍ *should commence* and ⟍⟍ *to commence*.

Accom-. 165. *Accom-* (or *accommo-*) is represented by ⟍ *k*, joined or disjoined; thus, ⟍ *accommodation*, ⟍ *accompany*.

Intro-. 166. *Intro-* is expressed by ⟍ *ntr;* thus, ⟍ *introduce*, ⟍ *introspection*.

126

Magna-, etc. 167. *Magna-, magne-* or *magni-* is expressed by a disjoined ⌒ *m;* thus, ⌐ *magnanimity,* ⌐ *magnetize,* ⌐ *magnify.*

Trans-. 168. *Trans-* may be contracted by omitting the *n;* thus, ⌐ *transfer,* ⌐ *transmit,* ⌐ *transgression;* but sometimes the full outline is preferable, as, ⌐ *transcend,* ⌐ *transit.*

Self- and Self-con- or Self-com-. 169. (*a*) *Self-* is represented by a disjoined circle *s* written close to the following stroke in the second vowel-place; thus, ⌐ *self-defence,* ⌐ *self-made.*

(*b*) *Self-con-* or *self-com-* is indicated by a disjoined circle *s* written in the position of the *con-* dot; thus, ⌐ *self-control,* ⌐ *self-confident.*

In- before Str, Skr, and H (up). 170. *In-* before the circled strokes ⌐ is expressed by a small hook written in the same direction as the circle; thus, ⌐ *instrument,* ⌐ *inscriber,* ⌐ *inhabit.*

Negative Words. 171. (*a*) The small hook for *in-* is never used in negative words, that is, where *in-* signifies *not.* In such cases *in-* must be written with the stroke *n;* thus, ⌐ *hospitable,* ⌐ *inhospitable;* ⌐ *humanity,* ⌐ *inhumanity.*

(*b*) Words which have the prefix *il-*, *im-*, *in-*, *ir-*, *un-*, are written in accordance with the following rules, so as to provide the necessary distinction between positive and negative words, and other pairs of words where distinction is required—

(*c*) By writing the downward *r* or *l* when the rules for writing initial *r* or *l* permit of this being done; thus, ⟋ *resolute*, ⟍ *irresolute*; ⟨ *resistible*, ⟍ *irresistible*; ⟍ *limitable*, ⟍ *illimitable*.

(*d*) By repeating the *l*, *m*, *n* or *r* in cases where a distinction cannot otherwise be obtained; thus, ⟋ *legal*, ⟋ *illegal*; ⟍ *mortal*, ⟍ *immortal*; ⟍ *noxious*, ⟍ *innoxious*; ⟍ *necessary*, ⟍ *unnecessary*; ⟍ *redeemable*, ⟍ *irredeemable*; ⟍ *radiance*, ⟍ *irradiance*.

Logograms. 172. Logograms, joined or disjoined, may be used as prefixes or suffixes; thus, ⟍ *almost*, ⟍ *understand*, ⟍ *undermine*, ⟍ *unimportant*.

Exercise 103

Read, copy, and transcribe

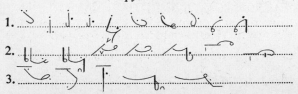

4. ....

5. ....

6. ....

Exercise 104

Write in shorthand

1. Competent, combat, common, compensate, compound, compact, compare.
2. Conductor, conflict, constant, convulsion, conserve, conscientious, contango.
3. Commissioners, incomplete, recognized, uncongenial, reconsider, incumbent.
4. *We*-were compelled, accompanying, accomplices, introducing, introduces.
5. Magnificent, magnifier, magnificence, transmission, translated, transmitter.
6. Self-possession, self-congratulation, instructor, inherent, inhumanly, insuperable.
7. Illiberal, immaterial, innocuous, unknown, reparable, irreparable, reclaimable, irreclaimable, *under*stood, *under*sell, *trade*-mark.

.... *selfish-ness;* .... *inscribe-d;* .... *inscription;*

.... *instruction;* .... *instructive.*

Exercise 105

Read, copy, and transcribe

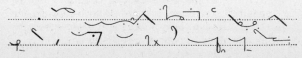

Exercise 106

Write in shorthand

We-thank-you for-your communication *and instruction* regarding-*the* lightning conductors *for-the* new Conservative Club *in* Conway Road. *The* slight misconception *has*-now *been* removed, *and your* recommendations *shall-be* carefully considered. *We-are having-the* corner-stones *inscribed this* week, *and-we-have*-no-doubt *that-you*-will-find-*the inscription* will satisfy *you*. We suggest *for-your* consideration *that-it-would-be instructive and* useful *to-have* a translation *of-the* Latin *inscription* printed *and* circulated before-*the* opening ceremony. *You*-will-not consider us *selfish* if-*we* arrange *for* a photograph *of-the* ceremony showing *our* name *as* contractors *for-the* work.

Summary

PREFIX	REPRESENTED BY
Initial *con-*, *com-*	A light dot.
Medial *con-*, *com-*	Disjoining the form immediately following the *con-*, etc.
Accom-	The stroke .... *k* joined or disjoined.
Intro-	The double-length ⌣ *ntr*.
Magna-, etc.	Disjoined ⌢ *m*.
Trans-	The sign for *trs*, or by the full form.
Self-	A disjoined circle *s* written in the second vowel-place.
Self-con-	A disjoined circle *s* written in the place of the *con-* dot.
In- before certain circled straight strokes	A small hook written with the Right motion.
Il-, *ir-*	Downward *l* or *r*, or by the repetition of the initial consonant.
im-, *in-*, *un-*	Repeating the ⌢ *m* or ⌣ *n*.
Logograms	May be used as prefixes or suffixes.

CHAPTER XXVIII

SUFFIXES AND TERMINATIONS

-Ing. 173. The stroke ⌣ is generally employed in the representation of *-ing*. Where this stroke cannot be written, or, where, if written, an awkward joining would result, a light dot is used to represent the suffix *-ing*. The dot *-ing* is written—

(*a*) After light straight downstrokes and downward *r*, as, ⟍ *paying*, ⎮ *tying*, ⎮ *etching*, ⏌ *hoeing*, ⟍ *hearing*, ⟍ *spluttering*.

(*b*) After circle *ns*, after *k* and *g* hooked for *f* or *v*, and after an upstroke finally hooked; as, ⟍ *prancing*, ⟍ *coughing*, ⟍ *waning*.

(*c*) After a half-length or a double-length stroke where no angle would be obtained by the use of the stroke ⌣, as, ⟍ *brooding*, ⟍ *fidgeting*, ⌢ *matting*, ⟍ *fielding*, ⌢ *muttering*.

(*d*) Generally after a contracted logogram; as, ⟍ *remembering*, ⌣ *coming*, ⟨ *thanking;* but the stroke ⌣ is employed in ⟍ *wishing*, ⌣ *calling*, ⟍ *having*, ⟍ *surprising*.

(*e*) The dot *-ing* cannot be used medially; therefore the stroke *ng* is written in *-ingly;* thus, ⟍ *admiring*, but ⟍ *admiringly;* ⟍ *deserving*, but ⟍ *deservingly*.

132

(*f*) Wherever *-ing* would be represented by a dot, *-ings* is indicated by a dash; thus, ⟋ *etchings*, ⟍ *scrapings*, ⟋ *plottings*, ⟍ *windings*, ⟋ *rinsings*.

-Ality, etc. 174. *-Ality*, *-ility*, *-arity*, *-ority*, *-elty*, and similar terminations are expressed by disjoining the stroke immediately preceding the termination; thus, ⟍ *formality*, ⟍ *barbarity*, ⟍ *novelty*, ⟍ *frivolity*, ⟍ *feasibility*, ⟍ *majority*.

-Logical-ly. 175. *-Logical* and *-logically* are expressed by a disjoined / *j*; thus, ⟍ *genealogical-ly*, ⟍ *mythological-ly*.

-Ment. 176. *-Ment* is, as a rule, expressed by ⟋ *mnt*; thus, ⟍ *sentiment*, ⟍ *agreement*. If this sign does not join easily, however, the contracted form ⟍ may be used; thus, ⟍ *imprisonment*, ⟍ *commencement*, ⟍ *refinement*, ⟍ *preferment*.

-Mental-ly-ity. 177. *-Mental*, *-mentally*, and *-mentality* are expressed by a disjoined ⟋ *mnt*; thus, ⟍ *fundamental-ly*, ⟍ *instrumental-ly-ity*.

-Ly. 178. *-Ly* is expressed by ⟋ *l*, joined or disjoined; thus, ⟋ *chiefly*, ⟍ *friendly*; or the hook *l* is employed; thus, ⟋ *deeply*, ⟍ *positively*.

-Ship. 179. *-Ship* is expressed by a joined or disjoined ⟋ *sh*; thus, ⟍ *friendship*, ⟍ *citizenship*, ⟍ *scholarship*, ⟍ *leadership*.

-Fulness and -lessness or -lousness. 180. (*a*) *-Fulness* is expressed by a disjoined ⌣ₒ *fs;* thus, ↗ₒ *usefulness,* ↘ₒ *carefulness,* ↘ₒ *gratefulness.*

(*b*) *-Lessness* and *-lousness* are expressed by a disjoined ⌢ *ls;* thus, ↗ₒ *heedlessness,* ↗ₒ *hopelessness,* ↗ₒ *sedulousness.*

-Ward, -wart, -wort; -yard. 181. *-Ward, -wart* or *-wort,* and *-yard* are expressed by a half-sized *w* and *y* respectively, as in the words, ↘ *backward,* ↗ *stalwart,* ↗ *brickyard.*

Compound Words. 182. Compounds of *here, there, where,* etc., are written as follows—

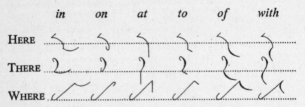

	in	on	at	to	of	with
HERE						
THERE						
WHERE						

Exercise 107

Read, copy, and transcribe

1. ....

2. ....

3. ....

4. ....

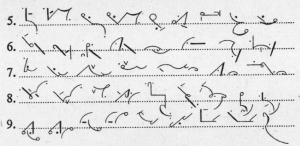

5.

6.

7.

8.

9.

Exercise 108

Write in shorthand

1. Sapping, tying, teaching, fearing, webbing, wading, lodging, shaking, flogging, loving, scathing, sowing, rushing, slaying, roaring.
2. Dispensing, enhancing, craving, surrounding, ballooning, opposing, menacing, puffing, disjoining, caning, concerning.
3. Pleating, obtruding, permitting, scaffolding, flitting, smothering, dissecting, smelting, sauntering, *speak*ing, castings.
4. Solubility, singularity, fatality, novelties, etymological, accompaniment, effacement, sentimentally, vainly, frankly, exhaustively.
5. *Chair*manship, clerkship, playfulness, credulousness, in*difference*, hereby, *there*about, whereunto.

PHRASES

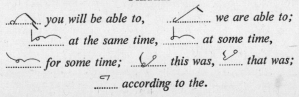

you will be able to,   *we are able to;*

at the same time,   *at some time,*

for some time;   *this was,*   *that was;*

according to the.

Exercise 109

Read, copy, and transcribe

Exercise 110

Write in shorthand

I-am-sorry *to* interfere *with-the* arrangements *for-the* announcement *of-the* concert season, *but* at-*the*-same-time I-am compelled *to* say *that* I-*think-the* form proposed *is*-not likely *to-have-the* effect *of* introducing new *members* to-*the* society. I-fear-*the* psychological effect *of-the* word*ing of-the* circular, *which-is more* like *a* command or *instruction* than *an* invitation. I-*think* it-will provoke *a* feeling *of* resentment *in-the*-minds *of-those* whom *you-are* addressing, *and* at-*the*-same-time convey *a* false impression. I-am conscious *of* no *selfishness in* communicating *with-you on-the* matter, *because-it-is quite* immaterial *to-me whether-the* membership *is large* or small; *but, as-the* instructor *and* conductor *of-the* choir, I-must, *in* self-defence, warn *the* committee against *a* possible misconstruction *of- their* circular. I-*think-you*-will-*be*-able-*to* induce *them to* change *it*. I-*have-been* wanting *to* see-*you for*-sometime, *and*-if-*you*-will *call* some-time *during-the com*ing *week* I-*shall-be*-glad *of a* little conversation *with-you*.

Revisionary Exercise (C)

I-*cannot quite under*stand *how you*-came *to* act *as you* did *in-the* court *today, nor how you could put-the* case against *that child with*-such *particular* force, missing no *opportunity that-you*-were able-*to* seize *to*-make-*the* poor *child* appear guilty *of-the* theft. *You*-may say *that, without-the* evidence *of-the gentleman whose* purse *was*-taken, *and without-the* statements *of-the* other *gentlemen who* said they saw-*the child put* her *hand into-the* old *gentleman's* pocket, *there-would* certainly *have-been* no case *for-the* jury. *But, surely, according-to-the* evidence *of-the guard called by-the* defence, *there-was more*-than *a* doubt *that-the* prisoner *was-the child* seen by-*the gentlemen who* testified. *The* guard told *a* straightforward tale, *and, though-you tried to* shake *his* evidence, *you* failed *to do*-so, except *towards-the* end, *when-he* admitted he-saw *a gold* coin drop apparently *from-the child's hands to-the* ground. I-*think-you*-were *a* little *short with-the* guard, *and* I-*was* glad *when-the people in-the* court *cheered his* final reply. They *chaired him, too,* at-*the* end *of-the* case, *under* protest by-*him and-his* friends. I-*do*-not *believe-the* poor *child* came out-*of-the yard, as* stated by-one-*of- your* witnesses, *and*-indeed I-*did*-not *believe a word of- that* witness's evidence. *It-was given in a* bad *spirit, in a* tone *which sent a* shiver through everyone *in-the* court. I-know *that* at-least *a third of-his* story about-*the school and-the wonderful instruction* he *had* received *there was* untrue. I-know *this because* I-went *to-the school myself and you*-will-find my name *inscribed on-the* roll *of* honour hanging *in-the large* hall. *It-is*-not *wonderful, therefore, that* I-*have a* doubt *of-that* man's *word. It-would-be rather more wonderful* if I-*believed* his story. I-*think that-he-is a selfish*, vindictive fellow, *and it-will-be instructive to* follow *his* future. *Any*way, I-*shall* set about *an* appeal *for-the child,* whom I-*believe to be* absolutely innocent *of-the* crime alleged against her.   (373 words)

Summary

SUFFIX	REPRESENTED BY
-ing	The stroke ⌣ where convenient; otherwise by a light dot.
-ings	The stroke ⌣ where convenient; otherwise by a light dash.
-ality, etc.	Disjoining the stroke immediately preceding the termination.
-logical-ly	Disjoining the stroke *l. j.*
-ment	The sign ⌢ *mnt,* where convenient; otherwise by ⌣ *nt.*
-mental-ly-ity	Disjoined ⌢ *mnt.*
-ly	The stroke ⌒ *l,* or by a form hooked for *l.*

-ship	The stroke ⟋ *sh*.
-lessness or *-lousness*	{ Disjoined ⌒ *ls*.
-fulness	Disjoined ⟍ *fs*.
-ward, etc., and *-yard*	{ Half-sized *w* and *y* respectively.

Compounds	{ Generally formed by joining the outlines for the separate words.

CHAPTER XXIX

CONTRACTIONS

Omission of Consonants. 183. (*a*) Where *p* is very slightly sounded, it may be omitted, as in ⌒ *prompt*, ⌐ *tempt*, ⌐ *assumption*, ⌐ *exemption;* but the *p* is represented in words like ⌐ *trumpet*, ⌐ *trumpeter*, where it is clearly sounded.

(*b*) *K* or *G* is omitted between *ng* and *t*, or between *ng* and *sh*, when no vowel occurs immediately after *k* or *g;* thus, ⌐ *adjun(c)t*, ⌐ *extin(c)tion*. In ⌐ *trinket*, ⌐ *blanket*, and similar words, in which a vowel follows the consonant, the *k* or *g* is retained. The *k* is also retained in past tenses, as ⌐ *inked*, ⌐ *winked*, ⌐ *banked*, ⌐ *linked*.

(*c*) Medial *t*, immediately following circle *s*, may be omitted in many words; thus, ⌐ *postman*, ⌐ *honestly*, ⌐ *tasteful*, ⌐ *mistake*, ⌐ *mistaken*, ⌐ *institute;* and in phrases like ⌐ *most important*, ⌐ *there must be*, ⌐ *your last letter*. In some words, however, the full form is quite as facile as the contracted form; thus, ⌐ *drastic*, ⌐ *elastic*, ⌐ *plastic*.

140

Exercise 111

Read, copy, and transcribe

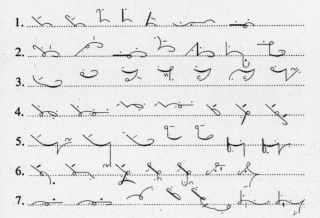

Exercise 112

Write in shorthand

1. Presume, presumptive, bump, bumped, tempt, tempter.
2. Temptation, contempt, contemptible, cramp, cramped, thump, thumped.
3. Consumption, consumptive, stamp, stamped, swamped, resumptive.
4. Indistinct, distinction, extinct, manifest, manifestly, adjustments.
5. Rest, restless, list, listless, dishonest, dishonestly, waste-pipe.
6. Text, textbook, trust, trustworthy, postcard, Post Office.

Exercise 113

Read, copy, and transcribe

Exercise 114

Write in shorthand

*We-are-much-*obliged *for-your-*letter *and* estimate
for-the elastic web. *But surely there-*must-*be* some
mistake *in-your* figures. Please-refer *to-your-*last-
letter *to* us, dated 26th October, *in-which-you-*gave us *a*
distinctly better price. Manifestly, *the* postponement
*of-the-*order *for a* week *cannot* possibly *have-*made so
*great a difference in-the-*price. *We* realize *that-the* web

is-the best-finish, *as-it-is most-important it-should-be,
but-you-*must-try *to-improve* upon *your* estimate, or
you-cannot hope *to-*receive-*the* order.   *You-*must-*be*
estimating, *we-think, on-the* assumption *that-the* web
is to be silk finished.   *That-is-*not so, *as you-*will-see *on*
referring *to-our* last-letter.   If-*there-is-to* be *a* resumption *of* business between-us, *your* estimate will-*have to
be* reconsidered.   *All-we* ask *for is a* web *with-the* best-
finish, *but* not silk, *and of a* tasteful design.   *What-can*
you offer *to* tempt us *to* pass *the* order *to-you?*

Other General Contractions. 184. Contractions for a
number of words in common use are formed by the
omission of a medial or final consonant or syllable.
These contracted words, together with the classes of
words contracted on the principles explained in the
present chapter, constitute what may be termed
General Contractions. A prefix or suffix may be
attached to a contracted outline, and in this way the
list of contractions may easily be extended; thus,

⟋⟍ *respect,* ⟍⟍ *disrespect,* ⟍⟍ *disrespectful,*
⟋⟍ *respective,* ⟍⟍ *respectively.* The halving
principle may be applied to contracted forms for
past tenses; thus, ⟍⟍ *endanger,* ⟍⟍ *endangered;*
but in many cases the same form may safely be employed for both present and past tenses; thus, ⟋⟍
respect-ed, ⟍ *suspect-ed.* Contracted outlines are
generally written on the line.

Omission of N

passenger	appointment
stranger	attainment
messenger	contentment
danger	assignment
dangerous	entertainment
contingency	enlightenment
emergency	abandonment
exigency	ironmonger
stringency	oneself

Omission of R

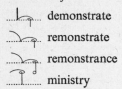

demonstrate	monstrous
remonstrate	manuscript
remonstrance	henceforward
ministry	thenceforward

Omission of -ect

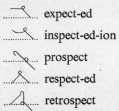

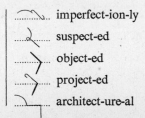

expect-ed	imperfect-ion-ly
inspect-ed-ion	suspect-ed
prospect	object-ed
respect-ed	project-ed
retrospect	architect-ure-al

Omission of kt before -ive

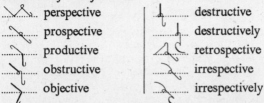

perspective		destructive
prospective		destructively
productive		retrospective
obstructive		irrespective
objective		irrespectively

Omission of K before -shun

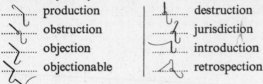

production		destruction
obstruction		jurisdiction
objection		introduction
objectionable		retrospection

Exercise 115

Write in shorthand

The *appointment of a stranger as Passenger* Super-intendent *is a* dis*appointment to-the* local candidates *for-the* position. *There-is a* rumour *of a* demonstration *of-*protest against *what-have-been called the monstrous* methods *of-the* administration *in-this-*matter. *There-is, however, great danger in a* form *of remonstrance that-*may provoke *a dangerous* outburst *in-*place *of-the-*present *contentment, and, with great respect to-the* leaders, *we-*fail *to* see *any prospect of-their* attaining *their object* if-*they* demonstrate *in-the* way suggested. *It-is* always *the* un*expected and* un*suspected contingency that-is* likely *to* happen, *and-we expect-the* present *emergency* will prove no exception *to-the* rule. *The introduction of a* policy *of obstruction* or *destruction*, or even *of* interference *with* reasonable *jurisdiction*, may-*be productive of* dis*contentment all-*round. *It-is to be* hoped every means will-*be* sought *for-the attainment of-the objective.*

Exercise 116

Write in shorthand

We-fear *there-is*-no *prospect of* success *for-those-who* raise *objection to-the appointment, and, quite irrespective of-the* merits *of-the respective* parties, *we-would* urge-*the abandonment of obstructive* measures *and-the entertainment of-the* suggested resort *to*-threats. Further *enlightenment is* necessary if matters *are to* proceed smoothly *henceforward. It-is* pleasant *to*-turn *from this-subject to-the* attractions *of-the* country-side, where *there-are* numerous *objects of entertainment and instruction for all who care to*-look *for-them. The* jerry builder *has*-not-yet begun *his destructive* work, *and-the monstrous things which* he *calls architecture, but which* cause dis*appointment and*-grief *to-the genuine architect, have*-not-yet appeared *to*-ruin-*the prospect. The* unspoiled beauty *of* Nature still remains *to* compel *our respect*ful admiration, *and to remonstrate in* silence against *those whose object is to*-make money, even *though it* involves *the destruction of-the-most* glorious *prospect.*

Exercise 117

Write in shorthand

(*a*) Please-send *a messenger to-the passenger* office *and* ask if-*there-is any danger of-the* train *being* late at Macclesfield. *The* present *emergency has* arisen through-*the* death *of-the* man *in*-charge *of-the* post-office, *and-the abandonment of-the stranger's* claim might bring-about-*the very contingency we-are* striving *to*-avoid. *We-had-the* same *emergency on-the appointment of-the* postmaster three-*years*-ago, *and-the entertainment* then arranged *had to be* abandoned *because-it-was* felt *that-it-would-be dangerous to* proceed. *The abandonment* caused dis*appointment*, *of*-course, *but* *contentment* followed *enlightenment as-to-the* cause *and* eventually *the attainment of-the* original *object was* secured.

(*b*) *The* demonstration against *the* administration *of-the* local funds *was*, *in-our-opinion*, *a monstrous* mistake, *and-we-shall remonstrate as* vigorously *as-we-can*. *The monstrosity in-the* shape *of an* effigy *of-the chairman of-the* administrative committee *was of-the-most objectionable* nature, *and*-only served *to* demonstrate *the* poor taste *of-those-who* designed *it*. I *should-have to*-write *a* long *manuscript* if I desired *to*-express my resentment properly, *and*-even then my *remonstrance would*-not-*be too* strong. I *should* like *to* assist *in-the* administration *of*-personal punishment upon-*the* men at-*the* head *of-this monstrous* business. *It-is* pleasant *to* know *that* no-one *from-the ministry was* concerned *in-the*-matter.

(*c*) *As-to-the architect's project for-the* alteration *of-the* club premises, I *rather suspect that-his* idea *of-the architectural* possibilities *is imperfect and*-incorrect. *With great respect to-him, because of-the imperfection of*-my acquaintance *with architecture*, I *respect*fully suggest *that-he-should* take counsel *with* someone *whose architectural* ability *would* entitle *him to*-express *an opinion*. I *quite expect-the architect* will consider *me* dis*respect*ful, *and*-I-am upset at-*the prospect of a* disagreement *with him*. My *object is to* secure *an* inspection *of-the* premises *as* they-*are*, and I-*believe-that* un*expected and*, indeed, un*suspected* possibilities may develop *as a* result. *There-can-be* no dis*respect in* suggesting *that a retrospective* view *of-the* case, so-*as-to* secure *a* proper *perspective, should-be* under-taken. *This-is* exactly *what* I suggested some-time-ago, *but it-was* considered *an* interference *with-the* administration, *and* no steps were taken.

Exercise 118

Write in shorthand

Irrespective entirely *of-the different* views *of-the respective* parties *to-the* discussion, I-am compelled *to* consider-*the* possible results *of-the obstructive* course taken by-*the* council. *There-can-be* no-doubt *that-the objective would-be more* easily attained if-these merely *destructive* methods were abandoned. They *can* only *be productive of*-mischief *in-the* case *of prospective* candidates *for* admission *to-the* society, *and-this whether we* consider-*the* matter *prospect*ively or *retrospect*ively. *A retrospective* examination will show *what-has* occurred *in-the* past, *in* similar *circumstances, and a prospective* consideration will show *what-is* likely *to* occur *in-the* future, if-*the respective* parties *are* allowed *to* follow *their-own* merely *obstructive* ideas. Each will-be *destructive of-the* other, *and*-will certainly act *destructively*, no matter *what* each may say. They *should-be* instructed *to* consider, *respect*ively *and* collectively, *the* effects *of-the* present methods *and* advised *to*-refuse *them*.

Exercise 119

Write in shorthand

The objection *to-the* obstruction *in-the* new bill *is*-not simply *a* personal matter. *The obstruction is objectionable on-several* grounds. *First, because it*-will certainly lead *to a destruction of-the* opposition *which-has-been* so *care*fully arranged, *and*, secondly, *because-the*-matter *is* one *which* falls *under* another *jurisdiction. The introduction of* various methods *of-production and* re*production has* no bearing *on-the* question, *as-the* least *retrospection would-have* shown *beyond* doubt. *It*-may sound dis*respect*ful, *but* my-*own* view

is that-the architect and-his friends, *who-are,* I-*suspect,
the* authors *of-the* bill, *are* simply unaware *of-the* real
circumstances of-the case, *and-have*-not *given-the project
the* consideration *it* deserves.

Summary

General contractions are formed by the omission of

p	in words where the *p* is only lightly sounded.
k or *g*	between *ng-t* and between *ng-sh*.
t	between circle *s* and a following consonant.
n	in words like *passenger,* *emer-gency,* etc.
r	in words like *remonstrate,* *demonstrate.*
-ect	in words like *expect-ed,* etc.
-kt	in words like *productive,* etc.

Derivatives are formed from contracted outlines by
attaching a prefix or a suffix, as in, *respect,*
disrespect, *respectively.*

CHAPTER XXX

FIGURES, ETC.

Figures. 185. Figures *one* to *seven*, and the figure *nine* are represented by shorthand outlines. All other numbers, except round numbers, are represented in the ordinary way by the Arabic numerals. In dealing with round numbers, the following abbreviations are used:

⁓ *hundred* or *hundredth*, as in 4 400;

(or (*thousand* or *thousandth*, as in 3(3,000;

⁓ *hundred thousand*, as in 4 400,000;

⁓ *million*, or *millionth*, as in 3 3,000,000;

⁓ *hundred million*, as in 7 700,000,000;

⟍ *billion*, as in 4⟍ *four billion*.

The principal monetary units are expressed as follows: ⟍ *pounds*, as in 2 £200, 6(£6,000. 5 £5,000,000; | *dollar*, (*dollars*, as in 15($15,000; ⟍ *francs*, as in 4 400 fr.; ⟋ *rupees*, as in 2⟋ Rs. 2,000,000.

⟍ written close after a figure represents *per cent*, as in 3⟍ 3%.

Accent, etc. 186. (*a*) Accent may be shown by writing a small cross close to the vowel of the accented syllable; thus, ⟋ *ar'rows*, ⟋ *arose'*.

150

(b) Emphasis is marked by drawing one or more lines underneath; a single line under a single word must be made wave-like, ⌇⌇⌇, to distinguish it from ⎯ k.

(c) The sign ⩥ indicates that the preceding remark is to be taken humorously.

Proper Names, etc. 187. In the few cases where it is necessary to indicate exactly the vowel following a diphthong, the separate signs should be used and not the triphone as explained in paragraph 35; thus, ⦚ Bryan, ⦚ Bryon, ⌐ Myatt, ⌐ Myott, ◁ Wyatt. Similarly, if it is necessary to indicate exactly the second of two consecutive vowels, the separate signs should be used and not the diphone; thus, ⌒ Leah, but ⌒ Leo; ∟ genii, ⌒ nuclei, △ radii. The necessity for the use of these separate vowel-signs will be found to arise but seldom.

Scottish, Welsh, and Irish Consonants and Vowels. 188. The Scotch guttural ch, and the Irish gh are written thus, ⌐ ch, as in ⌒ loch, ⌒ Loughrea, ⌒ Clogher. The Welsh ll by ⌒ ll; thus, ⌒ Llan.

Foreign Consonants and Vowels. 189. The German guttural ch is written thus, ⌐ ch, as in ⌐ ich, ⌐ Dach; French nasal ⌒, as in ⌒ soupçon; French and German vowels ⌒ jeune, ⌐ Goethe, ╪ dû.

Exercise 120

Write in shorthand

*The Chair*man, *in* moving-*the* adoption *of-the* report *and* accounts, dealing *first with-the* accounts *of-the* local holding company, said *it-would-be* noted *that-the* amount paid up *on-the* shares *was* increased by F.42,560, or £3,546; *this-was to-*keep pace *with-the* increase *in* capital costs *of-the* property, including extensions *during* recent *years*. Sundry creditors at £3,507 included £2,583 *for* Java income-tax reserve (*of-which* £1,666 appearing *to-the* debit *of-*profit *and* loss account *was* additional *for-the-year*), besides bonus due *to-the* staff *and-*some *trade* items. *The* outlay *on* capital account £3,714, included £2,746 *for a* new drying installation, smoke house, etc., *the balance being for* upkeep *of-the* immature area. They-*had* now *a* monthly capacity of 15,000 lb. sheet, *the* policy *of-the* board *being* to increase *their* output *of-this* quality *to* 50 per-cent *of-the* estate's whole output.

Their cash assets *in-*London *and* Java amounted *to* £16,712, *an* increase *of nearly* £5,000. *The* crop *was* 449,000 lb., *as* compared *with-the* restricted crop *of* 230,473 lb. *in-the* preceding *year*, *and* against *an* estimate *of* 394,000 lb., despite *the* fact *that for-the* last *two-*months *of-the-year* they-were *on a* restricted basis. *The* average net selling price *was a* fraction *under* 1s. 1d., against 1s. 4·35d. last-*year*. *Thanks, however, to a* reduction *from* 1s. 1·80d. *to* 8·92d., *in-the* total costs, *the* net profit per pound *was* 4·02d., or 1½d. above-*the* previous *year*. *It-was largely owing to-this* reduction *in* costs *that-*they-*had* made *a* net profit *of* £8,843, *over* 12 per-cent *on-the* issued capital. He thought-*the* shareholders *would* agree *that-this-was a* pleasing result.

CHAPTER XXXI

NOTE-TAKING, TRANSCRIPTION, ETC.

Note-Taking. 190. The inexperienced writer may sometimes find difficulty in turning over the leaves of his notebook. The following method may be usefully adopted—While writing on the upper half of the leaf, introduce the second finger of the left hand between it and the next leaf, keeping the leaf which is being written on steady by the first finger and thumb. While writing on the lower part of the page shift the leaf by degrees, till it is about half-way up the book, and, at a convenient moment, lift up the first finger and thumb, when the leaf will turn over almost of itself. This is the best plan when writing on a desk or table. When writing with the book on the knee, the first finger should be introduced instead of the second, and the leaf be moved up only about two inches. The finger should be introduced at the first pause the speaker makes, or at any other convenient opportunity that presents itself. Another method is to take hold of the bottom left-hand corner of the leaf with the finger and thumb, and on the bottom line being reached the leaf is lifted and turned over. Some reporters prefer a reporting book the leaves of which turn over like those of a printed book. When such a book is used there is less difficulty in turning over the leaves with the left hand. Whichever form of book is used, the writer should confine himself to *one side* of the paper till the end of the book is reached, and then turn the book round and write on the blank side of the paper, proceeding as before.

Unvocalized Outlines. 191. The essentials of accurate note-taking are rapid writing and facile reading, and it is to these objects that the following chapters are directed, special methods being developed for the formation of brief and legible outlines. The student is already familiar with a method of forming contracted outlines. He will find in succeeding pages further applications of that method, and also a method of abbreviation by Intersection, which gives distinctive forms of well-known combinations of words. Phraseography is also greatly extended, and compact outlines are provided for many technical and general phrases. Vocalization being a great hindrance to speed, Phonography from its beginning is so constructed that the necessity for the insertion of vowels is reduced to a minimum. By means of the principle of writing words in position, unvocalized outlines which are common to two or more words are as readily distinguished as are musical notes by means of the difference of place assigned to them on the stave.

Position-writing. 192. In speed practice, which should, of course, be pursued concurrently with the careful study of the advanced style as hereafter developed, the rules of position-writing should be carefully observed. After a short time this will become automatic. Even unique outlines that may appear to be independent of position are rendered still more legible by being written in accordance with the position-writing rules. At first a few vowels may be inserted, in order to promote clearness and to enable the writer to acquire the power of vocalizing quickly when necessary. But efforts should be made from the outset to write the outlines clearly and in position, and to make these, rather than vocalization, the factors on which reliance is placed for accurate reading. When a fair speed in writing has been reached the student should avail himself of opportunities of reporting public speakers, vocalizing but little even when there is ample time, so that the ability to dispense with vowels may be cultivated.

Practising the Rules. 193. Since perfect familiarity with the rules is essential to rapid writing, the aspirant for speed is advised to vary his dictation practice by writing from dictation the exercises which appear in ordinary type in the pages of the *Manual* or first part of the *Instructor*. Pitman Shorthand is a connected system, and the most elementary rules have been formulated with the needs of the fast writer in view all the time. There is an orderly development throughout the whole system, so that the advanced principles of abbreviation cannot be properly understood and instantaneously applied unless the elementary rules are understood and can be applied without hesitation. Practice in the writing of the exercises which illustrate the various rules has upon the shorthand student much the same effect as practising the scales has upon the advanced student of music. The more thoroughly the scales are studied and practised, the more easily will the musician play the most intricate passages in any musical composition. Similarly, the more familiar the speed writer is with the exercises given in illustration of the fundamental rules of the system, by means of repeated practice in writing exercises from dictation, the more easily and quickly will he become a fast and accurate writer of any matter he may be called upon to take in shorthand. It is well known that the most accomplished pianists are the most persistent and regular in their practice of difficult scales. The shorthand writer cannot do better than follow their example and apply their methods to his own subject.

Knowledge of Outlines. 194. The reading of printed shorthand in the advanced style is as important as writing practice, and should be practised daily. It gradually gives an extensive knowledge of outlines, and the power of reading unvocalized shorthand, as well as trains the student in the selection of the best outlines, and also considerably expedites the arrival of the time when the omission of practically all vowels may be ventured upon. When unvocalized shorthand can be read with facility, speed and self-reliance will be greatly increased. The student in reading his notes should observe whether he has omitted essential vowels or inserted unnecessary ones. The latter is as important as the former, because the loss of time occasioned by the insertion of unnecessary vowels may render the writer unable to keep pace with the speaker. An outline which has caused difficulty in writing or reading should be written in position several times, the word being repeated aloud simultaneously with the writing.

Knowledge of Contracted Forms. 195. It is impossible to lay too much stress upon the importance of an absolutely perfect knowledge of the grammalogues and contractions. It will be found that any ordinary piece of matter consists of about sixty per cent—and sometimes more—of words which are included in the lists of grammalogues and contractions given in this book. Easily written signs have been given to those words for the very reason that they are words in common use, and the student should know them with such thoroughness that he can write them at almost any speed at which they can be dictated. This familiar knowledge can only be obtained by repeated practice in writing from dictation the exercises which have been compiled for the purpose. The student cannot know these special word-forms too well. Fluency in writing and neatness in the formation of the forms will increase in proportion as his knowledge grows, and the general style of his shorthand notes will be improved as a result.

Method of Practice. 196. To a great extent the student must judge for himself as to his method of practice, but the following is recommended—Begin by taking down from dictation, well within your powers, for periods of five minutes, and with the insertion of none but necessary vowels. After half-an-hour's practice, read back to the dictator a passage chosen by yourself, and also one other, the choice of which should be left to him. Resume practice at an increased speed of ten words per minute, the same method of reading being pursued at the end of each half-hour. Continue the same speeds each evening until the higher becomes moderately easy, both in writing and reading. Then begin at the higher speed, and at the end of half-an-hour increase it by ten words a minute. Read a portion of the notes which were taken a day or two previously, to test your powers unaided by memory. Aim at keeping not more than two or three words behind the reader. After a time you should occasionally practise writing ten or a dozen words behind the reader, so as to acquire the power of doing so in emergencies. Ear and hand should work practically simultaneously in order to secure the best results. When a wrong outline has been written; ignore the fact and go on. You may correct it afterwards at your leisure. If several outlines are wrongly written, reduce the speed. The policy of hastening slowly was never more justified than it is in learning to take a note.

Regular Practice. 197. At first, particular attention should be given to the outlines, but imperceptibly the writing will become instinctive by practice, which should be regular and systematic. Practice of an hour a day is better than two, or even three, hours every second day. Practice in writing, and practice in reading both printed shorthand and your own notes will quickly give you confidence, which has its root in conscious ability to do the work required.

Varied Dictation. 198. The subject-matter taken down should be as varied as possible so that the writer's vocabulary may be extended, but special regard should be had to the object for which the art is being acquired. As to the size of the shorthand, that which is natural to the individual is the best for him; but the writing should not be cramped. A free style is necessary and should be cultivated. It will add greatly to the legibility of the notes if the large circles, loops and hooks are exaggerated in size. The pen should be held with only moderate pressure, and the whole hand, poised lightly on the little finger, should move with it. The common tendency to write sprawling outlines when writing at a high speed is distinctly bad. The immediate cause is mental stress, partly induced by anxiety lest a word should be omitted. It is obviously preferable to omit a few outlines rather than to risk the legibility of many. If the possibility of an occasional omission is not a source of fear, and if there is confidence in the ability to record, at all events the essential words of the speaker, the best chance is secured of recording everything. Even if something important has been left out, confidence must be maintained, or the rest of the note will suffer.

Concentration. 199. Concentration upon the work in hand is necessary even when the art of note-taking has been acquired, for unless the general trend of the discourse is followed, together with the grammatical construction of the sentences, the transcript, owing to looseness of speech met with everywhere, will sometimes be indifferent and possibly misleading. Special attention should be paid to the speaker's tone of voice and any peculiarities of speech or manner which may render his meaning clear, though he may not express himself properly. Any habit persevered in becomes automatic, and the mechanical writing of the shorthand characters is fortunately no exception to the rule. When experience has been gained, attention can be concentrated almost entirely on the matter; but as in writing an important letter in longhand some portion of the attention, slight, but nevertheless valuable, is devoted to the calligraphy and punctuation, so should this be the case in writing shorthand.

Punctuation in Note-taking. 200. Full stops should always be written if at all possible because of the great assistance it gives the note-taker in the transcription of his notes. Dashes should also be inserted where possible in order to indicate where the speaker drops the principal sentence and goes off at a tangent, and where he resumes it, if ever. The commas at the beginning and end of a parenthetical observation should be shown by a short space, the principal instance being where the noun and verb are separated as in the following sentence: "The soldier, being tired after the long day's march, quickly fell asleep." In such a simple case as this it is hardly necessary, but with long and involved sentences, it is of great assistance in analysing their construction to be able at once to locate the verb, which will very often be the second or third word after the second space. The following are examples: "The speaker, having discussed at length the arguments advanced by his opponent in the various speeches he had delivered during the week, earnestly urged his hearers not to be influenced by specious promises"; and "We, acting on behalf of the executive, who were of one opinion as to the necessity of prompt action in the matter, immediately issued a writ against the offender and succeeded in gaining substantial damages." As a corollary, it is obvious that a space should be left only where it has a definite meaning—a small space for a parenthesis or important comma, and a somewhat larger one for a full stop, if the stop cannot be written.

Reporting Technical Matter. 201. Where an engagement is expected for the reporting of highly technical addresses, or for a meeting at which speeches or discussions on highly technical matter have to be reported, it is obviously advisable that the shorthand writer should prepare himself beforehand as well as possible. If he does not already possess a fairly good knowledge of the subject-matter of the lecture or subject of discussion dealt with at which he is to exercise his professional skill, he should read up the subject so as to become more or less familiar with the terms which are likely to be used in connection with the engagement he has taken. Unless some such means are taken, it is likely that the shorthand writer's work will be unsatisfactory, both to himself and his clients. *Pitman Shorthand Writers' Phrase Books and Guides* have been compiled with the object of furnishing assistance in the application of shorthand to technical matters, and *Technical Reporting* gives valuable advice and suggestions for those wishing to be successful in this special branch of the shorthand-writing profession.

Summary

1. Exercise yourself in the use of a notebook.
2. Practise the reading of unvocalized shorthand.
3. Always write in position.
4. Practise the illustrative exercises from dictation.
5. Enlarge your knowledge of outlines by reading printed shorthand.
6. Read at least a portion of every note you take.
7. Vary your dictation matter as much as possible.
8. Pay attention to the subject-matter dictated or spoken.
9. Always indicate the end of a sentence.
10. Acquire a perfect knowledge of the contracted forms.
11. Read up the subject before undertaking a report of technical matter.
12. Practise note-taking every day.

CHAPTER XXXII

ESSENTIAL VOWELS

Vocalized Outlines. 202. There are certain word-outlines which should be vocalized to some extent. The following directions, therefore, should be carefully noted—

(*a*) In single stroke outlines having an initial and a final vowel, the final vowel should be inserted; thus, ⁀ *echo*, ⁀ *arrow*, ⁀ *area*, ⁀ *era*.

(*b*) An outline should be written in position notwithstanding that it has an initially or a finally joined diphthong-sign; thus, ⁀ *Isaac*, ⁀ *item*, ⁀ *review*, ⁀ *institute*, ⁀ *future*, ⁀ *ague*, ⁀ *renew*.

(*c*) Where an upward or a downward *r* or *l* does not indicate a preceding or a following vowel, the vowel-sign should be inserted; thus, ⁀ *aright*, ⁀ *erode*, ⁀ *irritable*, ⁀ *oracle*, ⁀ *aroma*; ⁀ *jolly*, ⁀ *jelly*, ⁀ *gilly*; ⁀ *billow*, ⁀ *early*.

(*d*) Generally speaking, vowels should be inserted—

(1) Where words of the same part of speech have similar outlines and the same position;

(2) Where a word is unfamiliar, or unfamiliar in the special sense in which it is used; and

(3) Where an outline has been written incorrectly, badly, or in the wrong position, in which case the insertion of a vowel is the quickest way of making the outline legible.

(*e*) It is also advisable to vocalize as fully as possible—

(1) Where the subject-matter is unknown; and

(2) Where the language is poetical, unusual, or florid, because in these instances the context is not as helpful as in other cases.

The following lists contain some of the more common words in which the vowels indicated by italic should be inserted in order to facilitate transcription; but after a little experience in shorthand writing the student will instinctively recognize other outlines in which distinguishing vowels should be inserted.

(1) *Insertion of an initial vowel*

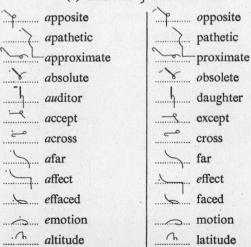

*a*pposite	*o*pposite
*a*pathetic	pathetic
*a*pproximate	proximate
*a*bsolute	*o*bsolete
*au*ditor	daughter
*a*ccept	except
*a*cross	cross
*a*far	far
*a*ffect	*e*ffect
*e*ffaced	faced
*e*motion	*m*otion
*a*ltitude	latitude

(2) *Insertion of a medial vowel*

adapt		adopt
extricate		extract
commissionaire		commissioner
exaltation		exultation
voluble		valuable
amazing		amusing
innovation		invasion
lost		last
layman		laymen
sulphite		sulphate
humanly		humanely

(3) *Insertion of a final vowel*

chilly		chill
monarchy		monarch
amicably		amicable
monkey		monk
manly		manual
enemy		name
anomaly		animal
snow		sun
liberally		liberal
radically		radical

Exercise 121

Read, copy, and transcribe

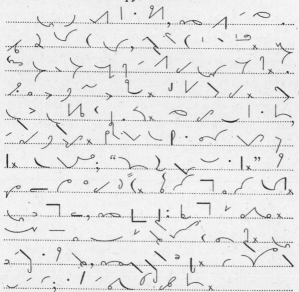

Exercise 122

Write in shorthand

(*In this and in the following exercise the vowels marked in italic should be inserted. Marked in divisions of thirty words each.*)

We should-neither *a*ccept any theories nor ad*o*pt any views, however v*o*luble the *a*dvocates of-such-may-be, except we-are convinced that-they-are authorized, and-have-been tested | and *a*ttested by-those upon whose veracity we-can rely, or unless our reason approves of-them and-we-have *a*mple proof that-though they-may-have some defects, | their ad*o*ption will-be valuable to us in-the-main, that-we-may employ them to-the benefit of-ourselves and others, and-that-they-will-be readily

recalled on | *o*ccasions of necessity. No matter how *a*pposite
the arguments may appear which-are *a*dduced to-move us from
an *o*pposite opinion, we should-be as *a*damant in-the face of |
any demand upon-the feelings, which-our reason does-not
sanction. Thus, any *a*ttempt to-tempt us to foolish actions will-
only *e*nd in-the failure of-the tempter. We- | have-been en-
do*w*ed with mental faculties far and *a*way above those with-
which-the lower *a*nimals are end*u*ed, in order that-we-may
protect ourselves from-our enem*i*es, and may | add to-our
happiness. It-is a fact, however, that-such-is-the *e*ffect of-
persuasion upon some persons of weak will that-they become
as mere wax in-the | hands of-those-who-would lure them to ruin.
With-such people it-seems only necessary for a fluent rogue to
*a*dvance an *a*lluring prospect of an *a*ffluent position at- | little
cost, and-they fall at-once, without a defence, into-the trap set
for-them. Is-not-this-the secret of almost every successful fraud
we-have-heard or | read of in-any-nation?   (275 words)

Exercise 123

Write in shorthand

There-are, *a*las, too-many persons who-make-it their vocation
or *a*vocation in life to dupe others less able than themselves.
They-have-no feelings of honour, or *e*lse | would-not prey on-
the failings of-those around. They despise veracity, and-their
greed for gold amounts almost to voracity. In order to obtain
wealth they-make light of- | every obstacle, and are slow to
*a*dmit themselves beaten. They-are *a*verse to honest labour,
and-yet they spare no pains to become versed in-the cunning
arts necessary to | extract money from-their victims, and to
extric*a*te themselves from-the consequences of-their illegal
actions. They devise a plot, and, under-the semblance of
*a*dvice, they *o*perate on-the | greed and-credulity of ignorant
persons, and-having thrown them off their guard, lead them into
foolish *a*dventures. Truly "A fool and-his money are easily
parted." We should-not | *a*ttach too-much importance to a
scheme because-it-is introduced with a flourish of fair words, nor
should-we touch any speculative *a*ffair without first subjecting
it to an | accurate examination. If-we could only examine the
*a*nnual returns of failures and analyse their-causes, we should-
find that many are *a*ttributable to an *u*tter absence of judgment
in- | the conduct of business, and an over confidence in-the
ni*c*ety and honesty of-others.   (225 words)

Summary

Vowels should be inserted—

(*a*) In single stroke outlines where a vowel is not indicated by position;

(*b*) In cases where a vowel is not indicated by an initial or a final stroke;

(*c*) In pairs of words occupying the same position but having a varying vowel;

(*d*) Where the language is of an unusual character.

CHAPTER XXXIII

SPECIAL CONTRACTIONS

Formation of Contractions. 203. In the Special Contractions dealt with in this chapter, the student is introduced to further methods of contracting outlines. The importance of having such contractions is shown by the fact that in ordinary language only a very limited number of words are used. Of these words at least 60 to 70 per cent are of frequent occurrence, and are, therefore, included in the grammalogues and contractions of Pitman Shorthand. An essential point in forming contracted outlines is to choose forms that are distinctive and legible at sight. With this end in view the special contractions are formed according to the following rules—

(a) By employing the first two or three strokes of the full outline, as in ⌍⌍ *perform*, ⌙ *advertisement*, ⌐ *expediency*, ⌒ *regular*, ⌒ *unanimity*, ⌒⌒ *henceforth*. (See sections 1–3.)

(b) By medial omission, as in ⌐ *intelligence*, ⌒ *sympathetic*, ⌙ *satisfactory*, ⌒ *influential*, ⌒⌒ *amalgamation*. (See section 4.)

(c) By using logograms, as in ⌒ *thankful*, ⌒ *something*, ⌒ *remarkable*. (See section 5.)

(d) By intersection, as in ⌙ *enlarge*, ⌲ *nevertheless*, ⌙ *notwithstanding*. (See section 5.)

Adjectives and Adverbs. 204. As a general rule the same contracted form may represent either an adjective or an adverb, but where a distinction is necessary the adverb should be represented either by writing a joined or disjoined *l*, or by writing the form for the adverb in full; thus, ⟍ *irregular,* ⟍ *irregularly;* ⟍ *substantial,* ⟍ *substantially.*

Contractions and -ing. 205. Dot *-ing* is generally used after contractions. In a few words such as ⟍ *distinguishing,* ⟍ *relinquishing,* and ⟍ *extinguishing,* where the stroke is clearly better, the stroke is used.

Arrangement of Lists. 206. The lists of contractions which follow are arranged according to the principles explained above, and the student should make himself thoroughly familiar with them. The portion of a word which is not represented in the contracted outline is shown in parentheses. This arrangement will help the student to memorize the contracted forms. Thus, ⟍ *pec* is the contraction for *peculiar-ity,* ⟍ *perf* for *perform-ed,* ⟍ *perfs* for *performance,* ⟍ *Feb.* for *February,* ⟍ *fam* for *familiar-ity,* and so on. The exercises which follow each list should be written from dictation until they can be taken down with ease and rapidity, and read back from the shorthand notes without hesitation.

SPECIAL CONTRACTIONS: SECTION 1

pec(uliar-ity)

perf(orm-ed)

perf(orms-an)ce

perf(or)mer

perp(endicular)

pub(lic)

repub(lic)

repub(lica)n

pub(lish-ed)

pub(li)sher

pub(lica)tion

prac(tice)

prac(tise-d)

prac(tic)able

prejud(ice-d-ial-ly)

prelim(inary)

prob(able-ly-ility)

profici(ent-cy-ly)

prop(ortion-ed)

propor(tionate)

subsc(ribe-d)

subsc(rip)tion

substan(tial-ly)

defici(ent-cy-ly)

descri(ption)

diffic(ulty)

disch(arge-d)

disting(uish-ed)

adver(tise-d-ment)

Exercise 124

Read, copy, and transcribe

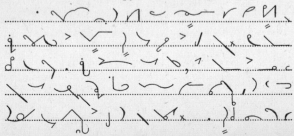

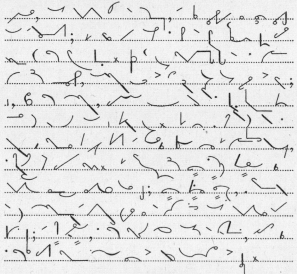

Exercise 125

Write in shorthand

In-the *preliminary* announcement *published* on-Thursday
the *public* were made aware of-the *deficiency* in-the income
of-the *Performers* Society which *performs* a good work in a
most | *practicable* manner. The offices of-the-society are
situated in a building which-is a fine example of-the *perpen-
dicular* architecture, but is in a state of decay. Lately there- |
has-been a discussion among-the-members on-the powers of-
the committee, and many divergent views were expressed by-
the-chairman and other members. As a tribunal the committee |
do-not always show a dignified attitude.

Among other observations, some of-which were extremely
strong in tone, the chairman, a person of-*prejudiced* views, said
there-were many *difficulties* | in-the way, but it-was-not at-all
im*probable* that our new patents would revive our trade in-the
South-American *Republics*, as-they-were *peculiar*ly applicable
to-the wants of-its people.   (154 words)

Exercise 126

Read, copy, and transcribe

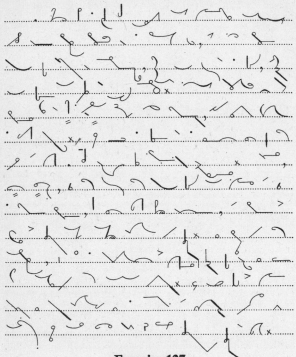

Exercise 127

Write in shorthand

The chairman, in-the-course-of his speech, said that to-seek-the preservation of-the concern when-the profits were so un-*substantial* and so dis*proportionate* to-the amount invested, | and when-the price of-the stock was so depreciated, was absurd, and it was inadvisable to-carry on-the company.

The *advertisements* in-the paper are out-of all- | *proportion* to-the news, which-is very *deficient*, and-we marvel at-the prosperity of-the *publication* and-the confidence of-the *publishers*. It-has often *subscribed substantial* amounts to | *public* funds, opened its columns for national *subscriptions*, and given *distinguished* services to-the cause of charity.

The *performer* who *performed* at-the theatre is a Russian, and-his artistic | *performance* of-the play brought out all-the *peculiarities* of-the Slav race, although-there-was a dis*proportion* in-his acting which-would render a long engagement im*practicable*.   (148 words)

SPECIAL CONTRACTIONS: SECTION 2

Jan(uary)		gov(ern-ed)
cap(able)		gov(er)nment
charac(ter)		fam(iliar-ity)
charac(ter)is(t)ic		fam(ilia)rize
commer(cial-ly)		fam(iliar)ization
cross-ex-(amine-d-ation)		Feb(ruary)
exch(ange-d)		finan(cial-ly)
exped(iency)		effici(ent-cy-ly)
expend(iture)		suffici(ent-cy-ly)
expens(ive)		manuf(acture)r
esp(ecial-ly)		math(ematical-ly)
esq(uire)		math(ematic)s
estab(lish-ed-ment)		math(ema)tician
immed(iate)		max(imum) (see *minimum* in section 4.)
impertur(bable)		
mag(netic-ism)		mechan(ical-ly)
manuf(acture-d)		metrop(olitan)
exting(uish-ed)		mor(t)g(age-d)

Exercise 128

Read, copy, and transcribe

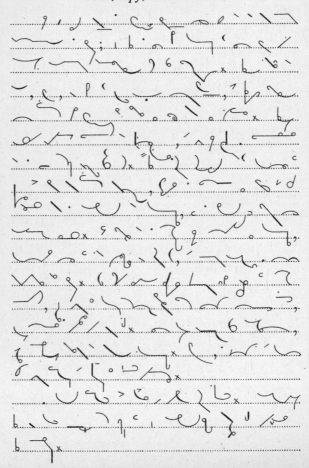

Exercise 129

Write in shorthand

At-the meeting of-the-directors today it-was stated that-the rates of-*exchange* in *January* and-*February* were favourable to *manufacturers* in-this-country. Regarding-the-matter | of *expediency*, to-discuss which the meeting was primarily called, it-was thought that-the plan suggested might prove very *expensive* and cause endless trouble in arranging-the necessary *mortgage*. | The chairman, John Ogden, *Esq.*, a *commercial* magnate, is a very *capable mathematician*, and he carries out all-his business with *mathematical* exactitude. He-is hoping that-the *mechanical efficiency* | of-the *establishment* may-be *sufficient* to-check any unnecessary *expenditure* during-the coming year. No-man is more *familiar* to-the-members of-the-*Exchange* than he, and-his | speeches at social functions are noted for-their humour, while-his placid manner is a *characteristic* which compels the admiration of all. He-is possessed of-great personal *magnetism*, and | it-is-due, undoubtedly to-his ability that-the company has an almost unassailable position which-has surprised those-who-are engaged in a similar *manufacture*. (176 words)

Exercise 130

Read, copy, and transcribe

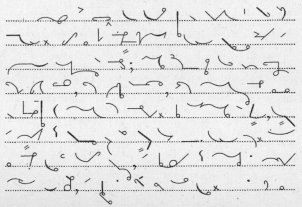

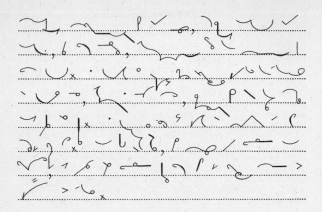

Exercise 131

Write in shorthand

The new book of essays by a member of-the-*Government* contains some very worthy sayings: "A person of-*character* is in*capable* of a mean action, and-is able-to- | *govern* himself under all-circumstances. We-cannot-be wise-men unless we *familiarize* ourselves, and sympathize, with human-nature. Our *familiarization* with new scenes and new peoples shows us the | in*sufficiency* of-our education." In-the-*immediate* future we-expect to see-the author at-the head of-the cabinet.

In dealing-with-the charge against the prisoner the *metro-politan* | magistrate passed the *maximum* sentence after a close *cross-examination* of-the offender, and-after several-witnesses had-been *cross-examined*, and despite the fact that-the-prisoner's action had-| been *governed* by *financial* troubles over-which he had no control. The magistrate is a man of-wide tastes, and-is one of-the prime movers in-our Agricultural Show, | and he-is regarded as an authority on-most-matters relating to-the land. His model farm is a splendid example of scientific farming, and it-is a source of-| amazement to-the farmers in-the district, who-are mostly satisfied with seeking for-the best-results by empirical methods.   (200 words)

SPECIAL CONTRACTIONS: SECTION 3

enthus(iastic-iasm)

incor(porated)

independ(ence-ent-ly)

indispens(able-ly)

individ(ual-ly)

inf(orm-ed)

inf(or)mer

interest

invest(ment)

negl(ect-ed)

negl(ig)ence

{ nev(er)
  Nov(ember) }

sensib(le-ility-ly)

elec(tric)

elec(tri)cal

elec(tri)city

recov(erable)

irrecov(erable)

ref(orm-ed)

ref(or)mer

reg(ular)

irreg(ular)

relinq(uish-ed)

rep(resent-ed)

rep(resenta)tion

rep(resentat)ive

respons(ible-ility)

irrespons(ible-ility)

organ(ize-d)

orga(ni)zer

organ(i)zation

certif(icate)

uni(form-ity-ly)

{ unan(imity)
  unan(imous-ly) }

yest(erday)

Exercise 132

Read, copy, and transcribe

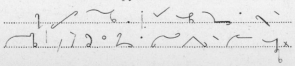

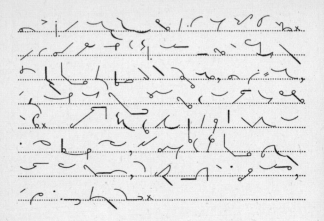

Exercise 133

Read, copy, and transcribe

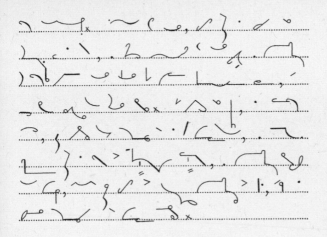

Exercise 134

Write in shorthand

Great-*interest* is manifested in-the *electric* apparatus at-the local exhibition, the *capable organizer* of-which is very *enthusiastic* in following-the development of *electricity* and-all *electrical* appliances.

Our *representative* on-the council is *responsible* for-the *negligence* of-the *reform*, and our committee is of-the *unanimous* opinion that in-the future its support cannot-be given | to-one who-has shown so-much *neglect* of-his duties, and it purposes nominating another and a better candidate for-the *November* elections.

Yesterday the *investment* was sanctioned by-| those *interest*ed in-the improvement of-the-association, and it-was hoped that-its previous position would soon be *recoverable*. When-the association becomes *incorporated*, its *certificate* should-be recognized | by-all similar *organizations*, some of-which have shown considerable opposition towards-it, and displayed an inexcusable temper when-the committee refused to-*relinquish*-the policy formulated several weeks-ago. | (150 words)

Exercise 135

Read, copy, and transcribe

Exercise 136

Write in shorthand

There-was a *unanimity* of opinion by-all-the *reformers* present that *organized* playgrounds were *indispensable* in-the education of children, and it-was resolved to-make a *representation* to-| the-council, and to ask it to introduce *uniformity* in-this-matter throughout-the county. This resolution was singularly unfortunate, as-it-was-the cause of-friction between these *individuals* | and-the-council.

Regular subscribers to-the institution showed arrogance at-the *irregular practices,* and many *informed*-the Board that-they-would withdraw their support if-such *irresponsible* actions were | allowed contrary to-all-the teachings of-the past. We-fear that no dis*interested* person was-the *informer* in-this-matter, and-*probably* he *represented*-the circumstances to be more | serious than they really are. The resignation of-the secretary, however, will-be demanded, as-his attitude amounts to insubordination, and-this will cause-the regret of all, no matter | what their *sensibility* may-be. The agenda of-the next Board meeting will-be far from un*interest*ing, and an apparently *irrecoverable* position may-be turned to-the advantage of-the | institution.   (181 words)

SPECIAL CONTRACTIONS: SECTION 4

Parl(iament)ary		defec(t)ive
pros(p)ec(t)us		execu(t)ive
tel(egraph)ic		exe(cut)or
tel(egr)am		exe(cutr)ix
satis(fact)ory		En(gli)sh
adm(inistrat)or		En(gli)shman
adm(inistratr)ix		En(g)land
ques(tion)ab(le-ly)		leg(islat)ive
fals(ific)ation		leg(isla)ture
amal(ga)mation		ar(bi)trate
amal(ga)mate		ar(bi)trator
m(inim)um		ar(bi)tration
symp(athet)ic		ar(bi)trary
inves(tig)ation		wheresoev(er)
insu(ran)ce		whereinsoev(er)
know(l)edge		whithersoev(er)
acknow(l)edge		u(ni)verse
in(con)siderate		u(ni)versal
in(fluen)tial-ly		u(ni)versality
int(elli)gence		u(ni)versity
int(elli)gent		howsoev(er)
int(elli)gible		whensoev(er)

Exercise 137

Read, copy, and transcribe

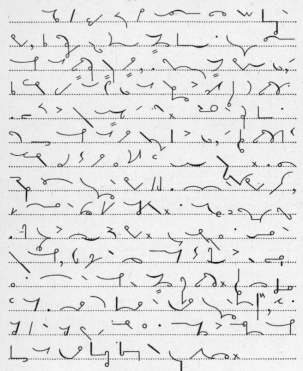

Exercise 138

Write in shorthand

One who *arbitrates* is called an *arbitrator*, and-there-is a growing tendency to-submit all disputes to *arbitration* by a third-party. Such decision would frequently save-the disputants | from being *arbitrary* and harsh towards one another

whereinsoever amends may-be-made. It-is thought by-some
that a *universal* language would foster the spirit of *arbitration*
throughout-the | *universe,* but as yet the attempts made to
formulate such a method of intercommunication have-not-been
very-*satisfactory.*   There-can-be   no-doubt that   *telegraphic*
communications, by-*telegram* and | wireless, work for-the-cause
of peace.

The *investigation* by-the *parliamentary* committee was *uni-versally acknowledge*d to be justified, and although-the *falsifica-tion* of the reports was *established,* there-were-| many un*sym-pathetic* remarks, reflecting adversely on-the supposed failings
of-members of-the *legislature,* by *influential* and un*influential*
newspapers. All *Englishmen,* however, should-be proud of-the
legislative bodies of | *England* and should-be *sympathetic*
towards all endeavours to effect any *intelligent* progressive.
reforms.   (164 words)

Exercise 139

Read, copy, and transcribe

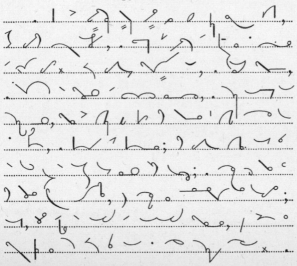

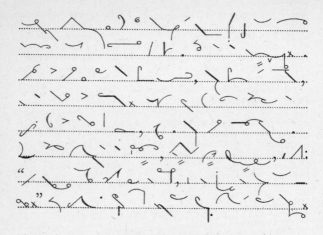

Exercise 140

Write in shorthand

At a quarterly gathering of-our scientific society the *university* lecturer said an *intelligible* reason could-be given for-his theory of economics, but-the *universality* of-its acceptance by | economists was-not-to-be expected in-our present state-of-*knowledge*. On a future occasion he-is to-lecture on-the-subject of a *minimum* wage for workers. He-| is *acknowledge*d to be a *capable* economist and a most excellent lecturer and writer on-the-subject for-which his name is famous.

The *prospectus* which-you forwarded *yesterday*, in | *acknowledg*ment of-mine of-last Monday, is un*questionably* very un*satisfactory howsoever* it-may-be considered. The *amalgamation* of two such prodigious concerns is very undesirable, and-the *intelligence* of-prospective | insurers should warn them of-the disadvantages of insuring under their tables. In-our company the *minimum* period for-such a policy of *insurance* is fifteen years, and it-is | *questionable* if-you-can secure better terms through any other *English* office. From-the-enclosed cutting you-will-find that-the *administrator* and *administratrix*, whom you-mention, were punished for | fraud in-connection with-the estate.   (186 words)

Special Contractions: Section 5

al(to)ge(ther)			un*principled*
*to*ge(ther)			n(o)t(withstand-ing)
(circum)stan-tial			de(nomi)nation-(al)
every*thing*			in(can)descent
*thank*ful			in(can)descence
some*thing*			en*large*
*remark*able			en*larger*
anything			in(con)ven(ient-ly-ce)
no*thing*			n(e)v(ertheless)
whatev(er)			irrem(ov)able
whenev(er)			rem(ov)able
misf(ortune)			

Exercise 141

Read, copy, and transcribe

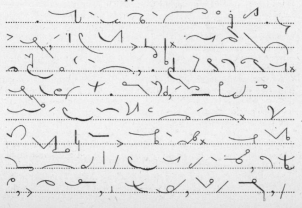

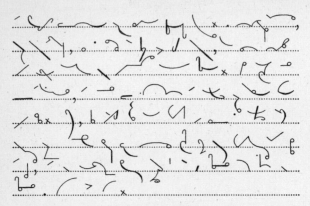

Exercise 142

Write in shorthand

Dear-Sir,

My committee have-considered your communication of-the 12th-inst., drawing attention to-several matters relating to-the *denominational* schools in-your district.

The *enlarge*ment of-the Cross | Street Schools received special consideration, and my committee are of-the opinion that *something* should-be done *immediate*ly in-this direction. To *enlarge* them again as-they-were *enlarged* ten | years-ago seems-to-be necessary, and it-is hoped to commence building operations during-the coming summer; and, to-save-time, my committee purpose giving the contract to-the | original builder of-the schools.

As-the whole of-the lighting of-the schools requires over-hauling, my committee have arranged for a report on-the matter, and-as-the *incandescence* | of-the mantles in-the offices here is very-*satisfactory*, it-is *probable* that similar *incandescent* lights will-be fitted throughout.

Notwithstanding your remarks, my committee think-there-will-be | no unfairness to-the voluntary-schools of-the district owing to-the recent Circular coming into force in-the autumn, and are of-the opinion that *nothing* should-be done | to hinder its working.

Yours-very-truly,   (187 words)

Exercise 143

Read, copy, and transcribe

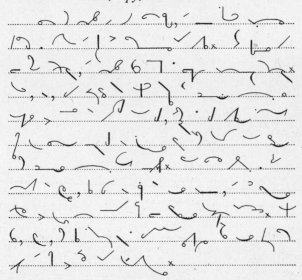

Exercise 144

Write in shorthand

Dear-Sir,

I-thank-you for-your *circumstantial* account of-the centenary celebrations in-your town, the reporting and sending of-which show much consideration on-your part. *Whenever* I-| can help you in similar circumstances, I-shall-be only too-pleased to-do-so.

It-is *remarkable* that-such an insignificant matter as-the one you-mention should give | offence in newspaper circles. One would-have-thought that-its very insignificance would-have-been *sufficient* to ensure its acceptance. Certainly it-is difficult to understand how *anything* of-the | kind could-be described as *unprincipled* and unmannerly. It-is a *misfortune* that-such a

quibble should-be raised and-I-hope that *everything* will-be-done
to-save any | *inconvenience* to-those *interest*ed in-the-press.
Nevertheless, I-do-not-think-the cause is *irremovable,* but rather
altogether removable, and-I-shall-be *thankful whatever* is done
to-bring-| the parties *together* again.

Yours-truly,   (156 words)

Summary

1. Special Contractions are formed as follows—
   (*a*) By employing the first two or three strokes of
   the full outline.
   (*b*) By medial omission.
   (*c*) By using logograms.
   (*d*) By intersection.
2. As a general rule the same contracted form may
   represent either an adjective or an adverb, but
   where distinction is necessary the adverb should
   be represented by a joined or disjoined *l*, or by
   writing the full form for the adverb.
3. Dot -*ing* is generally used after contractions, but
   the stroke is used in a few cases.

CHAPTER XXXIV

ADVANCED PHRASEOGRAPHY

Principles of Phrasing. 207. Bearing in mind the most important rules of phraseography, that all phraseograms must be recognizable at sight, easily written, and not too long, the various abbreviating devices are made to do service for words, or the forms of words are changed, or words are omitted altogether, with the result that an unlimited number of facile and legible phraseograms may thus be formed. The principles of phrasing are considered under the following heads—

(1) Circles, Loops and Hooks, (2) Halving, (3) Doubling, (4) Omissions.

Circles. 208. (*a*) The small circle, besides being used for *as, has, is, his,* as in ⟋ *it has been,* ⟍ *it is not,* may be used to represent *us,* as in ⟍ *from us,* ⟋ *please let us know.*

(*b*) The initial large circle may be used to represent the following—

    (1) *as we,*   as in   ℃ *as we think;*

    (2) *as* and *w,* ,, ,,   6 *as well as;*

    (3) *as* and *s,* ,, ,,   ℃ *as soon as.*

(*c*) The medial and final large circle may be used to represent the following—

    (1) *is* and *s,*   as in   ⟍ *it is said;*

    (2) *his* and *s,* ,, ,,   ⟍ *for his sake;*

(3) *s* and *s,*   as in ⌇ *in this city;*

(4) *s* and *has,*   ,,   ,,   ⌇ *this has been;*

(5) *s* and *is,*   ,,   ,,   ⌇ *this is.*

Loops. 209. (*a*) The *st* loop is used for *first,* as in
⌇ *at first cost,* ⌇ *Wednesday first;* (*b*) the *nst*
loop for *next,* as in ⌇ *Wednesday next.*

Hooks. 210. (*a*) The *r* and *l* hooks are used in
representing a few miscellaneous words, as in ⌇ *in
our view,* ⌇ *it appears,* ⌇ *by all means,* ⌇
it is only necessary, ⌇ *in the early part.*

(*b*) The *n* hook may be used for the following—

(1) *than,* as in ⌇ *older than;*

(2) *own,*   ,,   ,,   ⌇ *our own;*

(3) *been,*   ,,   ,,   ⌇ *I had been;*

(4) *on,*   ,,   ,,   ⌇ *carried on.*

(*c*) The *f* or *v* hook may be used for the following—

(1) *have,* as in ⌇ *who have;*

(2) *of,*   ,,   ,,   ⌇ *rate of interest;*

(3) *after,* ,,   ,,   ⌇ *Monday afternoon;*

(4) *even,* ,,   ,,   ⌇ *Monday evening;*

(5) in such phrases as ⌇ *at all events,* ⌇ *into
     effect.*

(d) The circle s and shun hook may be used for *association*, as in ⁓ₑ*medical association,* ⟋⟍*political association.*

Halving. 211. The halving principle is used for indicating the following—

(1) *it,*   as in ‿ *if it;*

(2) *to,*   „ „ ‿ *able to;*

(3) *not,*   „ „ ⌒ *you will not;*

(4) *would,* „ „ ⌇ *this would be;*

(5) *word,* „ „ ⌇ *this word;*

(6) in such phrases as ⟋⟍*from time to time.*

Doubling. 212. Besides strokes being doubled for *there, their,* in a few cases they may be doubled for *other* and *dear,* as in ⌒ *some other,* ⌒ *my dear sir.*

Omissions. 213. These are arranged under (a) Consonants, (b) Syllables, (c) Logograms.

(a) Consonants may be omitted as indicated in the following phrases—

⟋ *mos(t) probably,* ‿ *in (f)act,*

⟍ *in this (m)anner,* ⌒ *animal (l)ife,*

⟍ *in (r)eply.*

(b) The syllable *con* may be omitted, as in ⟋ *I will (con)sider,* ⟍ *we have (con)cluded.*

(*c*) The signs omitted are chiefly logograms—

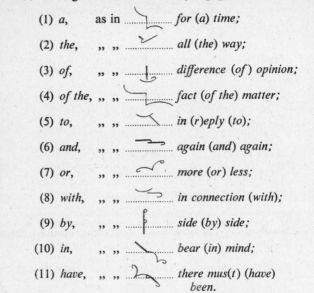

    (1) *a,*   as in .... *for (a) time;*

    (2) *the,*   ,, ,, ... *all (the) way;*

    (3) *of,*   ,, ,, ... *difference (of) opinion;*

    (4) *of the,* ,, ,, ... *fact (of the) matter;*

    (5) *to,*   ,, ,, ... *in (r)eply (to);*

    (6) *and,* ,, ,, ... *again (and) again;*

    (7) *or,*   ,, ,, ... *more (or) less;*

    (8) *with,* ,, ,, ... *in connection (with);*

    (9) *by,*   ,, ,, ... *side (by) side;*

   (10) *in,*   ,, ,, ... *bear (in) mind;*

   (11) *have,* ,, ,, ... *there mus(t) (have)*
                                         been.

The student should seek to understand thoroughly the principles on which the phraseograms in the following lists are formed without seeking necessarily to commit the lists to memory. The lists are by no means complete. As stated above, the examples given merely show the general lines on which the phrases are formed, and the student in the course of his practice will find many opportunities of phrasing if he will keep in mind the general principles as illustrated above, and in the pages which follow. The exercises which follow each list should be written from dictation until they can be taken down with ease and rapidity.

ADVANCED PHRASEOGRAPHY: SECTION 1

agree with the	notwithstanding such
all circumstances	notwithstanding that
and in all proba-bility	on either hand
as fast as	on either side
as it were	on the other hand
as much as were	on the other side
as the matter	on these occasions
brought forward	on this occasion
by and by	on this matter
by the by	peculiar circum-stances
by some means	per annum
dealing with the	per cent
discuss the matter	percentage
every circumstance	quite agree
I am certain that you are	quite agreeable
I am inclined to think	so that we may
I am persuaded	take the liberty
I am very glad	there were
I think it is necessary	those which we are now
I think that you are	those who are
in all circum-stances	those who were
in his own opinion	through the world
in the meantime	to bring the matter
in this country	very satisfactorily
in this matter	you will agree
in this respect	you will probably

Exercise 145

Read, copy, and transcribe

Exercise 146

Write in shorthand

Dear-Sir,

I-am-very-glad to notice-that by-some-means you-are hoping to-have-the new proposal brought-forward at-the-next meeting of-the-directors, and-| I-am-persuaded that in-the-meantime you-should-not discuss-the-matter with anyone, because-it-is-necessary to-be very cautious in-all-circumstances as on-this-occasion. | You-will-probably do what-can-be-done to-make-the case complete, so-that-we-may-have every-circumstance detailed that-is in-our-favour. I-think-that-you-| are-aware of-the importance of-having ready a definite scheme if-we-would-be successful, but as-the-matter is of-such vital importance to-us, I-take-the-| liberty of-emphasizing-the point. Awaiting your-reply, we-are, | Yours-truly,   (132 words)

Exercise 147

Read, copy, and transcribe

Exercise 148

Write in shorthand

Dear-Sir,
I-am-certain-that-you-are-not fully conversant with-the-matter, or you would-not urge those-who-were present on-these-occasions to-bring-the question | to-the notice of-the meeting. On-either-side there-are those-who-are always ready to hurry business as-fast-as they can, notwithstanding-that there-is-no-advantage | gained by unnecessary haste. By-and-by, I-am-inclined-to-think-that you-will-agree-with me on-this-matter, and-then you-will regret that-you unduly hastened-| the passing of-the rules with-which-we-are-now | dealing. Yours-truly,

(103 words)

ADVANCED PHRASEOGRAPHY: SECTION 2
(*Circles, Loops and Hooks*)

from us		it is only necessary
please inform us		it can only be
to us		it may only be
as we have		they will only be
as we can		longer than
as we cannot		more than
as we do		any longer
as we think		no longer than
as we shall		rather than
as we may		smaller than
as well as usual		going on
as well as can be		at all our own
as soon as we can		have been expected
as soon as they		have been informed
it is said		have been returned
for his sake		who have not
in this century		out of doors
in this city		rate of interest
in this subject		state of affairs
of this statement		Thursday afternoon
this has been		Thursday evening
at first cost		at all events
Wednesday next		into effect
in our view		incorporated association
in our statement		medical assocn.
it appears		political assocn.
it appears that		traders' assocn.
by all means		

Exercise 149

Read, copy, and transcribe

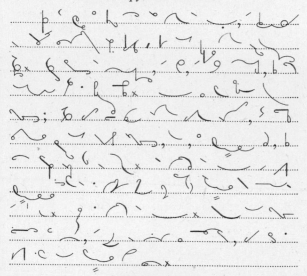

Exercise 150

Write in shorthand

We-have-been-informed of-the-proposed meeting of-your county-association on-Wednesday-next, and to-us it-appears-that as-soon-as-the members realize the state-of-| affairs they-will-be only too-glad to postpone a definite decision. We-are of-the opinion that-there-are many who-have-not agreed-with-the attitude of-the | executive, and who do-not-wish the proposals to be carried into-effect. At-all-events, at-all-our-own recent county gatherings, which-have-been rather smaller-than usual, | there-has-been much objection to-several proposals on-this-subject, and as-soon-as-we-can, we-are having a postal vote as-we-cannot decide certain matters without | knowing-the opinion of-members who-have-not-been in attendance to-express any views on-the-questions.   (138 words)

Exercise 151

Read, copy, and transcribe

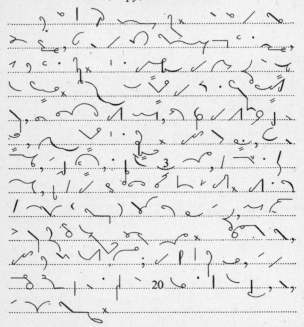

Exercise 152

Write in shorthand

It-will-take longer-than we-expected to-finish the premises for-the political-association, but-we-shall-be-able-to get all-the out-of-doors work finished before-| the winter sets in; and-then it-can-only-be a matter of weeks for-the completion of-the interior. Anyway, we-shall-be no-longer-than we-can | help. When finished, the building will-be one of-the | handsomest in-this-city.   (73 words)

Exercise 153

Read, copy, and transcribe

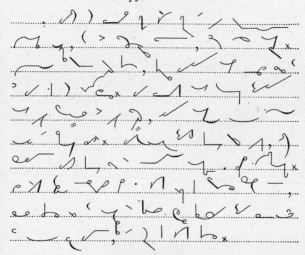

Exercise 154

Write in shorthand

In-our-statement at-the Traders'-Association on-Thursday-evening it-will-only-be necessary to-mention briefly the high-rate-of-interest to be charged for-the loan on-| the new buildings, as-we-shall-have a full discussion of-the whole matter at-the-next meeting. All-the voting cards have-been-returned and-in nearly all-cases | the vote is in-favour of-the-present president continuing in office.

We-shall-be-able-to purchase the materials at-first-cost, and as-we-do a very large | turnover our profits should exceed, rather-than fall below, those of-last-year. As-well-as-can-be estimated beforehand, we-shall-have to increase our stocks at-all-our-| own depôts, and as-we-may also require a new depôt at Acton, we-shall-be-obliged to increase-the initial order. In-view of-this we-shall-expect prices | to be much lower-than-the old rates.   (158 words)

ADVANCED PHRASEOGRAPHY: SECTION 3
(*Halving Principle*)

as if it were	I trust not
by which it was	I was not
if it is not	you cannot
if it be not	you may not
if it were	you must not
in which it is	you should not be
in which it has appeared	you were not
of which it has been	you are not
of which it must be	I would
able to make	if it would be
able to think	they would
I am able to think	they would be
I am unable to think	they would not be
we are able to make	we would
you will be able to	few words
I cannot be	in our words
I cannot say	many words
I cannot see	at any rate
I hope you will not	at all times
I may not be	at some time
I shall not be	at the same time
	for some time
	from time to time
	some time ago

Exercise 155
Read, copy, and transcribe

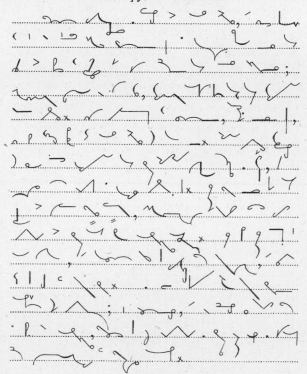

Exercise 156
Write in shorthand

Dear Mr. Scott,

    For-some-time past I-have-been unable-to write to-you as I-have desired and-as I-promised you when you-were here. I-hope-│ you-will-not-be annoyed at-my apparent neglect.

You-should-not-be, and-I-am-sure you-will-not-be when you-are-aware of-the-reason for-my | silence. I-have-no-doubt you-will-remember that I-was-not well previous to-your visit, but I-am-sorry to-tell-you I-have-been under-the care | of Dr. Brown ever-since-the day you left. Indeed, you-were-not gone an hour when I-had to-send for-the physician. I-do-not-know what-was-the | cause of-my illness; I-cannot-say that I-am-aware of anything to-which-it-may-be due. I-know of nothing to-which-it-can-be traced. At-| all-events, it-has-been very severe, and, for-some-time, my recovery was considered hope-less. Of-course, I-am-not yet out-of-the-wood, and-I-must-not | boast, but I-think I-am fairly on-the road to complete recovery. You-will-be-sorry to-learn that I-am-not yet strong enough to-leave my room, | but-you-must-not suppose that I-am in danger. I-trust I-shall-be-able-to-make an effort to visit you some-time during-the coming month. At-| any-rate, I-am hoping so. I-must leave off for-the-present, but will write again very-soon.

                    Very-truly-yours,

                         THOMAS MAKIN.   (264 words)

Exercise 157

Read, copy, and transcribe

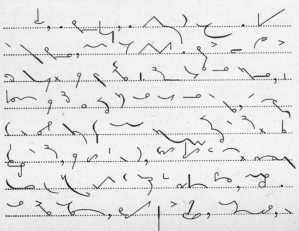

Exercise 158

Write in shorthand

Dear Mr. Scott,

Since I wrote-you last I-have-heard that-you-were injured slightly in a railway accident. Is-this true? I-trust-not. If-it-is, you-| are-not likely to be improved by-my-letter. If-it-is-not you-will pardon my mentioning the report. In-any-case, you-might send me word, and-if-| you-can spare-the time, perhaps you-will come over on-Monday. If-you-cannot arrange this, please inform me from-time-to-time how you-are getting on with-| the new business, to-which-it-appears you-are devoting yourself. If-it-be as successful as you-were inclined-to-think you-will-be very fortunate, and-if-it-| be-not quite so profitable as you hoped, it-will still have proved an interesting experiment. At-all-events, it-was well worth a trial. At-the-same-time, you-| should-not work too hard. If-you do you-must-not-be surprised to-find your health giving way. I-have-no-doubt of-the ultimate success of-your patent, | and-if-it-were-necessary, I could arrange to invest a considerable amount in-the business. I-cannot-do anything in-the-matter of-the shares you spoke about until | I-have-seen-you again. I-cannot-see that-there-is any hurry about-the affair. If-it-does happen that-the shares are all taken-up before I-make | application I-shall-not mind very-much. I-am-trusting, however, that-you-will-be-able-to pay me a visit on-Monday and explain matters. I-have staying with | me an old friend who-has-been out to South-America for three-years on business matters, and-I-am-sure you-will-be delighted with-his conversations on-the | customs and manners of-the natives.

Yours-truly,
Thomas Makin.   (310 words)

Advanced Phraseography: Section 4
(*Doubling Principle*)

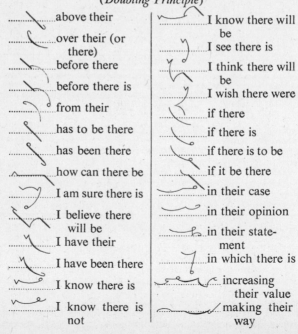

above their	I know there will be
over their (or there)	I see there is
before there	I think there will be
before there is	I wish there were
from their	if there
has to be there	if there is
has been there	if there is to be
how can there be	if it be there
I am sure there is	in their case
I believe there will be	in their opinion
I have their	in their statement
I have been there	in which there is
I know there is	increasing their value
I know there is not	making their way

more than their		some other
pending their decision		some other way
shall be there		some other respects
then there are		or some other
they have been there		in other words
though there is		in order
upon their		in order that
we have their		in order to
we have been there		my dear sir
whenever there is		my dear madam
by some other means		my dear friend
		my dear fellow citizens

Exercise 159

Read, copy, and transcribe

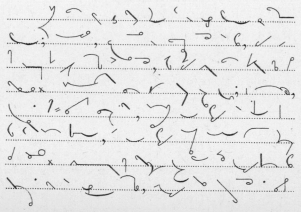

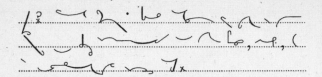

Exercise 160

Write in shorthand

I-know-there-has-been a great-deal said, as-well-as written, about-the interest attaching to-the study of phrase and-fable, but I-know-there-has-not-| been sufficient said, in-view-of-the importance of-the-matter, and-I-know-there-will-be a great-deal-more both said and written before-the subject is exhausted. | Whenever-there-is a subject of interest to-the general reader, and a desire expressed for information upon-it, there-will-be-found someone ready and willing to obtain-the | necessary knowledge and impart it to-others. As-we-have-seen, too, the work is from-time-to-time generally executed as-well-as-it-can-be, and-the-results | made known in-the very shortest time possible. This-is a great convenience to-most of-us, as-we-have-not-time to devote to-research in-these-subjects.   (149 words)

Exercise 161

Read, copy, and transcribe

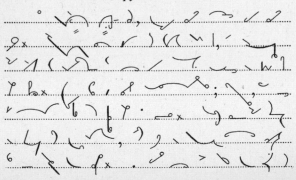

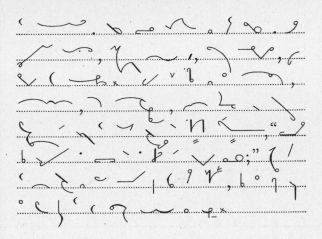

Exercise 162

Write in shorthand

I-think-there-is room, indeed, I-am-sure-there-is room for-something-more on-the-topic I-have-mentioned before it-can-be-said that-the public is | tired of-it. There-are-some-people, however, who know very-little of-the origin and meaning of-many peculiar expressions of-frequent occurrence. For-their-sake, for-their-satisfaction | and-pleasure, as-well-as for-the educational advantage it-would-be to-them, I-wish-there-were some-means of-bringing before-their notice some of-the books already | published on-this-subject. (94 words)

Exercise 163

Read, copy, and transcribe

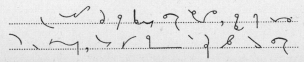

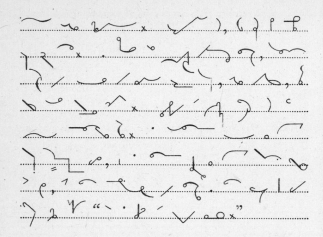

Exercise 164

Write in shorthand

I-know-there-is a variety of opinion, however, on almost all-questions, and-if-there-be any of-my-readers who doubt-the benefit to be derived from such | a study as I-have referred to, and-if-they assert that, in-their-opinion, it-would-be a waste of-time as-well-as money to-procure such books, | I-ask-them, for-their-own sake and-for-that of-other-people in-their-position, who-may look at-the matter from-their own view, to-weigh-the following- | points as carefully and as-soon-as-they can. How often do we come across such phrases as "toad-eater," "salted accounts," etc., and-though-their meaning, from-their position | in-the-sentence, may-be pretty clear, should-we-not-have some difficulty in saying how they came to-have-their present significa-tion? Have-we-not all occasionally read some | phrase, or heard some allusion which-we-did-not-understand, and-have-we-not sometimes lost the beauty of a passage through our want of knowledge? I-think-there-will- | be few who-will dissent from this.   (187 words)

ADVANCED PHRASEOGRAPHY: SECTION 5
(*Omissions: Consonants and Syllables*)

I have (r)eceived

in other (r)espects

in (r)eply

we have (r)eceived

almos(t) certain

jus(t) been

jus(t) received

las(t) week

las(t) month

last year

mos(t) probably

mus(t) be

nex(t) week

there mus(t) be

you mus(t) be

you mus(t) not be

very please(d) indeed

in (f)act

in (point of f)act

telegra(ph) office

wor(th) while

in the (m)anner

and in like (m)anner

and in the same (m)anner

and in the same (m)anner as

in this (m)anner

nex(t mon)th

this (mon)th

as far as poss(ible)

as much as poss(ible)

as soon as poss(ible)

as well as poss(ible)

as if it were poss(ible)

jus(t) poss(ible)

betwee(n) them

foundatio(n) stone

o(n)e another

towards o(n)e another

industrial (l)ife

I (h)ope

I (h)ope you are satisfied

and the (con)trary

cannot be (con)sidered

for (con)sideration

fully (con)sidered

further (con)sidered

further (con)sideration

I have (con)cluded

in (con)clusion

into (con)sideration

it is (con)sidered

it may be (con)sidered

little (con)sideration

mus(t) be (con)sidered

necessary (con)clusion

necessary (con)sequence

ought to be (con)sidered

satisfactory (con)clusion

shall be (con)sidered

shall be (taken into con)sideration

should be (con)sidered

some (con)sideration

take (or taken) (into con)sideration

that (con)clusion

unsatisfactory (con)clusion

we have (con)cluded

were (con)sidered

which will be (con)sidered

which will be (taken into con)sideration

Exercise 165

Read, copy, and transcribe

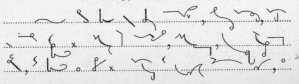

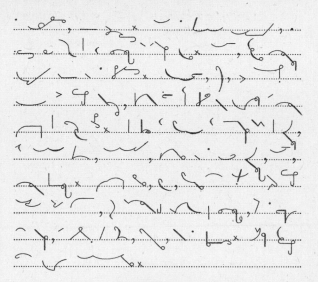

Exercise 166

Write in shorthand

Dear Mr. Brown,

I-have-received your communication of-the 12th-inst., and-I-am-very-pleased-indeed to inform-you that-you-are almost-certain to-hear from-me | in-the affirmative next-week. Most-probably you-will-be asked to-come here the last-week in-the-last-month of-the-year, but-you-must-not-be surprised | if-you-are-requested to-give your lecture at an earlier date. Your lecture in-the autumn of-last-year was a great success; in-fact, unparalleled in-the history | of-our literary organization. This-month and next-month we-are to-have a series of-lectures on-the industrial-life of-our cities in-the nineteenth-century, and it- | is-just-possible that-we-may-have a famous economist as chairman at-the opening gathering. We-have-concluded that-these problems ought-to-be-considered without-delay, especially as | economic questions are very-pressing just-now.

Yours-very-truly,　　　(160 words)

Exercise 167

Read, copy, and transcribe

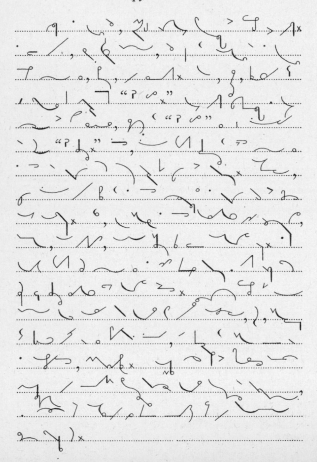

Exercise 168

Write in shorthand

My-dear-Sir,

I-hope-you-will-think-it worth-while to-consider, as-far-as-possible, the alteration of-the date of-the laying of-the foundation-stone, and- | I-am-sure a little-consideration will lead you to a decision that will materially enhance the chances of a successful gathering. Is-it worth-while ignoring-the wishes of | a small but influential section of-your supporters in-this-manner when a slight alteration would-be of advantage? In-other-respects I-think no-fault can-be-found with- | the arrangements.

Very sincerely yours,   (95 words)

Exercise 169

Write in shorthand

Dear-Sirs,

We-have-received your-letter of-the 9th-inst., respecting consignments, and your-requests shall-be-considered in-the-same-manner-as your previous communications on-such-matters. | Our Mr. Burton is away at-present in-the-north of-Scotland. We-expect him back tomorrow, however, when-the whole-question shall-be-taken-into-consideration, and an | early-reply forwarded to-you. Doubtless a satisfactory-conclusion can-be arrived at which-will-be-considered agreeable to all concerned.

Yours-truly,   (83 words)

Exercise 170

Write in shorthand

In concluding my report, I-would point-out that-there-are many-circumstances which-will-be-taken-into-consideration on a future occasion, but of-which it-is-considered unwise | to-speak now. One necessary-conclusion, however, is-that only in-the-manner I-have indicated is-it possible to arrive at anything like a true estimate of-the-motives | of-these men towards-one-another, and to judge impartially of-the letters which passed between-them. The incident at-the telegraph-office is-the-most-important.   (87 words)

Advanced Phraseography: Section 6
(Omissions: Logograms)

.... as (a) rule

.... at (a) loss

.... in (a) few days

.... in (a) great (m)easure

.... in such (a) (m)anner as

.... for (a) moment

.... to (a) great extent

.... about (the) matter

.... all over (the) world

.... all (the) circumstances

.... at (the) present day

.... at (the) present time

.... by (the) way

.... for (the) first time

.... I will (con)sider (the) matter

.... in (the) first instance

.... in (the) first p(l)ace

.... in (the) sec(ond) place

.... in (the) th(ird) place

.... in (the) las(t) place

.... in (the) nex(t) p(l)ace

.... into (the) matter

.... notwithstanding (the) (f)act

.... on (the) (con)trary

.... on (the) o(n)e hand

.... on (the) subject

.... in (the) circumstances

.... what is (the) matter

.... as (a) matter (of) course

.... as (a) matter (of) (f)act

.... expression (of) opinion

.... in (con)sequence (of)

.... in (r)espect of

.... on (the) part (of)

.... out (of) place

.... short space (of) time

.... do you mean (to) say

.... expect (to) receive

.... face (to) face

.... from first (to) last

.... having (r)egard (to)

.... in (r)ef(eren)ce (to)

.... in (r)ef(eren)ce (to) which

in (r)elation (to)

in (r)eply (to)

in (r)espect (to)

it appears (to) me

it appears (to) have been

it seems (to) me

ought (to) have been

ought (to) have known

regret (to) say

regret (to) state

we shall be glad (to) hear

we shall be glad (to) know

wi(th) (r)ef(eren)ce (to)

wi(th) (r)ef(eren)ce (to) which

wi(th) (r)egard (to)

wi(th) (r)elation (to)

wi(th) (r)espect (to)

Exercise 171

Read, copy, and transcribe

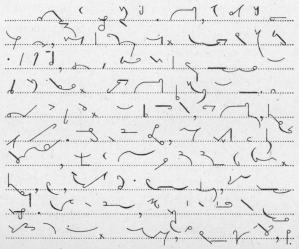

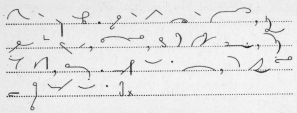

Exercise 172

Write in shorthand

In-consequence-of the short-space-of-time at our-own dis-posal, and-having-regard-to all-the-circumstances under-which-the order was-given, we-are at-a-loss | to understand-the reason for-the delay in-the delivery of-the-machine which ought-to-have-been here a week ago. We-shall-expect-to-receive it in-a- | few-days without fail. We-are face-to-face with a difficulty which-appears-to-have-been in-a-great-measure and to-a-great-extent brought about by-those- | who ought-to-have-known better, and-we-shall-be-glad if-you-will look into-the-matter for-us, notwithstanding-the-fact that-you-are so busy yourself. The | enclosed-statement gives you our position in-reference-to-the difficulty, and-we-shall-be-glad-to-have your expression-of-opinion on-the-matter at an early date.   (149 words)

Exercise 173

Read, copy, and transcribe

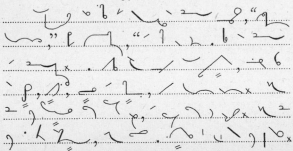

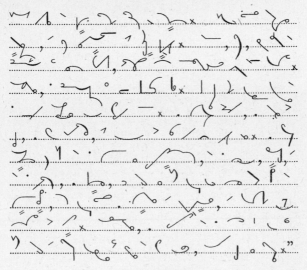

Exercise 174

Write in shorthand

Dear-Sirs,

In-reply-to-yours of-the 11th-inst., we-regret-to-state that under-the-circumstances we-cannot-accept-the mere apology on-the-part-of your-client. | This conduct of-your-client has-been a source of annoyance for a considerable time, and-in-spite-of our requests that-such conduct should cease, and not-withstanding-the-fact | that legal proceedings have-been threatened, the statements of-which-we complain have continued. From-first-to-last we-have-been face-to-face with inconvenience in-consequence-of your- | client's attitude. Under-the-circumstances, and having-regard-to what-has happened an apology is out of the question. On-the-contrary, we-shall-be compelled to-seek redress in- | the law-courts in-respect-of your-client's statements, and shall instruct our solicitors to-take action forthwith, unless your-client is prepared to pay-the amount of damages claimed. |

                    Yours-truly,   (152 words)

Exercise 175

Write in shorthand

The lecturer said: It-appears-to-me that at-the-present-time many of-the changes taking-place all-over-the-world are-the outcome of inviolable laws working for- | the-progress of-mankind. As-a-rule, man is apt to overlook-the silent working of-the laws of-the universe in-reference-to-which he-appears, as-a-matter- | of-fact, very-little concerned, or his interest lasts but for-a-moment when some striking incident compels his attention. Generally speaking, he takes things as-a-matter-of-course, | and, as a necessary-consequence-of this attitude, at-the-present-day the beauties of nature are a closed-book to a vast majority of-the inhabitants of-the globe. |

I-will-consider-the-matter and deal-with-the subject as briefly as-possible. In-the-first-place, it-seems-to-me that in-relation-to-the authorship there-is- | no-ground for supposing it to be doubtful. In-the-second-place, the statements in-the book are supported by contemporary accounts. In-the-third-place, all-the other known | works of-the author are of-unimpeachable accuracy. Therefore, from-first-to-last, I-think-the criticisms are entirely out-of-place, and-I-cannot-understand what-is-the-matter | with-the reviewer that-he-should make such a violent attack, on-the-one-hand, upon-the probity of-our author, and-on-the-other, upon-the accuracy of-his | statements.

(241 words)

Exercise 176

Read, copy, and transcribe

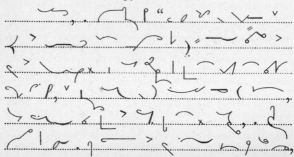

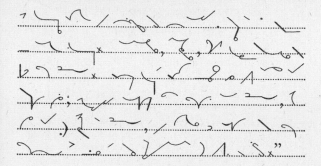

Exercise 177

Write in shorthand

For-the-first-time in-the history of-the company, said-the speaker, we-have to-report an adverse balance. In-the-first-instance, we-have-had a serious strike | at-the works, but-you-will-be-glad-to-know-that all disputes have-been amicably settled. In-the-next-place, we-have-had some very heavy law expenses with- | reference-to our existing patents, and-with-reference-to-which a statement appears in-the report. In-the-last-place, our annual turnover has-not-been up to expectations, though, | by-the-way, it slightly exceeds-the figures of-last-year. You-will-be-glad-to-hear that our new manager has introduced several excellent reforms which-will bear fruit | in-the-near-future.

It-would-be out-of-place for-me in-the short-space-of-time at-my disposal to-try to-go fully into-the details of- | the-accounts. Moreover, we-expect-to-receive, very-shortly, a further report from-the auditors. Having-regard-to-the present state-of-affairs, and-in-consequence-of certain criticisms, we- | think-it best, under-the-circumstances, to-have an independent investigation, and-the auditors have-been asked to-give a frank expression-of-opinion in-reference-to-the affairs of- | the Company. The position is a difficult one. On-the-one-hand we-are-told-that as-a-matter-of-course the business ought-to be prosperous, yet as-a- | matter-of-fact, the contrary is-the case. What-is-the-matter we-hope to-hear from-the auditors, who-are looking into-the-matter, and who-are expected to- | report in-a-few-days.   (275 words)

ADVANCED PHRASEOGRAPHY: SECTION 7

(Omissions: Logograms)

.... again (and) again

.... dee(per) (and) deeper

.... high(er) (and) higher

.... lower (and) lower

.... fast(er) (and) faster

.... less (and) less

.... more (and) more

.... Mr. (and) Mrs.

.... near(er) (and) nearer

.... nor(th) (and) south

.... east and west

.... over (and) over again

.... over (and) above

.... here (and) there

.... qui(cker) (and) quicker

.... rates (and) taxes

.... time (and) space

.... ways (and) means

.... side (by) side

.... bear (in) mind

.... borne (in) mind

.... all parts (of the) world

.... fact (of the) matter

.... facts (of the) case

.... for (the) purpose (of)

.... history (of the) world

.... out (of the) question

.... peculiar circumstances (of the) case

.... more (or) less

.... one (or) two

.... right (or) wrong

.... six or seven

.... sooner (or) later

.... three or four

.... two (or) three

.... up (to the) present

.... up (to the) present time

.... in accordance (with)

.... in accordance (with) the

.... in accordance (with) the matter

.... in connection (with)

.... in connection (with) the

.... in connection (with) their

Exercise 178

Read, copy, and transcribe

Exercise 179

Write in shorthand

Ships of immense proportions are nowadays found in-all-parts-of-the-world, and docks have-to-be-made deeper-and-deeper in-order-to accommodate the huge vessels which- | are constructed to-carry more-and-more and to-travel faster-and-faster as time advances. Distance between-us and-foreign parts is becoming less-and-less, and north-and- | south, and east-and-west are being brought nearer-and-nearer, so-that-the desire long-since expressed has almost-been accomplished, and-time-and-space have-been practically annihilated | by-the progress of science and-the ingenuity of-man.   (100 words)

Exercise 180

Write in shorthand

Owing to-the peculiar-circumstances-of-the-case such a course as you suggest is out-of-the-question, and you-will-have to-follow the procedure in-accordance-with | precedent. Further, you-must endeavour to secure Mr.-and-Mrs. Brown as witnesses, as their evidence is absolutely-necessary. The fact-of-the-matter is that-you have failed to | bear-in-mind the really essential features in-connection-with-the case and-have chiefly borne-in-mind one-or-two quite subsidiary points. Side-by-side with-this, you | have unfortunately displayed a more-or-less vindictive spirit, which, in-our-opinion, can-only-be prejudicial to-the success of-your claim.   (113 words)

Exercise 181

Read, copy, and transcribe

Exercise 182

Write in shorthand

Over-and-over-again we-have-complained of-the rates-and-taxes in-connection-with our concern, and sooner-or-later we-shall-have to-discuss ways-and-means of | a successful agitation for-their reduction. Up-to-the-present-time we-have-been very heavily handicapped in-this-respect, and judging from-the present outlook our resources will-be- | called-upon more-and-more in-the-immediate future, unless-we-are-enabled to obtain-the relief we-think-we-are entitled to. Again-and-again, during-the-last six- | or-seven years there-have-been outcries against the upward tendency of-these local levies, and-in-connection-with-their collection many have urged that-the facts-of-the-case | required-the immediate attention of-the authorities. The history-of-the-world shows that-this-matter of-rates-and-taxes has always-been a sore point with people of-every- | clime and nation, and-whether right-or-wrong, it-is a fact that a great-many have suffered imprisonment rather-than pay what they-have deemed unjust impositions.   (178 words)

Exercise 183

Read, copy, and transcribe

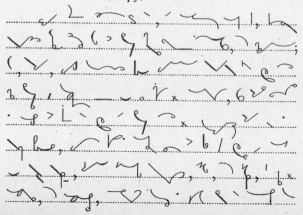

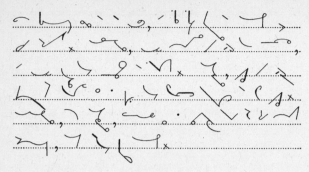

Summary

1. Abbreviations are utilized in advanced phraseography, as follows—
   (a) The small circle for *as, is, us*.
   (b) The large circle initially for *as we, as* and *w, as*
       and *s;* medially for *is* and *s, his* and *s, s* and
       s; finally for *s* and *has, s* and *is*.
   (c) The loop *st* for *first*, the loop *nst* for *next*.
   (d) The *r* and *l* hooks for a few miscellaneous words.
   (e) The *n* hook for *than, been, on*, and *own*.
   (f) The *f* or *v* hook for *have, of, after, even*, and in
       a few common phrases.
   (g) The circle *s* and *shun* hook for *association*.
   (h) The halving principle for *it, to, not, would, word*,
       and in a few common phrases.
   (i) The doubling principle for *there, their, other,*
       dear.
2. The following may be omitted—
   (a) Consonants not essential to phraseograms.
   (b) The syllable *con-*, and a few other common
       syllables.
   (c) Any logogram or logograms providing the
       phraseogram is legible.

CHAPTER XXXV

INTERSECTIONS

The Use of Intersections. 214. The method of intersecting, or writing one stroke through another, is utilized for the brief, distinctive, and rapid indication of official titles, of persons or associations of various kinds, and of frequently-occurring colloquial phrases, etc. Where intersection is impracticable, the method of writing one stroke in close proximity to another is adopted instead; thus, ⟨shorthand⟩ *political party,* ⟨shorthand⟩ *party question,* ⟨shorthand⟩ *Labour Party,* ⟨shorthand⟩ *Party Bill.* When the word to be indicated by an alphabetic stroke is to be read first, the stroke is struck first, and the rest of the outline is cut through, or written in close proximity to it. The examples which follow illustrate the manner in which similar phrases may be dealt with.

P is employed to represent **party,** as in

⟨shorthand⟩	birthday party	⟨shorthand⟩	parliamentary party
⟨shorthand⟩	children's party	⟨shorthand⟩	party government
⟨shorthand⟩	garden party	⟨shorthand⟩	political party

Pr is employed to represent **professor,** as in

⟨shorthand⟩	Professor Jackson	⟨shorthand⟩	Professor of Chemistry
⟨shorthand⟩	Professor Morgan	⟨shorthand⟩	Professor of Commerce
⟨shorthand⟩	Professor Peake	⟨shorthand⟩	Professor of Music

B is employed to represent the following—
  (*a*) **bank,** as in

⟍⌣	bank bills	⤬	City Bank
⟍	Bank of England	⌢⤬	Mercantile Bank
⟍	bank pass book	⟍⤬	Penny Bank
⤬	bank rate	⟋⤫	savings bank

  (*b*) **-bankment,** as in

⤬	sea embankment	⌐⤫	Thames Embankment

  (*c*) **bill,** as in

⟍⤫	Finance Bill	⤬	Education Bill

T is employed to represent **attention,** as in

⟍	best attention	⤓	my attention has been called
⟍	careful attention	⟋	necessary attention
⤬	early attention	⤬	special attention
⤬	early attention to the matter	⤓	your attention

D is employed to represent **department,** as in

⌐⟋	Department of Agriculture	⟍	Government department
⌐⤬	electrical dept.	⤓	life department
⤓	engineering dept.	⟋	shipping dept.
⤓	foreign dept.	⤓	silk department

CH is employed to represent **Chancery,** as in

⤬	Chancery appeal	⫽	Chancery Judge
⤬	Chancery proceedings	⤓	into Chancery

J is employed to represent **Journal,** as in

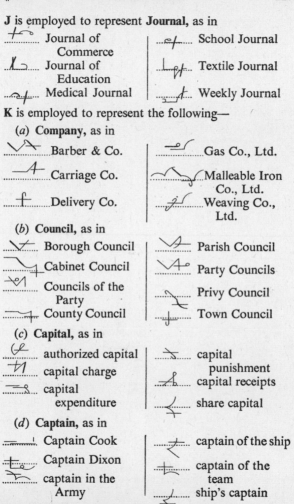

Journal of Commerce	School Journal
Journal of Education	Textile Journal
Medical Journal	Weekly Journal

K is employed to represent the following—

(*a*) **Company,** as in

Barber & Co.	Gas Co., Ltd.
Carriage Co.	Malleable Iron Co., Ltd.
Delivery Co.	Weaving Co., Ltd.

(*b*) **Council,** as in

Borough Council	Parish Council
Cabinet Council	Party Councils
Councils of the Party	Privy Council
County Council	Town Council

(*c*) **Capital,** as in

authorized capital	capital punishment
capital charge	capital receipts
capital expenditure	share capital

(*d*) **Captain,** as in

Captain Cook	captain of the ship
Captain Dixon	captain of the team
captain in the Army	ship's captain

Kr is employed to represent the following—

(*a*) **Colonel**, as in

.... Colonel Anderson | .... Colonel Jackson

(*b*) **Corporation**, as in

.... investment
       corporation
| .... Corporation of
       Leeds

G is employed to represent **government**, as in

.... British Govern-
       ment
| ....government
       official

...........French Govern-
       ment
| ....municipal
       government

F is employed to represent **form**, as in

.... entry form | ....form of Govern-
       ment

.... form of acknow-
       ledgment
| ....form of the report

.... form of agreement | ....medical form

.... form of bequest | ....necessary form

V is employed to represent **valuation**, as in

.... low valuation | ....valuation of the
       site

.... valuation of the
       property
| ....site valuation

TH is employed to represent the following—

(*a*) **Authority**, as in

.... authority of the
       manager
| ....military
       authorities

.... authority of the
       representative
| ....sanitary authority

.... legal authority | ....well-known
       authority

.... local authority | ....written authority

(*b*) **Month,** as in

⋎	for a month		many months ago
	in a month's time		some months ago

S is employed to represent **society,** as in

	dramatic society		Society of Compositors
	Hearts of Oak Society		Society of Musicians
	medical society		Temperance Society

M is employed to represent the following—

(*a*) **Mark,** as in

	auditor's mark		official mark
	high-water mark		private mark
	low-water mark		save the mark!
	mark of respect		to mark time

(*b*) **Major,** as in

	Major Anson		Major Jones
	Major General		Sergeant Major Jones

N is employed to represent **national,** as in

	national affair		national dividend
	national bank		national finance
	national defence		national reserve
	national desire		national revenue
	national disaster		national society

L is employed to represent the following—

  (*a*) **liberal,** as in

.... Liberal Club	.... liberal discount
.... Liberal Party	.... liberal payment
.... Liberal policy	.... liberal view

  (*b*) **limited,** as in

| .... Pears' Limited | .... Lupin Limited |

R (down) is employed to represent **arrange-d-ment** in colloquial phrases like the following—

.... better arrangement	.... it was arranged
.... I shall arrange	.... please make arrangements
.... if you can arrange	.... we will arrange the matter

R (up) is employed to represent the following—

  (*a*) **railway,** as in

.... Metropolitan Ry.	.... railway rates
.... railway company	.... railway ticket
.... railway facilities	.... railway time
.... railway official	.... railway time table

  (*b*) **require, required, requirement,** as in

| .... to meet the requirements | .... do you require |
| | .... if he required |

Sr (up) is employed to represent **conservative,** as in

| .... Conservative Club | .... Conservative Party |
| .... Conservative Government | .... Conservative policy |

Exercise 184

Read, copy, and transcribe

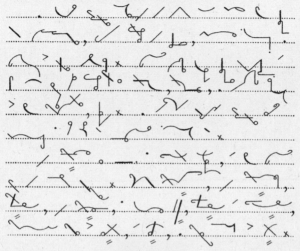

Exercise 185

Write in shorthand

Messrs. Barber-and-Co., the New Carriage-Company, and-the Dorset-Supply-Company, are to be converted into limited-companies. The annual reports of-the Malleable-Iron-Co.,-Ltd., Smith,- | Brown-and-Co.,-Ltd., and-the Weaving-Co.,-Ltd., all bear testimony to-the prosperity of-trade during-the past year. A Government-official, a well-known railway-official, and | a clerk in-another Government-department have all advised me to-take shares in Lee's-Brewery-Company, but, as a member of a temperance-society, I-do-not like-the | idea. The local-authorities have invited the committee of-the Agri-cultural-Society to arrange a show here, and-the local Society-of-Musicians has undertaken-the charge of-the musical- | arrangements. It-is hoped the committee will-arrange-the-matter. Please-make-arrangements to-come over on-the first-day if-possible.   (142 words)

Exercise 186

Read, copy, and transcribe

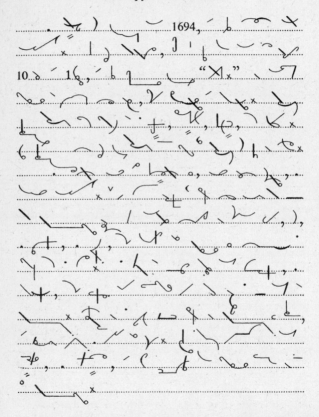

Exercise 187

Write in shorthand

We give a liberal-discount on all cash-orders. The committee treated him in a liberal-manner and allowed him a most liberal-payment for-his services at-the Liberal- | Club. On-the-authority-of-the-representative we-are-bound-to-say that-the valuation-of-the-site is a very unsatisfactory-one in-view of-the yearly-valuation which- | has-been made for-the last twelve years.

Our national-society is very-much interested in national-affairs, and it-is desirous of securing the strengthening of-our national-defence. | The other evening Major-Jones opened a debate on capital-punishment, and-after an interesting discussion in-which Captain-Dixon, Colonel-Beach and Professor-Peake took-part, we-regret-to- | say that a majority voted for-its retention.　　　　　　　　　　　　　　　　　(128 words)

Summary

An intersection is formed by allocating a definite word or words to an alphabetic stroke when intersecting, or written in close proximity to, another stroke, as follows—

P	= *party*	F	= *form*
Pr	= *professor*	V	= *valuation*
B	= $\begin{cases} bank \\ -bankment \\ bill \end{cases}$	TH	= $\begin{cases} authority \\ month \end{cases}$
		S	= *society*
T	= *attention*	M	= $\begin{cases} mark \\ major \end{cases}$
D	= *department*		
Ch	= *Chancery*	N	= *national*
J	= *journal*	L	= $\begin{cases} liberal \\ limited \end{cases}$
K	= $\begin{cases} company \\ council \\ capital \\ captain \end{cases}$	R(down)	= *arrange-d-ment*
Kr	= $\begin{cases} colonel \\ corporation \end{cases}$	R(up)	= $\begin{cases} railway \\ require-d \\ requirement \end{cases}$
G	= *government*	Sr(up)	= *conservative*

CHAPTER XXXVI

BUSINESS PHRASES

Phraseography in Business. 215. When the require-ments of particular businesses have to be met, the principles of phrasing and intersecting may be given a special application according to the purpose for which they are required. Thus, while in a general sense ⟍ *p* intersected indicates the word *party*, it may be used to represent the word *policy* in an insurance office, and the word *pump* in an engineer's office. This allocation of a special meaning to an alphabetic stroke and a further application of the rules of phrasing are set out in the following lists. The following are intended to suggest similar phrases to be met with in various branches of business.

GENERAL BUSINESS

	account sales		declare a dividend
	additional cost		directors' report
	additional expense		discount for cash
	at your earliest convenience		early convenience
			enclose-d herewith
	best of my ability		faithfully yours
	best of our ability		five per cent
	best of their ability		five per cent per annum
	best of your ability		from the last report
	bill of exchange		
	bill of lading		goods not to hand
	board of directors		I am directed to inform you
	by passenger train		I am directed to state
	by return of post		

I am in receipt of your esteemed favour

I am in receipt of your favour

I am in receipt of your letter

I am instructed

I am instructed to inform you

I am instructed to state

I am requested to inform you

I beg to acknowledge receipt of your favour

I beg to acknowledge receipt of your letter

I beg to call attention

I beg to enclose herewith

I enclose herewith

I have to acknowledge receipt of your letter

I have to call attention

I regard

I regret

in reply to your esteemed favour

in reply to your favour

in reply to your letter

in your reply to my letter

not yet to hand

ordinary rates

postal order

referring to our invoice

referring to our letter

referring to your favour

referring to your letter

referring to yours

registered letter

respectfully yours

under bill of sale

we beg to quote

we respectfully request

your esteemed favour

your favour

your obedient servant

yours faithfully

yours obediently

yours respectfully

yours sincerely

Exercise 188

Write in shorthand

Dear-Sir,

In-reply-to-your-favour of-the 16th-inst., we-regret that-we-cannot undertake-the responsibility of adopting your sugges-tions with-regard-to-the machine. We-are | willing to-execute the repairs to-the best-of-our-ability, and-on-the lowest-terms possible, but as we stated in-our last-letter, the methods you-propose would- | be attended with great risk to-the rider. If-you decide to-leave-the-matter to-us you-might inform-us by-return-of-post, and-we-will put-the | work in-hand at-once, so-as-to-be-able-to dispatch-the machine by-goods-train on-Saturday. We-need hardly-say that-we pay-the best-price for | all-the-materials we use, and-we guarantee them to-be of-the best-quality obtainable. Referring-to-your-letter of-the 9th-inst., we-have-done our best to | induce-the carriers to-quote special-rates for-the-goods consigned to-you, but-they decline to-make any reduction on-the ordinary-rates unless-the traffic is-consider-ably increased. | With-reference-to-our statement-of-account for last quarter, we-beg-to-call-attention to-the fact that-the balance due has-not-yet-been received, and- | we-will-thank-you for a cheque or a postal-order for-the-amount at-your-earliest-convenience. We-shall-give early-consideration to-your inquiries for-the special tandem, and-will- | forward-the specifi-cation desired as-soon-as-convenient.

                              Yours-faithfully,   (250 words)

Exercise 189

Write in shorthand

Dear-Sir,

I-am-in-receipt-of-your-letter of-the 24th, and I-regret-to-state that I-am-unable-to give-you-the information you-require. I- | can-assure-you I should-be-pleased to-do-so if-it-were-possible. I-am-surprised to-hear from-you that-the funds of-your-society are in-such | a bad-way. I-regard-the objects of-the-society as most praiseworthy, and I-cannot-understand how it-is that public support should-be withheld. I-enclose-cheque for | ten-pounds as a subscription, and shall-be-glad to-give-the same-amount next year. I-am-much-obliged-to-you for-the copy of-the report.

                              Yours-faithfully, | (120 words)

Exercise 190

Write in shorthand

Dear-Sir,

I-brought your-letter before-the Board-of-Directors at-their-meeting yesterday, but after some discussion they-were-obliged to postpone further-consideration of-the-matter until | the next Directors'-meeting, which-will-be held on-the last Tuesday-afternoon of-this-month. I-think-the Directors would-be-glad if-you would kindly set-forth your- | proposals more fully than is done in-your-letter. The first-cost of-the-material is very-low, but-the question of-the additional-cost of-preparing it for-sale, | and-the additional-expense which-will-probably be incurred in advertising it is sure to be taken-into-consideration by-the-Directors, and-if they-had your estimate of-what- | the total expenditure is likely to amount to, it-would-no-doubt help them in coming to a decision. If-you-will make-an-appointment for-some day next-week | I-shall-be-glad to see-you, and it-is-just-possible that I-may-be-able-to give-you some further-particulars. Meanwhile, I-have-the-pleasure to enclose | copy of-the-Directors'-Report published last-month.

Yours-faithfully,   (190 words)

Exercise 191

Write in shorthand

Dear-Sirs,

In-reply-to-your-letter of-yesterday, we-beg-to-state that-the bill-of-lading and-the bill-of-exchange were forwarded to-you by-first-post | on Tuesday-morning last, in registered-letter, addressed as-usual, and-we-are-surprised that-they-have-not reached you. We-will make inquiries here, and-in-the-meantime, if- | you-receive-the letter kindly inform-us by wire at-once. Referring-to-our-letter of-the 27th ult., and your-reply to-same, we-have written-the works | pressing-them to-give early-attention-to-the-matter and to-make-the necessary-arrangements for forwarding-the goods to-the finishers as-soon-as-ready. We-have-instructed the | latter to-give-the-material the best-finish, and-we-have-no-doubt they-will-do-so. We-have-also mentioned your complaint as-to-the finish of-the last | consignment, and-we-are-assured that special-care will-be-taken to-prevent a repetition of-the-mistake in-the future.

Yours-faithfully,   (173 words)

CHAPTER XXXVII
POLITICAL PHRASES

Phraseography in Political Matter. 216. The following phrases are illustrative of the kind commonly met in taking notes of political speeches, etc. The shorthand writer should keep himself informed in regard to the political questions of the day, and familiarize himself with the phrases which almost invariably accompany the introduction of any special legislation. The list of phraseograms here given will serve as models for similar phrases.

POLITICAL

⌐	Act of Parliament	⌐	First Lord
	at the first reading		freedom of the press
	at the second reading		freedom of trade
	at the third reading		Home Rule Party
	British Constitution		hon. and learned member
	British Empire		hon. gentleman
	Cabinet meeting		hon. member
	Chairman of Committee		hon. member for Preston
	Chancellor of the Exchequer		House of Commons
	colonial preference		House of Lords
	Commissioner of Works		Houses of Parliament
	Conservative Party		

Imperial Parliament

in committee of supply

in the House of Commons

in the House of Lords

Labour Party

Leader of the House

Leader of the Opposition

Leader of the Party

Liberal Party

Liberal Unionist

Liberal Unionist Party

Local Government Board

Lord of the Admiralty

Lord of the Treasury

member of Parliament

my hon. and gallant friend

my hon. friend

National Insurance Act

nationalization of railways

naval estimates

Parliamentary Committee

party leaders

plenipotentiary

Postmaster-General

Prime Minister

President of the Board of Agriculture

President of the Board of Trade

President of the Local Government Board

proportional representation

ratepayers

right honourable

right hon. gentleman

Secretary of State

Secretary of State for the Colonies

Secretary of State for the Home Department

Secretary of State for War

Secretary for War

Tariff Reform

United Kingdom

United States

Exercise 192

Write in shorthand

The right-hon.-gentleman, the member-for-Preston, speaking in-the-House-of-Commons, on Tuesday-evening, on-the-proposal to increase-the numerical strength of-the Army-and-Navy, | referred to-the extraordinary growth of-the British-Empire during-the-last fifty years. He asserted with-much vigour that freedom-of-trade, freedom-of-the-people, and freedom-of- | the-Press, were-the rule in every-part of-His-Majesty's dominions, and he declared that every free-trader was bound to-give-the measure his support. His Majesty's-Government | had given most careful-consideration to-this-matter, and Ministers in both Houses-of-Parliament were quite unanimous in-the conviction that-such a measure was-necessary for-the safe-guarding | of-the vast interests committed to-their care. His right-honourable-friend, the Secretary-for-War, had shown exactly how-the proposed increase would-be distributed, and-the Chancellor-of- | the-Exchequer, the First-Lord-of-the-Treasury, and-the First-Lord-of-the-Admiralty had each advanced weighty reasons for-the adoption of-the-proposal. It-was-not a | party-question, and he trusted that-the right-honourable-gentleman, the Leader-of-the-Opposition, would-not attempt to-make party-capital out-of-it. It-was true, as-the | President-of-the-Board-of-Trade and-the Secretary-of-State-for-the-Home-Department had both candidly admitted, there-were several minor details of-the-measure open to amendment, | but-they-would, no-doubt, be amended in-committee, when-the Chairman-of-Committee would-give honourable-members, and especially the honourable-and-learned-member for Bath an opportunity of | debating these-points. The Leader-of-the-Opposition took exception to-the-manner in-which-the proposal had-been brought before-the House, and declared that sound reasons had-not- | been advanced for-its adoption. As Leader-of-the-Party in Opposition he claimed that fuller discussion should-be given to-the-measure before-the Government pressed it forward to | a division. The Secretary-of-State-for-War replied for-the-Government, and-the-motion was carried by a very large majority.   (352 words)

Exercise 193

Write in shorthand

Topics of-considerable interest were discussed at-the district conference of-the Labour-Party. There-was much praise for-the National-Insurance-Act. The question of-the nationalization-of-railways | in-the United-Kingdom raised a lengthy and-interesting discussion. With-regard-to proportional-representation it-was asserted that-it-was opposed by party-organizers because it-would open-the | way to-government by groups which-would-be contrary to-the traditions of-the-British-Constitution. Much objection was-taken to-the increase in-the naval-estimates for-the- | current year, and-some speakers averred that our plenipotentiaries abroad might do more to-check-the desire for increased armaments. The condition of-the working-classes in-the United-States | and-Germany was-given as an argument against tariff-reform, while it-was argued that-the whole question of colonial-preference could-only-be satisfactorily settled by an Imperial-Parliament. | (150 words)

Exercise 194

Write in shorthand

The Treasury had consented to enlarge-the land-department. There-would-be one additional Sub-Commissioner and-four Assistant Sub-Commissioners. The Treasury had also sanctioned an additional clerical staff to-the | number of eleven persons. A matter of-great importance and difficulty at-the beginning of-this work had-been-the obtaining of-suitable land. A great-deal of-land was | expressly excluded by-the Act. In-some-places there-was-not enough suitable land for all-the applicants, and-there-were cases in-which-the only remedy for congestion was- | the migration of-some of-the applicants to other-parts of-Scotland. There-were various causes which-made rapid progress impossible in-the-first year, but-these-would diminish as | time went on. He hoped the Board would-be-able-to bring into use for small-holders land which now was either not cultivated or not being used to-the | best-advantage. During-the past century a large area of arable cultivation had passed into permanent pasture, and he hoped it-would-be possible to-place many small landholders on | land of-that kind—a process which-would increase-the number of-men maintained on-the soil. As-to deer forests, there-were two-cases in-which owners had offered | to negotiate for a settlement, and-there-were several other cases in-which negotiations were going on. The question of compensation might make-the taking of a small piece of- | land in-the-middle of a deer forest an extremely costly business. The first report showed that by-the end of-the-year, subject to-the decision of-the Land | Court, arrangements had-been made to-provide for 500 applicants, and-since-then a great-deal of work had-been-done. Many hundreds of-cases were in various stages | of development. The Board were anxious, not-only to-find land for small holdings, but also to assist their successful cultivation by giving the holders opportunities of-practical instruction and | demonstration, of-learning the best-methods of-cultivation, of keeping up-the quality of-their stock, and-by encouraging poultry and everything which-would-make-the small holdings profitable. Co-operation | amongst small-holders was-making satisfactory progress, and-the-Board were at-present in communication with-the Scottish-banks for-the-purpose-of seeing whether-they could offer better credit | facilities.   (391 words)

CHAPTER XXXVIII

BANKING AND STOCKBROKING PHRASES

Phraseography in Banking and Stockbroking. 217. The shorthand writer engaged in banking or stock-broking will meet with many terms peculiar to these branches of business, and he should equip himself with suitable and easily written phraseograms for their rapid representation. It will not be sufficient, however, for him to know the shorthand outlines for these phrases. He should make himself master of the meanings of the terms and their correct use. A study of the following lists will enable him to frame similar contractions for any phrase not included in the lists.

BANKING

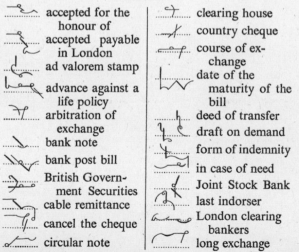

accepted for the honour of

accepted payable in London

ad valorem stamp

advance against a life policy

arbitration of exchange

bank note

bank post bill

British Government Securities

cable remittance

cancel the cheque

circular note

clearing house

country cheque

course of exchange

date of the maturity of the bill

deed of transfer

draft on demand

form of indemnity

in case of need

Joint Stock Bank

last indorser

London clearing bankers

long exchange

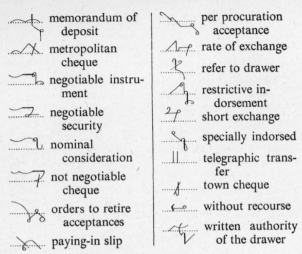

memorandum of deposit

metropolitan cheque

negotiable instrument

negotiable security

nominal consideration

not negotiable cheque

orders to retire acceptances

paying-in slip

per procuration acceptance

rate of exchange

refer to drawer

restrictive indorsement

short exchange

specially indorsed

telegraphic transfer

town cheque

without recourse

written authority of the drawer

Exercise 195

Write in shorthand

My-brother and-I are in Joint-Stock-Banks in-London. He-is in-the foreign-department and consequently he-is specially acquainted with-such expressions as arbitration-of-exchange, | course-of-exchange, rate-of-exchange, long-exchange, short-exchange, cable-remittance and telegraphic-transfers, and a draft-on-demand. The phraseology used in-connection-with bills is very interesting | to-him, and-in dealing-with a bill he-has, of-course, to note the date-of-the-maturity-of-the-bill, whether it-is specially-indorsed, or has a | restrictive-indorsement, or has on it the words without-recourse, or in-case-of-need. Bills are sometimes accepted-for-the-honour-of any party thereon, or accepted-payable-in- | London, or they-have a per-procuration-acceptance. A bank may-receive orders-to-retire-acceptance. I-am specially concerned with cheques which-may-be town-cheques, metropolitan-cheques, or | country-cheques, paying-in-slips, various bank-notes and circular-notes. Our-bank occasionally consents to-grant an advance-against-a-life-policy and accepts deeds accompanied by a memorandum- | of-deposit.   (182 words)

Exercise 196

Write in shorthand

I-understand-the significance of a nominal-consideration, which-is given for-the-purpose-of avoiding paying ad-valorem-stamp duty, a deed-of-transfer, a negotiable-instrument, and a | negotiable-security, among-which last British-Government-Securities take a premier place. A form-of-indemnity is used in-connection-with-the loss of documents, and-in other matters. Sometimes | I-have to-write on a cheque "refer-to-drawer," and occasionally a cheque is-not honoured without-the written-authority-of-the-drawer, or-the advice to "cancel-the- | cheque" is received. I-have to pay particular attention to a "not-nego-tiable"-cheque. Without-the Clearing-House the London-clearing-bankers would-be unable to-cope with-the huge | number of cheques which pass daily through-their banks, the daily average being about £50,000,000. The amount of-labour, both physical and mental, represented by-this vast sum, | is indeed wonderful. There-are four clearings each day: Metro-politan, Town (morning), Country, Town (afternoon), at-each of-which-the respective-cheques are cleared. The busiest days are-the fourth | of-the-month when so-many bills are payable and-the Stock-Exchange settlement days.   (195 words)

STOCKBROKING

bearer shares	cum dividend
blank transfer	cumulative prefer- ence shares
buying for control	day to day money
capital liabilities	demoralized markets
carry-over facilities	directors' · qualification
concentrating plant	dwts. per ton
consolidated annuities	ex-dividend
convertible gold bonds	first mortgage debentures

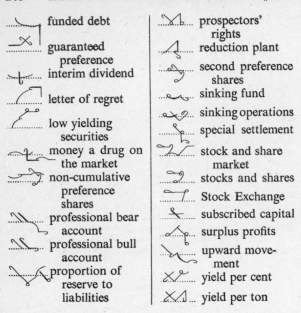

funded debt

guaranteed preference

interim dividend

letter of regret

low yielding securities

money a drug on the market

non-cumulative preference shares

professional bear account

professional bull account

proportion of reserve to liabilities

prospectors' rights

reduction plant

second preference shares

sinking fund

sinking operations

special settlement

stock and share market

stocks and shares

Stock Exchange

subscribed capital

surplus profits

upward movement

yield per cent

yield per ton

Exercise 197

Write in shorthand

The young investor is apt to be nonplussed by-the business vocabulary of-the stockbroker. If-he reads the financial articles on-the stock-and-share-markets he-will come | across such expressions as buying-for-control, carry-over-facilities, day-to-day-money, money-a-drug-on-the-market, demoralized-markets, professional-bear-account, professional-bull-account, and upward- | movement. In-the-mining market section he-will read of-prospectors'-rights, concentrating-plant, reduction-plant, sinking-operations, and-the report of a year's working will mention dwts.-per-ton, | yield-per-ton, and yield-per-cent. He probably knows little of-directors'-qualifications, and-is liable to be misled into buying low-yielding-securities. Among-the various investments there- | are consolidated-annuities or consols, a funded-debt of-the-government, cumulative-prefer-ence-shares, non-cumulative-preference-shares, first-mortgage-debentures, second-preference-shares, and so on. He-may come | across blank-transfers and bearer-shares, and-have to study the subscribed-capital, the capital-liabilities, the proportion-of-reserve-to-liabilities and-the surplus-profits of going concerns.

(179 words)

Exercise 198

Write in shorthand

He-will-have to pay special-attention to-the sinking-fund, an amount which-is annually set aside out-of revenue and-invested with-the interest accruing to-provide, at | a future date, for-the redemption of a loan or a series of debentures, or for recouping the gradual shrinkage in value by exhausting the known profit-bearing resources of | a mine or similar undertaking. When taking-up stocks-and-shares he-will, of-course, be influenced by interim-dividends, and-whether-the stocks-and-shares are cum-dividend or ex- | dividend, and-in-some-cases after much trouble and-some worry he-may-receive a letter-of-regret. In-the-case-of companies being floated he-must notice if-the | Stock-Exchange is giving a special-settlement. Certainly the investment of-money so-as-to produce a satisfactory return is-no easy-matter, and-whether convertible-gold-bonds or guaran-teed- | preference-shares are held, it-is-necessary to-exercise the greatest caution. Even-the most astute investor may-be deceived at-times by prospectuses, and balance-sheets may fail to- | reveal the true state-of-affairs of a company.   (189 words)

CHAPTER XXXIX

INSURANCE AND SHIPPING PHRASES

Phraseography in Insurance and Shipping. 218. The following lists of phrases in common use in insurance and shipping are only a small selection of the total number of such-like phrases to be met with daily in either of these important branches of business. The shorthand-writer entering upon work in either an insurance or a shipping office should immediately set about familiarizing himself with the terms he will be called upon to write in shorthand and with their meanings. His value to his employers and his chances of promotion will depend largely upon his intelligent understanding of the terms employed and his unceasing efforts to extend his knowledge of the business.

INSURANCE

Accident Insurance Co.

approximate rate of premium

automatic sprinklers

bonus year of the company

casual employment

claim for compensation

combined accident and disease policy

damage by fire

damage to premises

damage to tyres

date and term of insurance

dislocation of the wrist

fire insurance

immediate benefit

in full discharge of all claims

incombustible materials

Insurance Co.

interim bonus

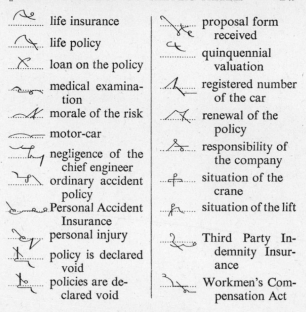

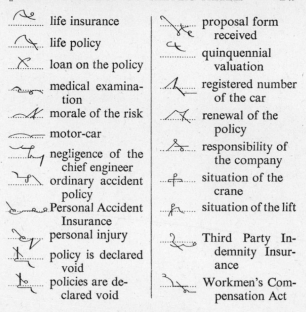 life insurance

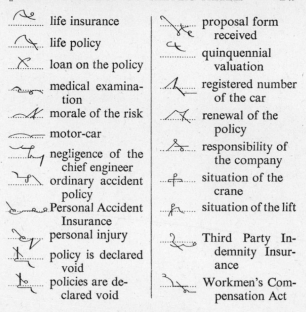 life policy

 loan on the policy

 medical examination

 morale of the risk

 motor-car

 negligence of the chief engineer

 ordinary accident policy

 Personal Accident Insurance

 personal injury

 policy is declared void

 policies are declared void

 proposal form received

 quinquennial valuation

 registered number of the car

 renewal of the policy

 responsibility of the company

 situation of the crane

 situation of the lift

 Third Party Indemnity Insurance

 Workmen's Compensation Act

Exercise 199

Write in shorthand

The operations of insurance-companies now cover a very extended field and are continually growing consequent upon legislative enactments and improved methods of-locomotion. There-is-the Workmen's-Compensation-Act | which deals with accidents arising out-of and-in-the-course-of employment, and-claims-for-compensation are made for minor-accidents such-as-the dislocation-of-the-wrist and | unhappily also for fatal accidents. Often this compensation is paid in a lump-sum in-full-discharge-of-all-claims. Evidence of a definite contract or arrangement must-be shown | in-the-case-of casual-employment before compensation can-be claimed. Third-Party-Indemnity-Insurance is concerned with-the liability of-persons to-third-parties in-respect-of personal-injury | and damage-to-property.

(124 words)

Exercise 200

Write in shorthand

The rate-of-premium depends on-the *morale*-of-the-risk. In-the-matter of-motor-car insurance there-are-considerations of damage-by-fire and damage-to-tyres, and- | in-all-cases the registered-number-of-the-car must-be given. Then there-is indemnity for accidents in-connection-with lifts, cranes and hoists in-which-the situation-of- | the-cranes, and-the situation-of-the-lifts are of-much importance. Personal-Accident-Insurance may-be covered by an ordinary-accident-policy or a combined-accident-and-disease-policy. | Fire-insurance covers damages-to-premises by fire, and among other precautions automatic-sprinklers are insisted upon where there-are other-than incombustible-materials. Life-insurance is often associated with | a medical-examination and policies-are-declared-void and-the responsibility-of-the-company ceases if material facts are hidden by-the insured.   (143 words)

Exercise 201

Write in shorthand

Most insurance-companies have what-is termed-the bonus-year-of-the-company, and-some declare an interim-bonus. A quinquennial-valuation is taken by life-offices when bonuses are | declared and-provisions made for shareholders'-dividends where-the office is a proprietary one. It-is-true that-the holders of-life-policies payable with bonus pay a higher premium | than-the holders of-life-insurance-policies payable without bonus, but it-is-not correct to assume that-the holders of bonus-policies merely receive back in-the form of | bonus the excess premiums paid to-the Life-Insurance-Company. If a life-office could predict exactly its future mortality experience, rates of interest realizable, and rates of-expense, it | could fix its premiums so-that it-would show neither profit nor loss. One-of-the-most attractive features of-life-insurance is-its simplicity. There-are-no legal costs | or charges to be faced, there-are-no trying and complicated investigations to-be-made, requiring the skill and experience on-the-part-of-the principal personally or by deputy, | and-the business of obtaining a life-policy can-be completed in-the-course-of a very-few hours, without incurring a single farthing of unproductive expense.   (207 words)

SHIPPING

advances against shipment

advances on acceptances

bill of lading in set of four

Board of Trade regulations

cable exchange rate

captain's receipt for documents

case of total loss

cash against bill of lading

Chamber of Commerce

charter party

constructive total loss of cargo

consular invoice

cost, insurance and freight (*c.i.f.*)

documents of title

indorsed and confirmed

errors and omissions excepted (*e. & o. e.*)

foreign general average

free of general average

free on rail (*f.o.r.*)

free on board (*f.o.b.*)

London office of the bank

Marine Insurance Act

marine insurance policy

Merchant Shipping Act

nature and cause of damage

not responsible for the damage

Port of London Authority

remit draft on Paris

remit proceeds of bill

salvage charges

shipping documents enclosed

telegraphic codes

to be approved by the underwriters

value to be declared

voyage policy

weight subject to correction

York-Antwerp Rules

Exercise 202

Write in shorthand

The Port-of-London-Authority extends its sway over-the greatest and richest highway of-commerce ever-known to history, and it-is continually improving the conditions of shipping on- | the Thames. In matters relating to shipping the Board-of-Trade-regulations have-to-be carried-out, while-the various chambers-of-commerce seek to-improve and modify any enactments | affecting the interests of-their-members. The Merchant-Shipping-Act, the York-Antwerp-Rules, and-the Marine-Insurance-Act have an important bearing on-the importation and exportation of-produce. | When goods are exported various documents are used according-to-circumstances. Among-these documents may-be a bill-of-lading-in-set-of-four, an invoice, marked *e.-&-o.-* | *e.*, a consular-invoice, and a marine-insurance-policy, which-may-be a voyage-policy.

(135 words)

Exercise 203

Write in shorthand

These documents, which-are frequently accompanied with a bill-of-exchange, form-the documents-of-title. If an advance-against-shipment is required, the documents-of-title, including-the Consular-invoice, | are forwarded to-the London-office-of-the-bank. The advice should-be marked "shipping-documents-enclosed." If a bill-of-exchange is sent through-the bank for-collection, any | special-instructions as to-the proceeds should-be given; for-instance, remit-proceeds-of-bill to-London; or, remit-draft-on-Paris. Sometimes a charter-party is employed, and for | all-these a captain's-receipt-for-documents is given. A shipper's prices may-be *f.-o.-b.*, *f.-o.-r.*, or *c.-i.-f.*, and insurance may-be free-of-general-average, or according-to foreign- | general-average. In-all-cases risks must-be approved-by-the-underwriters or they-will-not-be responsible-for-the-damage which-may occur. In making a claim the nature- | and-cause-of-damage must-be given, and-there-may-be a case-of-total-loss or constructive-total-loss. If salvage is-necessary the ship, freight, and cargo must | each pay its-own share of-the salvage-charges. Consignees may-be written to by post with shipping-documents-enclosed.

(207 words)

Exercise 204

Write in shorthand

Arrangements are often made for bankers to-make advances-against-shipments, or advances-on-acceptances. The banker forwards the documents to-his agent abroad who presents-the bill-of-exchange | for acceptance or payment upon-which-the agent will surrender the shipping-documents. The London-office-of-the-bank will-be advised and-the shipper will-be credited with-the | margin, or difference between-the advance made and-the amount-of-the-bill. Instructions are often given to remit-draft-on-Paris, to remit-proceeds-of-bill by telegraphic-transfer, | or to cable-exchange-rate, and telegraphic-codes are employed. These usually consist of key-words or figures, each word or group of figures representing a complete sentence.

(118 words)

CHAPTER XL

TECHNICAL AND RAILWAY PHRASES

Phraseography in Engineering and Railway Offices.
219. There is no more difficult form of note-taking than that to be met with in the offices of electrical and mechanical engineers or certain departments of railway work. Special care is, therefore, necessary on the part of the shorthand writer undertaking such work. It is not, of course, to be expected that he should have a great deal of technical knowledge; but it is very desirable that he should endeavour to acquire at least a general knowledge of the difference in meaning of terms which are more or less similar in sound. He will find that the terms used are dictated at a fairly rapid rate, and that his outlines for them must be clearly and easily written. Very much more extensive lists of phrases are given in the publishers' series of Shorthand Writers' Phrase Books, to which the shorthand writer entering for the first time the office of an engineering concern or a railway is referred.

ELECTRICAL AND ENGINEERING

	alternating current		discharge resistance
	automatic apparatus		discharge chamber
	Bessemer steel		earth currents
	block signal		eddy currents
	civil engineer		electric current
	combustion chamber		electrical engineer
	current density		energy current

......*.......	energy resistance	......\.......\......	primary coil
......⊥.......	exhaust valve	......~⌐.......	primary currents
......λ.......	free charge	......⌐/.......	railway engineer
......⊶.......	heating apparatus	......∬.......	residual charge
......ℓ.......	high resistance	......×.......	resistance board
......ℓ.......	high voltage		resistance of copper circuits
......⌐.......	induction coil	......∧ℓ⌐.......	rotary converter
	lever and weight safety valve	......∧×.......	rotary transformer
	low pressure cylinder	......∿........	secondary coil
......K.......	low voltage	......∿_/.......	secondary current
	mechanical stokers		sight feed lubricator
	monophase generator		spring balance safety valve
......×.......	no voltage attachment		vacuum brake
......⌐.......	pressure gauge		water cooling plant
......~×.......	primary battery		

Exercise 205

Write in shorthand

The history of engineering is a very fascinating subject, and-the remains of-remote antiquity, as exemplified in-the pyramids of Egypt, and-of Stonehenge in-our-own island, testify | to-the early skill of-men in matters relating to engineering. It-was about-the middle of-the 18th-century that-the-profession of engineering originated, and today it- | is-one of-the foremost in-the-world. There-are many subdivisions such-as military, mining, mechanical, civil, railway, sanitary and electrical, and-as electricity is-now so generally applied | it-is-necessary for-most engineers to be electricians also. Electricians must understand what-is-meant by earth-currents, eddy-currents, electric-currents, alternating-currents, residual-charge, resistance-board, rotary- | transformer, or rotary-converter.   (124 words)

Exercise 206

Write in shorthand

The railway-engineer is concerned, more-or-less, with block-signals, heating-apparatus, Bessemer-steel, and vacuum-brakes, while-the mechanical-engineer pays special-attention to automatic-apparatus, combustion-chambers, | exhaust-valves, low-pressure-cylinders and high-pressure-cylinders, mechanical-stokers, sight-feed-lubricators and water-cooling-plants. He-has to-consider-the advantages and disadvantages of-the lever-and- | weight-safety-valve and-the spring-balance-safety-valve, and also of-the surface-condenser, which-is a device employed for condensing exhaust-steam without mixing-it with cold-water. | The method is-now universally used in marine engines.

(99 words)

Exercise 207

Write in shorthand

Among other things, the electrical-engineer should-know-that power delivered from-the monophase-generator is pulsating, that from-the multiphase-generator is constant; that current-density is-the amount | of current per unit of area of a cross-section of a conductor; that an induction-coil is an apparatus used for obtaining a very-small-current at a very | high-voltage from a battery-current of low-voltage, and hence really a trans-former especially adapted to work a continuous-current from a few cells; that a primary-coil is- | that coil of an induction-coil, transformer, etc., through which flows a primary-current, with-the original-current, whose fluctuations are to be utilized in-order-to induce another or | secondary-current in-the secondary-coil of-the apparatus; and-that copper-loss is-the waste of-energy through-the resistance-of-copper-circuits in electric-plant, the energy being | dissipated in-the form of heat. The dynamo is a reversible machine, that-is-to-say, it-may-be used either as a dynamo or as a motor. In-the- | first-case, the machine is driven by a steam-engine or gas-engine or turbine, and gives out electrical-energy. In-the-second-case, electrical-energy is imparted to-the | machine.

(211 words)

RAILWAY

break down plant

British Railways

Charing Cross Station

chief mechanical engineer

defective signal

diesel engine

dining car

district traffic manager

driver's report

engine driver

fast passenger train

first class compartment

general manager

goods traffic committee

high pressure of steam

King's Cross Station

locomotive and engineering committee

locomotive department

locomotive superintendent

loss in transit

main line

Paddington Station

passenger brake van

passenger traffic committee

passenger train

passengers' luggage

permanent way committee

railway directors

railway executive

railway manager

railway receiving station

St. Pancras Station

sleeping saloon

Station Master

superintendent of the line

telegraph superintendent

third class compartment

traffic manager

Exercise 208

Write in shorthand

We left King's-Cross-Station on time, but owing-to a defective signal near Grantham we suffered a delay of fifteen minutes. We-were being hauled by-one-of-the | latest diesel engines, and-the engine-driver, who had-the Chief-Mechanical-Engineer in-the cab with him, made up most of-the time before-the train reached Berwick. His | speed, at-times, was well over 70 miles-an-hour. For a heavy passenger-train this-was a fine perform-ance. On-our arrival at Edinburgh I-had a chat with- | the engine-driver, and he told-me that-the locomotive was capable-of a much higher speed, but he had to-reduce speed fairly frequently because-of permanent-way "slows." | The Station-Master, and-the Locomotive-Superintendent, who then came forward, showed great interest in-the driver's and-the Chief-Mechanical-Engineer's account of-the performance of-the locomotive.   (149 words)

Exercise 209

Write in shorthand

For-purposes-of administration the work of a railway is divided into many-departments under-the-control of-the general-manager, who ultimately settles all disputes. Then there-are-the | chief-mechanical-engineer, who-is-the head of-the locomotive-department which-has very complicated matters to negotiate, the traffic-manager, the locomotive-superintendent, the superintendent-of-the-line, the | telegraph-superintendent, and so on; while various committees, such-as-the goods-traffic-committee, the locomotive-and-engineering-committee, the passenger-traffic-committee and-the permanent-way-com-mittee decide important- | matters concerning-the working of-the line. The settlement-of-claims made by-clients of-the railways is a very difficult problem, and often leads to actions in-the-law- | courts.   (121 words)

Exercise 210

Write in shorthand

To cope with-these and other-matters, such-as-the rating of-the railway by public bodies, a staff of fully-qualified solicitors is employed by-each-company. The very- | important and complicated work of-the equitable division of-receipts for-the carriage of passengers and goods, demurrage on wagons, etc., is performed at-the Railway-Clearing-House. Long-distance | passenger-trains may-have sleeping-saloons and dining-cars, and many companies have discontinued second-class-compartments on all-trains. Nearly all passenger-trains have a passenger-brake-van for | passengers'-luggage and merchandise and perishables for quick transit.   (99 words)

CHAPTER XLI

LEGAL PHRASES

Phraseography in Legal Work. 220. The law has, to a large extent, a vocabulary and terminology of its own, and the shorthand writer engaged upon legal work, whether in taking notes of correspondence and of documents, or as note-taker in courts, must have a fairly wide acquaintance with the peculiar style of language employed. The court reporter must also be familiar with quite a number of leading cases, because reference to these is of everyday occurrence, and ignorance of them would make his work difficult, if not, indeed, impossible. Neatness of outline formation in legal note-taking of any description is of the utmost importance, and absolute accuracy of transcription is essential. No pains, therefore, should be spared by the writer to make himself thoroughly efficient, both in general knowledge of the matter he will be sure to meet with in the course of his work, and in regard to the actual writing of his shorthand notes.

LEGAL

	affidavit		counsel for the defence
	Articles of Association		counsel for the defendant
	bankrupt		counsel for the plaintiff
	bankruptcy		counsel for the prisoner
	breach of promise of marriage		counsel for the prosecution
	Central Criminal Court		
	Chancery Division		Court of Criminal Appeal
	circumstantial evidence		

Court of Appeal
deed of settlement
deed of trust
deed of assignment
Divisional Court
documentary evidence
Ecclesiastical Court
employers' liability
equity of redemption
examination in chief
executor
executrix
false pretences
Habeas Corpus
heirs, executors, administrators and assigns
heirs, executors, administrators or assigns
High Court of Justice
judgment summons
jurisprudence
justice of the peace
learned counsel
learned counsel for the defence
learned judge
legal estate

legal personal representative
Lord Chancellor
Lord Chief Justice
marriage settlement
may it please your honour
memorandum of association
my learned friend
official receiver
official writer
originating summons
power of attorney
Probate, Divorce, and Admiralty Division
Queen's Bench
Queen's Bench Division
Queen's Counsel
real estate
recognisance
reversionary bonus
trust funds
verdict for the defendant
verdict for the plaintiff
voluntary conveyance
will and testament
your worship

Exercise 211

Write in shorthand

Re SMITH, a Bankrupt

T. B. GILL, Esq.

Dear-Sir,

The action brought by-the Official-Receiver to-test the validity of-the Bill-of-Sale given to-you by | Mr.-Smith, came on for trial today in-the Queen's-Bench-Division of-the High-Court-of-Justice, before Mr. Justice Bright. I-regret-to-say that-the learned-judge, | after hearing the arguments on both-sides, decided against you on-the ground that-the document is-not in-accordance-with-the form prescribed by-the Act-of-Parliament relating | to Bills-of-Sale. You-will-remember-that I-have many-times pointed out to-you that-the Bills-of-Sale Act is so obscurely worded that great-numbers of | Bills-of-Sale prepared by-the-most eminent conveyancers have-been set aside on-the-same-ground. It-is open to-you to-carry-the matter to-the Court-of- | Appeal, but I-do-not advise that course.

Yours-truly,   (160 words)

Exercise 212

Write in shorthand

Mr. Walter Morton's progress at-the Bar has-been unusually rapid. He-was called in 1947. Before he had-been two-years at-the Bar | he had-been counsel-for-the-plaintiff in an action for breach-of-promise-of-marriage, and counsel-for-the-defendant in actions in-the Probate,-Divorce,-and-Admiralty-Division; | he had appeared in-the Ecclesiastical-Court and twice before-the Lord-Chief-Justice in Habeas-Corpus cases. In every-instance he-was successful. If-he represented-the plaintiff the | result was a verdict-for-the-plaintiff, and-if-he represented-the defendant the result was a verdict-for-the-defendant. He-is respected in-the High-Court-of-Justice | for-his thorough-knowledge of-the Common-Law, and-is always heard with marked attention in-the Divisional-Court. He argued with great ability a novel point raised on a | commercial-summons in-the Queen's-Bench last-week. He-has-been retained in an important action on a bill-of lading, and also in-several assessment appeals arising out-of- | the recent quinquennial-valuation. He-is an authority on-the vexed question of employers'-liability.   (195 words)

Exercise 213

Write in shorthand

Those-who heard his arguments the other-day as-to-the difference between-the meaning of-the two phrases, "heirs,-executors,-administrators,-*and*-assigns," and "heirs,-executors,-administrators,-*or*-assigns," | will-not soon forget his keenness. He-was equally brilliant lately when a notary-public was sued in an action for negligence. As-he refuted the arguments of-the learned- | counsel-for-the-defendant, "my-learned-friend" must-have felt overwhelmed. In-consequence-of the death of-his-father, under whose will-and-testament he inherits considerable personal-estate and | real-estate he-is-not dependent upon his profession. People are already speculating as-to when-he-will-be-made a Queen's-Counsel. He-has-been nominated as a Justice- | of-the-Peace for Surrey, his father's county. He-is-the prospective candidate for a very large constituency in-the-North of England and he-is in great demand as | a political speaker. There-is-no-doubt that at-the first opportunity he-will-be elected to-represent-the constituency in-Parliament. His intimate friends are hopeful that in-due | time he-will fill the highest judicial position in-the land, and-they feel sure he-would-be an ornament to-the office.   (203 words)

CHAPTER XLII

THEOLOGICAL PHRASES

Sermon Reporting. 221. Very many students of shorthand make an opportunity of practising the art by taking notes of the sermons delivered in the various places of worship in their neighbourhood. There are peculiar difficulties in this kind of note-taking, because of the necessity for taking notes without a firm rest for the notebook. A piece of stiff cardboard, or of thin wood, attached to the back of the notebook will be found to answer the purpose of a knee-rest very well, and practice will make the note-taking under these conditions a fairly easy task. The writer must guard against allowing the neatness of his notes to be affected by the unusual conditions under which they are taken.

THEOLOGICAL

....	Almighty God	....	covenant
....	archbishop	....	ecclesiastic-al
....	atonement	....	Episcopal Church
....	baptize-d-st-m	....	Episcopalian
....	Calvinism	....	Epistle to the Corinthians
....	Catholic faith	....	Established Church
....	Children of Israel	....	evangelical
....	Christ Jesus	....	everlasting life
....	Church and State	....	Feast of Tabernacles
....	Church of England		

fellow-creature

fruits of the Spirit

glad tidings

goodness of God

gospel of peace

Greek Church

Heavenly Father

Holy Scripture

Holy Word

House of Israel

in Jesus Christ

in the presence of God

in the providence of God

in the sight of God

in the words of the text

Jewish dispensation

kingdom of Christ

kingdom of God

kingdom of heaven

knowledge of Christ

Lord and Saviour Jesus Christ

Lord Jesus

minister of the gospel

Methodism

my beloved brethren

my text

New Testament Scriptures

Nonconformist

Nonconformity

Old Testament

passage of Scripture

Presbyterian

resurrection of Christ

Revised Version

Right Reverend

Right Rev. Bishop

Roman Catholic

Roman Catholic Church

Sabbath day

Sermon on the Mount

tabernacle

transubstantiation

United Free Church of Scotland

Virgin Mary

Wesleyan Methodist

world without end

Exercise 214

Write in shorthand

Humanity owes much to-the Church-of-Christ, in-which-the true children-of-God have-been animated by-the Holy-Spirit to Christian-faith and-practice, and-to-the | advocacy of-the gospel-of-peace and-the promotion of a love-of-our fellow-creatures in every child-of-God. Though-the relations of Church-and-State in various | lands have-not-been always what could-be desired, yet in-the-providence-of-God the fruits-of-the-Spirit have-been revealed, so-that in-the-Church the knowledge- | of-Christ has increased, and-in-the-world in-the-providence-of-God there-has-been an extension of-the kingdom-of-Christ. The blessing of-the divine Head-of- | the- Church, and-the outpouring of-the Holy-Spirit, have-been often asked on foreign-missions and home-missions, as-well-as on Sunday-school work, and other methods in- | which Christian activity has manifested itself to-bring into-the kingdom-of-God the ignorant and indifferent, by taking to-them a knowledge-of-Christ and-of-the Holy-Word, | by bringing to-them the glad-tidings of-the goodness-of-God and a know-ledge of-the kingdom-of-heaven, and of-Him who-is at-the-right-hand-of- | God.

The minister-of-the-Gospel selected a passage in-the-word-of-God from-the Revised-Version, and-said that in-the-words-of-the-text, or in my- | text, taken from St.-Paul's-Epistle to-the Collossians, they-would-find authority for-his addressing-them not as my-beloved-brethren, my-brethren, or my-dear-friends, but as- | he proposed to-do in-the-sight-of-God, and feeling that-they-were in-the-presence-of-God, as faithful brethren in-Christ, accepting the Catholic-faith, looking to- | the-same Heavenly-Father, having-the-same trust in Almighty-God, and believing in an everlasting-God, world-without-end, the ruler over heaven-and-earth for-ever-and-ever. | (330 words)

Exercise 215

Write in shorthand

Christianity as represented in-the-Christian-Church is-the religion of-the European race, the principal bodies engaged in-its maintenance or dissemination being-the Roman-Catholic-Church, the Greek- | Church, the various national Established-Churches, the Free-Churches, and many other organizations which find their faith and-practice in-the New-Testament-Scriptures. There-are, at-the-same-time, | scattered among-the nations-of-the-earth, descendants of-the Children-of-Israel who obey the Mosaic-law, observe-the Sabbath-day, the Feast-of-Tabernacles, and-the Festival of- | the Passover, and-find spiritual guidance in-the Old-Testament.

Our-Lord-Jesus-Christ was-born under-the Jewish-dispensation, and-with-his parents visited Jerusalem in-his twelfth year. | Here he-was found by Joseph and-his mother, the Virgin-Mary, among-the great-ones of-the House-of-Israel. John the Baptist bore testimony that-the Lord-Jesus- | Christ was-the Lamb-of-God, and at-the first call of-the disciples, testimony was-borne that-the Lord-Jesus was-the Son-of-God. At-the second call, | the first four in-the Apostolic College were chosen. Among-the-words of-the Lord-and-Saviour recorded in-the Gospels, the Lord's-Prayer is-the-most widely known and | used; and-of our-Saviour's teaching, the Sermon-on-the-Mount is perhaps most generally quoted. The institution of-the Lord's-Supper is recorded by three of-the Evangelists, and- | the-last discourses of-the Lord-and-Saviour-Jesus-Christ by St.-John.   (253 words)

CHAPTER XLIII

SPECIAL LIST OF WORDS

222. (*a*) The fact that the English language contains very many words which have a similar consonantal structure was early recognized by the Inventor of Pitman Shorthand, and provision was accordingly made in the system for the easy differentiation of these words by distinguishing outlines, so that the writer would have no difficulty either in the writing or in the transcription of these similarly constructed words. It is, indeed, mainly this inherent power of readily distinguishing similar words that makes Pitman Shorthand at once legible and capable of being written with extreme rapidity.

(*b*) It will be found that the application of the ordinary rules of the system provides distinguishing outlines in the great majority of cases, but where this is not so, distinction is obtained by the insertion of a vowel or, in a few cases, by placing the outline out of position, or by writing a full outline instead of applying an abbreviating principle. In studying the following list of outlines, the student should seek to appreciate fully the reasons for the various forms and positions. Where a line contains more than one word, the first word is the root word, the others being derivatives. The list of words here given is not, of course, exhaustive. The student may easily compile further lists for himself and, proceeding upon the method here illustrated, he may at one and the same time test his vocabulary and enlarge it by starting with a few root words and from them building up lists of words formed from them by the addition of prefixes and suffixes.

Exercise 216

Read, copy, and transcribe

1. Compatible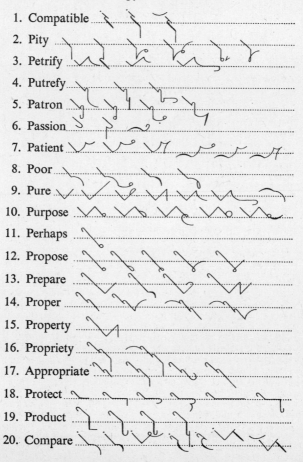
2. Pity
3. Petrify
4. Putrefy
5. Patron
6. Passion
7. Patient
8. Poor
9. Pure
10. Purpose
11. Perhaps
12. Propose
13. Prepare
14. Proper
15. Property
16. Propriety
17. Appropriate
18. Protect
19. Product
20. Compare

Exercise 217

Write in shorthand

Is-it compatible with fairness to-call-the trader a useless
member of society, one that stands between producers and takes
toll of-the-goods that are exchanged? That-is | a proper ques-
tion, for-we-have-seen-that, although money intervenes in-order-
to facilitate exchange, the appropriate fact is-that commodities
are exchanged for commodities, the pure wheat of | Canada for-
the railway-material of Warwickshire, the beef of-the Argentine
for-the woollens made and-prepared in Bradford. The farmer
of-the far-stretching fields beyond Winnipeg works, | perhaps,
for-the-purpose-of feeding-the operatives in an engine-shop at
Birmingham. Men tend cattle on-the great plains of-South-
America so-that British workers may-be- | the better fed. And-
the poorest worker here toils for-those separated from-him by
wide areas of sea and land. It-is-not improper or inaccurate to
say that- | we-are all exchanging services. We-may ask with
perfect propriety, is a middleman, a trader, necessary? We-are-
prepared to say that-he-is; it needs little thought or | comparison
of argument to-bring home to-ourselves how indispensable the
trader's work is. The proposition is almost self-evident. When,
as happened occasionally during-the pitiable days of-the war, |
the Government felt constrained to-take into its-own-hands the
distribution of-some commodity—petrol, or meat, or accommodation on-board steamers—it-was obliged to appoint armies
of | officials who did, after a certain amount of-preparation and-
training, what traders had done cheaply and smoothly before.
The work was, of-course, incompatible with their intentions in |
early-life, but it-was important, and required patience to-carry it
through. There-is-no essential difference between-the work of-
the-trader and-the work of another man. | The trader is helping
to-move products—and to-move things is-the only act that-man
is capable of; the trader helps-the commodity along its lengthy
journey from- | its production to-its consumption. The trader
seeks to-place commodities where-they shall-be of-most service
for-men. That is-his purpose or business in life. He-must- |
know where-the best and cheapest commodities are to be had;
he-must-know also where-these commodities will satisfy-the
keenest demand.   (383 words)

Exercise 218

Read, copy, and transcribe

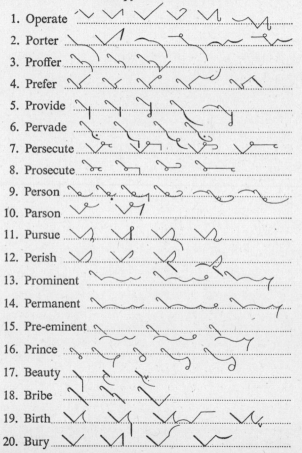

1. Operate
2. Porter
3. Proffer
4. Prefer
5. Provide
6. Pervade
7. Persecute
8. Prosecute
9. Person
10. Parson
11. Pursue
12. Perish
13. Prominent
14. Permanent
15. Pre-eminent
16. Prince
17. Beauty
18. Bribe
19. Birth
20. Bury

Exercise 219

Write in shorthand

We-are all sellers and buyers. Parson or layman, prince or peasant, we-are all either providers or consumers of things. We proffer services or offer goods to others and- | if-we-are keen we-prosecute a person who illegally tries to-prevent us from carrying-on our legitimate business. We live by exchanging, by bargaining; and-for-our-own | sakes it behoves us to acquire some skill in-the operation or making of bargains. This-is true whether-we-are exporters or importers, manufacturers or merely dealers. In-any-event, we | sell our services and so buy money. This money we change into those-things we-desire most—and which-are provided by-others—into-the necessaries and comforts of-existence, | a beautiful house, an extensive library of-permanent value, or whatever we-may prefer to add to-our reasonable enjoyment of-life. In agriculture itself, people are ceasing to-produce- | the things they consume; the farmer sells his milk-and-cream and buys butter, or contents himself with-the substitute that tropical Africa has lately added to-our tables; he | sells his cattle and buys beef of-the butcher who carves an ox fed on-the pampas of-South-America; he no-longer makes even his-own flour. The essential, | all-pervading fact of-our economic life is exchange. Apart from agriculture, we should-be unable-to produce sufficient to sustain-the simplest life, and-we should perish. By-means- | of exchange and-the co-operation it brings-about, we-are-enabled to-produce enough to satisfy a very complex life. We go to-the-market with our goods, perishable or | imperishable. Our goods may-not-be embodied in commodities that can-be weighed or measured; they-may-be, and usually are, merely proffered services. But-whether-we offer our services | for-the permanent or temporary accommodation of others—or whether-we-have visible and tangible commodities—pairs of boots, or pounds of bacon, or attractive ties, or succulent fruits—makes | no difference. It-is-our supply, and-this-is-the course to pursue if-we-would-be a seller of what we-have. In-our minds we attach a minimum | price to-it, what-the auctioneer calls a reserve price. Unless we get that-price we-shall withdraw from-the market, and-no briber can bribe us to-sell at | a figure below that-price.   (395 words)

Exercise 220

Read, copy, and transcribe

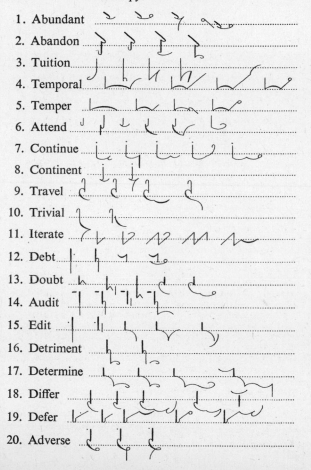

1. Abundant
2. Abandon
3. Tuition
4. Temporal
5. Temper
6. Attend
7. Continue
8. Continent
9. Travel
10. Trivial
11. Iterate
12. Debt
13. Doubt
14. Audit
15. Edit
16. Detriment
17. Determine
18. Differ
19. Defer
20. Adverse

Exercise 221

Write in shorthand

Unless a business-man has an abundant knowledge of-the fundamental art of-calculating he-will-be hopelessly outclassed in-the keen competition of-modern-times, and might even have | to abandon a business-life. An apparently trivial amount, a tiny fraction may-make-the difference between profit-and-loss and turn a favourable amount into an adverse balance. In | no branch of commerce is-this more evident than in transactions with-the continent and other-parts-of-the-world. So-many factors have-to-be-taken-into-consideration that-the | middleman, by whose offices such transactions are settled, must calculate to a nicety. He-cannot afford to-make a rough estimate, or leave-the-matter to an inefficient man or | woman. Men or women inexperienced in figures would-be useless in-such offices. He carries on-his business of bill-broking—of buying from those-who-have credit abroad and selling | to-those-that seek credit—largely on borrowed money for-which he pays interest. He-cannot charge very high for-his services for two-reasons. Other brokers are available; and- | there-are other-ways of settling debts than-the buying of a draft to-send abroad. The debtor may procure gold and himself dispatch it, or he-may send a | security to-his foreign creditor—a railway-debenture, a municipal bond, a mortgage on-land, though he-would-not-be indifferent as-to-the choice. For in a sense we- | can, in-these-days, so closely identified is property with-the legal title to-it, export our fields and-factories, our railroads and canals, to pay for our imports. However, | a debtor resorts to-the export of-gold or securities only as a temporary measure, when-the bills-of-exchange are at-a-price he judges exorbitant. What-is this | exorbitant price which determines his choice? It-is a price beyond that-which he-would-be-required to pay for gold and-for-the-expenses of-sending it to-his | creditors, or for-the security that-would in-the foreign-country command enough credit to cancel the debt. When-we-are guided, as normally we-are, by economic considerations, we | elect the cheaper instrument for performing a necessary operation; we-do-not give good-money when poorer will suffice. That-would-be detrimental to-our business, as-the audited accounts | would afterwards show.   (393 words)

Exercise 222

Read, copy, and transcribe

1. Diverse
2. Decease
3. Disease
4. Dear
5. Agent
6. Act
7. Cause
8. Access
9. Excise
10. Exercise
11. Cultivate
12. Column
13. Culminate
14. Calumny
15. Create
16. Carry
17. Credence
18. Credit
19. Accord
20. Guide

Exercise 223

Write in shorthand

The view taken of-the very diverse changes and chances of-life varies with different people, and-with-the same people at different times. Some there-are who-would perform- | the same journey, work at-the-same desk, have lunch at-the-same table day after day, year in and year out. They-are, apparently, merely mechanical agents, and-nothing | short of sickness, culminating in chronic disease, would alter their habits. They cultivate a disinclination to-exercise their undoubted right to change. They prefer routine to-risk, and are appalled | when-they consider-the uncertainties that dog their paths from one cause or another. They carry-on, accordingly, in-the-same-way, year after year, until their decease. Our modern | trade facilities have, indeed, removed from tolerably civilized societies many of-the risks of famine or scarcity or sudden death or ruin that-men ran in ruder times. We-have | a security of-person and-property such-as was-not enjoyed in-the best days of-the Roman peace; and-the cheapness and ease of-transport enable-the surplus of- | one area to-supply-the deficiency of another. Modern conditions have created a different atmosphere, and-we-are, in a sense, very different creatures. We-are freed from-the drawback | of-which Mill speaks: "In poor and backward societies, as in-the-East, and-in Europe during-the Middle-Ages, extraordinary differences in-the-price of-the-same commodity might | exist in-places not very distant from each-other, because-the want of-roads and canals, the imperfection of-marine navigation, and-the insecurity of communications generally, prevented things from | being transported from-the places where-they-were cheap to-those where-they-were dear. The things most liable to fluctuations in-value, those directly influenced by-the seasons, were | seldom carried to any great-distances. Each locality depended, as-a-general-rule, on its-own produce and-that of-its immediate neighbourhood. In-most years, accordingly, there-was, in- | some part or-other of any large country, a real dearth. . . . In modern-times there-is-only dearth where there formerly would-have-been famine, and sufficiency everywhere when anciently | there-would-have-been scarcity in-some-places and superfluity in others."   (372 words)

Exercise 224

Read, copy, and transcribe

1. Good 
2. Guard 
3. Grade 
4. Grant 
5. Guarantee 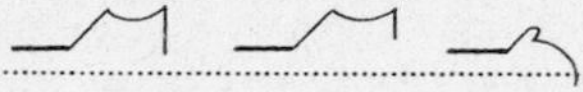
6. Factor 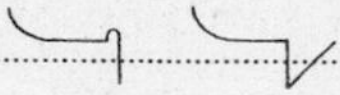
7. Favour 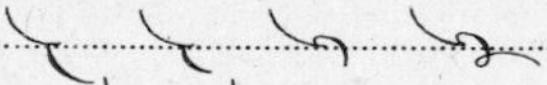
8. Fall 
9. Felon 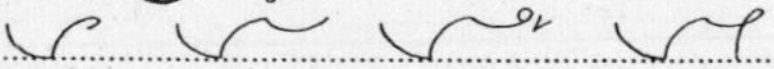
10. Fortune 
11. Four 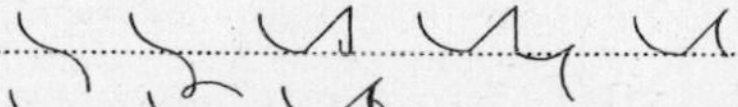
12. Far 
13. Further 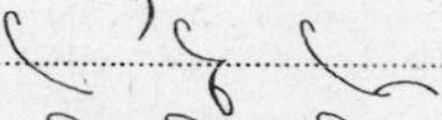
14. Fresh 
15. Form 
16. Farm 
17. Firm 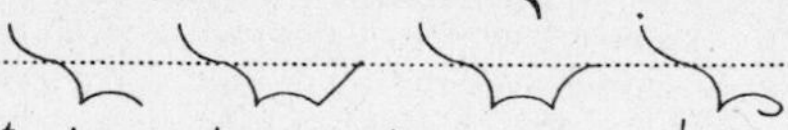
18. Evident 
19. Confide 
20. Avoid

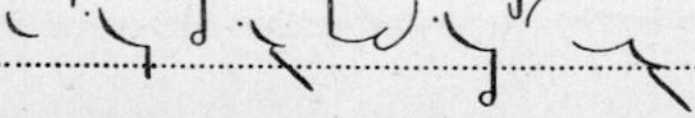

Exercise 225

Write in shorthand

It-is evident that-we-shall hardly succeed in-our business-relations unless we-understand something of-the law that guards and guarantees our legal rights, and-in-the-last | resort enforces the performance of bargains. We-must in-our duties as ordinary-citizens have-some degree of knowledge in-the-laws in-order-that-we-may protect ourselves against | the felonious acts of felons or would-be felons. In matters of business we-need to-have a keener appreciation of-our rights-and-obligations, or we-shall-probably fall | into serious mistakes and, possibly, lose our whole fortune. Certainly we-are-not to-suppose that-men act honourably in business merely because they-are constrained by-the law. Merchants, | factors, agents and owners of factories perform their contracts without thinking about-the possibility of a law-suit, even as-they respect-the property of-their neighbours from-other motives | than a dread of punishment for thieving. Confidence in-the honesty of others there-must-be, or business would-be-impossible. Contracts were performed long-before there-was a law | of contracts; and numberless bargains are effected that-the law would-not-think of enforcing. Much of-our mercantile law is, in-fact, simply the custom of-merchants made authoritative | and applicable to all-grades of business. What men have-found convenient to-do, what-has conduced to-the smooth working of buying and selling, has-been adopted and made | effective, and few seek to-avoid their obligations. The merchants enjoyed special privileges and-were subject to special duties; and-their usages were binding only upon them. These usages were | a body of customs by-which trade was facilitated and-they-were more firmly established as time passed. Recognized as binding by-the merchants this body of customs was gradually | incorporated into-the law that-everyone, whether merchant or farmer, factor or agent, is constrained to observe. Such law is, as-was declared by a judge of a case in | 1875, "neither more-nor-less than-the usages of-merchants and-traders. They-have-been ratified by-the decision of-courts-of-law, which, upon such usage being | proved before them, have adopted them as settled law." In-the-present tendency to-consolidate the law, most of-the usages are contained in-the Sales-of-Goods-Act of | 1893.   (393 words)

Exercise 226

Read, copy, and transcribe

1. Inevitable
2. Value
3. Avail
4. Convulse
5. Evolution
6. Violent
7. Converse
8. Support
9. Separate
10. Situate
11. Station
12. Structure
13. Consider
14. Secret
15. Secretary
16. Secrete
17. Sacred
18. Consist
19. Short
20. Emigrate

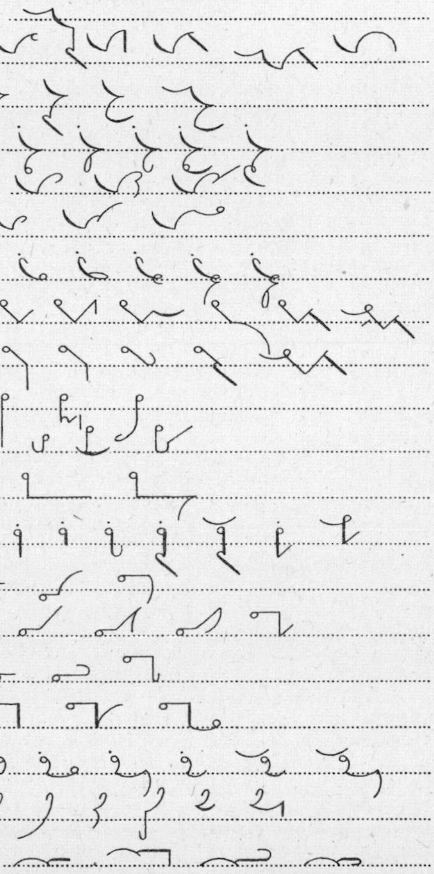

Exercise 227

Write in shorthand

The assuming of risks, the shouldering of responsibility for bearing losses that-may arise, is incident to all business and it-is inevitable. However far one pushes the invaluable practice | of insurance, this-will-not avail entirely, and something must needs be left to chance. Nor, on-the whole, would it-be good for-man if chance were altogether eliminated | from-life and separated from business. Uncertainty adds considerable piquancy to a drab existence though, of-course, nobody desires convulsive or violent changes for-the-sake-of variety. Though-we- | are, taking-us all-round, a very cautious race there-are-never wanting among-us those willing to-take-the chances inseparable from business. And taking one with another the | risk-takers profit because, since more are ready to devolve risk from themselves than are ready to assume it, they can put a premium upon-their services. Those services are | real. What people call "remuneration for risk" is really earned. Unless plans were made for a more-or-less distant future, no progress would-be possible; but as-soon-as | futurity comes into-the account, chance enters too. The Time Element—"the changes and chances of-this mortal life," as-it-is expressed—implies uncertainty. A natural instinct prompts us | to-consider enjoyments now as more eligible than enjoyments that are to-come. Few future events are quite free from uncertainty; gilt-edged securities of-the-most unblemished reputation fluctuate in- | value, as anyone with secretarial experience will-know. The man that sinks a mine, even though-he acts upon-the advice of a geological expert, runs-risks; for geology itself | is-not-yet infallible. The emigrant frequently risks a good-deal. The rubber planter in Ceylon takes risks of-political upheavals that-might conceivably sweep away his property rights, | takes some risk that-the secret researches of scientists may devise a suitable substitute, takes risks of-market, of-weather, of any number-of factors that no foresight can predict. | Even when-we-take seats in-the luncheon car, signifying by-the act that-we accept-the offer of-the railway-company to-provide a good meal for five-shillings, | we run risk of not getting the meal we anticipate. The company, too, runs some risk; for-we-may-be short of-money, or we-may-have-no money to | pay, or having it, may evade payment.   (397 words)

Exercise 228

Read, copy, and transcribe

1. Immigrate
2. Murder
3. Define
4. End
5. Need
6. Ingenious
7. Ingenuous
8. Labour
9. Elaborate
10. Learn
11. Write
12. Rot
13. Regret
14. Regard
15. Refer
16. Rough
17. Revere
18. Human
19. Heart
20. Hard

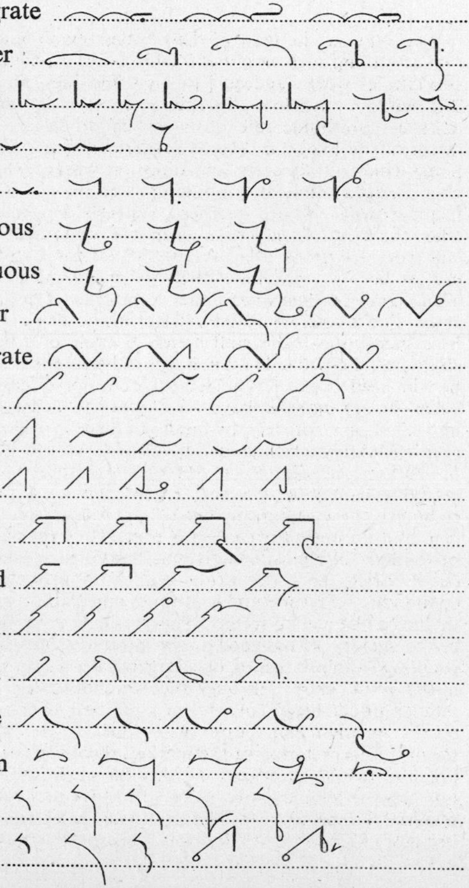

Exercise 229

Write in shorthand

By-no-means the least of-the business-man's many duties is-that of-finding such an outlet for-his goods as will enable him to continue at work. Indeed | this-is sometimes his hardest task. The weekly payments of-wages in-the factory are dependent upon-the profitable sale of-the calico or cutlery made in-the factory; the | regular salaries of-clerks and-travellers, of ware-house workers, labourers, and-transport workers cease if-there-is a prolonged difficulty in-finding customers. Certainly the factory owner, whose overhead expenses | are-not much less when-the factory is idle than when-it-is working at full pressure, will work for stock even if sales fall off for awhile. But he- | cannot lay up stock indefinitely. An end must come to-that. There-comes a time when either work must stop or products be sold. The wholesale dealer will-not dislocate | his organization by dispensing with-his staff merely because of a brief period of slackness; he-will hold on in hopes of better times coming when-he-will need them. | The retailer does-not discard his helpers when-the spring sales have given place to a dearth of visitors into-his shop. Any lengthy failure to dispose of-goods is, | however, inevitably accompanied by unemployment, unemployment of workers, of capital, and-of business ability. However re-grettable it-may-be, we-must regard this as a fact. We-may elaborate the | argument, but labour it as-we-may, there-is-the fact, and-no ingenuity can get over-it. How then are markets to be-found? The most effective method of increasing | sales is a cut in price, or a rise of-the quality or attractiveness of-the commodity. This method is at-times applicable; and when-it-is, there-is a | benefit all-round. The consumer gains in-the quantity or-the quality of-the-goods; the producer has-the advantages resulting from production on a larger scale. From-the customer | in-the retail shop; through-the warehouseman, to-whom-the retailer offers bigger orders on condition of-more favourable terms; to-the-manufacturer who looks to-the warehouseman for an | interpretation of-the-market, there-is exerted a constant pressure to-reduce prices. Neither-the ingenious manufacturer nor anyone else can fix these at-his whim or caprice. The material | incentives to increased purchases need only to be brought effectively to-the notice of prospective buyers.

(406 words)

Exercise 230

Read, copy, and transcribe

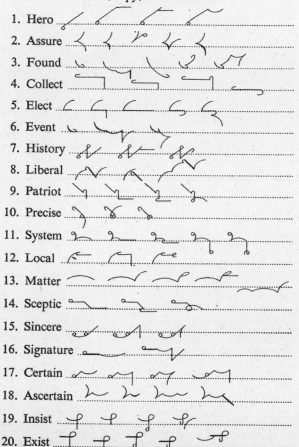

1. Hero
2. Assure
3. Found
4. Collect
5. Elect
6. Event
7. History
8. Liberal
9. Patriot
10. Precise
11. System
12. Local
13. Matter
14. Sceptic
15. Sincere
16. Signature
17. Certain
18. Ascertain
19. Insist
20. Exist

Exercise 231

Write in shorthand

To an extraordinary extent the modern business-man is dependent upon-the banker and-the banking system. One enthusiastic writer, proud of-the dominating influence exercised by-the banks, insists | that-the cessation even for a day or-two of-the banker's activities would certainly cause a complete paralysis of-the economic life of-the nation. Such a cessation would | assuredly be-found to-produce swifter and-more far-reaching effects than-the strike of-the-most effective Labour Union. The merchant works by-means-of-the credit facilities he enjoys, | and he-would-have-no facilities either to-collect or to pay his accounts. Unable-to discount-the bills he held, unable-to cash the cheques paid to-him, he-could- | not meet-the obligations constantly falling due, and must eventually become bankrupt. His signature on a cheque would-be useless. The manufacturer making for a market distant in-time-and- | place, depends upon-the support of-the banks; and-that support failing he-must cease work, no matter how sincerely he-might desire to-carry-on. Whether money is scarce | or plentiful, whether overdrafts are hard or easy to obtain, is-a-matter of supreme importance to-the trader. The stock he-has bought is carried-on credit; if-the | banker, the interpreter of-the financial state-of-the country, restricts-the credit then-the trader is obliged to unload, to-sell his stock with as little sacrifice as-possible. | He-could-not exist without-the liberal help of-the banker. The picture drawn of-the banker's work is little exaggerated. True, the banker is only a middleman; he connects | the people who save with-the people who-are-able-to employ savings in-the creation of wealth. In-our-country, at-any-rate, people have a deep-rooted confidence in- | the security of-funds entrusted to others. They-are willing to deposit with bankers and content themselves with moderate-interest upon-their deposits, the rate-of-interest being precisely ascertainable | at-any-time. Unwilling or unable-to use their accumulated savings themselves, they provide-the means whereby-the banker meets the needs of-those-that work and-trade on borrowed- | capital. This-is absolutely-certain. There-is-no room for scepticism on-the-matter. "Our people," says Bagehot, "are bolder in-dealing-with their money than any continental nation."   (389 words)

CHAPTER XLIV

SHORTHAND IN PRACTICE

In taking notes of a speech, the employment of certain significant marks will be found necessary or desirable, in order to facilitate the production of a correct verbatim transcript or a good condensed report, or to prevent misunderstanding. The use of these signs is described below—

Mishearings, etc. 223. When a word has not been heard distinctly, and the shorthand writer is uncertain whether he has written the right one or not, a circle should be drawn round the character, or a cross (×) placed under it. When the note-taker has failed to hear a word, the omission should be indicated by a caret ( ) placed *under* the line. Should a portion of a sentence be so lost, the same sign should be employed, and a space left blank corresponding to the amount omitted. Or the longhand letters *n h* (*not heard*) may be written.

Errors. 224. In cases where a reporter has failed to secure a correct note of a sentence, this may be indicated by an inclined oval, thus O (*nought* or *nothing*). When it is noticed that the speaker has fallen into an error, the mark × should be made on the margin of the notebook.

Reference Marks. 225. When verbatim notes of a speech are taken, but only a condensed report is required, a perpendicular stroke should be made in the left-hand margin of the notebook to indicate an important sentence or passage which it is desirable to incorporate in the summary. The end of a speech or the completion of a portion of a discourse may be indicated by two strokes, thus ∥ . When the reporter

suspends note-taking, but the speaker proceeds, the words *continued speaking* may be written.

Quotations, etc. 226. Quotations from well-known sources, such as the Bible or Shakespeare, familiar to the reporter, need not be written fully if time presses. It will suffice to write the commencing and concluding words with quotation marks and a long dash between, thus "*The quality of mercy ——— seasons justice.*" A long dash may be used to denote the repetition of certain words by a speaker, instead of writing them each time, as in the familiar passage, "*Whatsoever things are true, ——— honest, ——— just,*" etc.

Examination of Witnesses. 227. In reporting the examination of witnesses in questions and answers, the name of each witness should be written in longhand. The name of the examiner may be written in shorthand before the first question. If the judge, or other person, intervenes with questions during the examination, his name must be written before the first question; it need not be repeated, but care must be taken to write the name of the original examiner when he resumes his questions. Various methods may be employed for dividing questions from answers, and the answer from the succeeding question, but, whatever plan is employed, it should be one which is absolutely distinctive. When a document is put in, write *document*

between large parentheses, thus {⌐⌐}. When a

document is put in and read, write {◺◹}.

Applause, Dissent, etc. 228. The following words, descriptive of the approbation or dissent of an audience, should be enclosed between large parentheses : ⌇ *hear,* ⌇ *hear, hear,* ⌇ *no,* ⌇ *no, no,* ⌇ *sensation,* ⌇ *applause,* ⌇ *chair,* ⌇ *cheers,* ⌇ *laughter,* ⌇ *up-roar,* ⌇ *hisses.* The adjective, or adjectives, descriptive of the kind of applause must be written after the first word. For example, what would be described as *loud and continued applause* would be written ⌇ ⌇ ⌇ in reporting.

Reference Books. 229. In most offices the short-hand writer will find some reference books. But he will soon discover that it is needful to have on his own bookshelf or in his desk certain books of reference for his own use. The most indispensable work is undoubtedly a good English Dictionary. *Pitman English and Shorthand Dictionary* will be found to answer the purpose. Next in importance, if his work is of a literary character, will be a guide to all proper names in biography, geography, mythology, etc.

Business Knowledge. 230. It may not be out of place to observe that the more thoroughly equipped the shorthand writer is in the matter of general knowledge the more accurate and reliable will his shorthand prove to be. If, in addition to the necessary dexterity in the writing of shorthand, he possesses a good knowledge of business and other matters, it is obvious that his work will be performed with much greater ease and satisfaction to himself and to his employers. He should consult *Pitman Business Catalogue* for suitable books on business.

OUTLINES FOR THE NAMES OF SOME CITIES
AND TOWNS

Adelaide		Liverpool
Belfast		London
Birkenhead		Madras
Birmingham		Manchester
Bombay		Melbourne
Bradford		Middlesbrough
Brisbane		Montreal
Bristol		Newcastle-on-Tyne
Calcutta		Norwich
Canberra		Nottingham
Cape Town		Ottawa
Cardiff		Plymouth
Cork		Portsmouth
Derby		Preston
Dublin		Pretoria
Dunedin		Sheffield
Edinburgh		Singapore
Gateshead		Southampton
Gibraltar		Stoke-on-Trent
Glasgow		Sunderland
Halifax		Swansea
Hong Kong		Sydney
Huddersfield		Wellington
Hull		Winnipeg
Johannesburg		Wolverhampton
Leeds		

GRAMMALOGUES

Arranged alphabetically

a *or* an	cold	his
accord-ing	come	hour
advantage	could	how
ah!	dear	however
all	deliver-ed-y	importance-ant
and	deliverance	impossible
any	difference-t	improve-d-ment
are	difficult	in
as	do	influence
aught	doctor, Dr.	influenced
awe	during	information
aye	eh?	inscribe-d
balance	equal-ly	inscription
be	equalled	instruction
because	first	instructive
been	for	is
behalf	from	it
belief-ve-d	general-ly	itself
beyond	generalization	justification
build-ing	gentleman	language
but	gentlemen	large
call	give-n	largely
called	go	larger
can	gold	liberty
cannot	great	Lord
care	guard	me
cared	had	member
chair	hand	mere
chaired	has	more
cheer	have	most
cheered	he	Mr.
child	him	much
circumstance	himself	myself

near	should	told
next	significance	too
nor	significant	toward
northern	signification	towards
number-ed	signify-ied	trade
O! oh!	southern	tried
of	speak	truth
on	special-ly	two
opinion	spirit	under
opportunity	subject-ed	usual-ly
ought	subjection	valuation
our	subjective	very
ourselves	sure	was
over	surprise	we
owe	surprised	what
owing	tell	when
own	thank-ed	whether
particular	that	which
people	the	who
pleasure	their	whose
principal-ly	them	why
principle	themselves	wish
put	there	wished
quite	therefore	with
rather	thing	within
remark-ed	think	without
remember-ed	third	wonderful-ly
satisfaction	this	word
school	those	would
schooled	though	writer
selfish-ness	thus	yard
sent	thyself	year
several	till	you
shall, shalt	to	young
short	to be	your

GRAMMALOGUES. *Arranged phonetically*
(*Numbers refer to the position of the outline*)

3 put	2 deliverance
2 special-ly, 3 speak	1 advantage, 3 difficult
3 principle, principal-ly	1 much, 2 which
3 people	2 chair, 3 cheer
1 surprise	1 chaired, 2 cheered
1 surprised	1 child
1 particular, 2 opportu-	1 large
2 spirit [nity]	1 larger
2 be, 3 to be	1 largely
2 subject-ed	2 general-ly
2 subjective	2 generalization
2 subjection	2 justification
1 liberty, 2 member, remember-ed, 3 number-ed	1 gentleman, 2 gentlemen
3 belief, believe-d	1 can, 2 come
1 behalf	1 because
2 been	2 care
1 balance	1 accord-ing, 2 cared
2 build-ing	1 call, 2 equal-ly
2 it	1 called, 2 equalled, cold
3 itself	2 school
2 truth	2 schooled
1 tried, 2 toward, trade	1 quite, 2 could
2 towards	1 cannot
2 tell, 3 till	1 inscribe-d
2 told	1 inscription
2 circumstance	1 go, 2 give-n
2 satisfaction	1 signify-ied-ficant
2 instructive	1 significance
2 instruction	1 signification
1 had, 2 do, 3 different--ence	1 guard, 2 great
1 Dr., 2 dear, 3 during	2 gold
2 deliver-ed-y	1 for
	2 from

2 have | 1 myself, 2 himself
2 several | 1 most
1 over, 3 however | 1 more, remark-ed,
1 valuation | 2 Mr., mere
2 very |
| 1 important-ance,
1 thank-ed, 2 think | 2 improve-d-ment
2 third | 1 impossible

1 though, 2 them | 1 in, any, 3 own
1 those, thyself, 2 this, | 1 influence
   3 thus | 1 influenced, 2 next
2 themselves | 1 nor, 2 near
2 there, their | 2 opinion
3 within | 1 northern
2 southern | 1 information
1 that, 2 without | 1 hand, 2 under
3 therefore | 1 sent

1 has, as, 2 his, is | 1 language, owing,
2 first | 2 thing, 3 young

2 was, 3 whose | 2 Lord

2 shall, shalt, 3 wish | 2 your, 3 year
2 wished | 1 yard, 2 word
2 selfish-ness | 2 are, 3 our, hour
3 sure | 3 ourselves
1 short | 2 rather, writer

2 usual-ly | 2 we
2 pleasure | 2 whether
1 me, 2 him | 2 wonderful-ly

VOWELS

Dots ....: a, an, ... the; ..... ah!
  ..... aye, eh?

Dashes ....: of, ... to; ..... all,
  ..... two, too; ..... on, ... but;
  ..... O, oh! owe, ... he; ..... and,
  ..... should; ..... awe, ought,
  aught; ..... who.

DIPHTHONGS

..... how;

..... with, ... when; ..... what,

..... would;

..... beyond, ... you, ... why.

SPECIAL LIST OF CONTRACTIONS

Arranged alphabetically

A

acknowledge
administrator
administratrix
advertise-d-ment
altogether
amalgamate
amalgamation
anything
arbitrary
arbitrate
arbitration
arbitrator

B

bankruptcy

C

capable
certificate
character
characteristic
circumstantial
commercial-ly
cross-examination
cross-examine-d

D

defective
deficient-ly-cy
denomination-al
description
difficulty
discharge-d
distinguish-ed

E

efficient-ly-cy
electric
electrical
electricity
England
English
Englishman
enlarge
enlarger
enthusiastic-iasm
especial-ly
esquire
establish-ed-ment
everything
exchange-d

.... executive
.... executor
.... executrix
.... expediency
.... expenditure
.... expensive
.... extinguish-ed

F

.... falsification
.... familiar-ity
.... familiarization
.... familiarize
.... February
.... financial-ly

G

.... govern-ed
.... government

H

.... howsoever

I

.... identical
.... identification
.... immediate
.... imperturbable
.... incandescence
.... incandescent
.... inconsiderate

.... inconvenience-t-ly
.... incorporated
.... independent-ly-ce
.... indispensable-ly
.... individual-ly
.... influential-ly
.... inform-ed
.... informer
.... inspect-ed-ion
.... insurance
.... intelligence
.... intelligent-ly
.... intelligible-ly
.... interest
.... investigation
.... investment
.... irrecoverable-ly
.... irregular
.... irremovable-ly
.... irresponsible-ility

J

.... January

K

.... knowledge

L

.... legislative
.... legislature

M

.... magnetic-ism

.... manufacture-d

.... manufacturer

.... mathematical-ly

.... mathematician

.... mathematics

.... maximum

.... mechanical-ly

.... metropolitan

.... minimum

.... misfortune

.... mortgage-d

N

.... neglect-ed

.... negligence

.... never

.... nevertheless

.... nothing

.... notwithstanding

.... November

O

.... organization

.... organize-d

.... organizer

P

.... parliamentary

.... peculiar-ity

.... perform-ed

.... performance

.... performer

.... perpendicular

.... practicable

.... practice

.... practise-d

.... prejudice-d-ial-ly

.... preliminary

.... probable-ly-ility

.... proficient-ly-cy

.... proportion-ed

.... proportionate-ly

.... prospectus

.... public

.... publication

.... publish-ed

.... publisher

Q

.... questionable-ly

R

.... ratepayers

.... recoverable

.... reform-ed

reformer
regular
relinquish-ed
remarkable-ly
removable
represent-ed
representation
representative
republic
republican
responsible-ility

S

satisfactory
sensible-ly-ility
something
subscribe-d
subscription
substantial-ly
sufficient-ly-cy
sympathetic

T

telegram
telegraphic

thankful-ly
together

U

unanimity
unanimous-ly
uniform-ity-ly
universal-ly
universality
universe
university
unprincipled

W

whatever
whenever
whensoever
whereinsoever
wheresoever
whithersoever

Y

yesterday

INDEX

The figures refer to the paragraphs, except where the page is mentioned.

KEY
TO
PITMAN
SHORTHAND
INSTRUCTOR

KEY TO EXERCISES

Exercise 2

1. p, b, t, d, ch, j, k, g, w, y, h (down), h (up), r (up).
2. r (down), p, h (up), d, h (down), b, y, t, ch, r (up), k, j, g.
3. f, v, th, TH, s, z, sh, zh, m, n, ng, l, r (down).
4. r (up), m, l, v, th, ng, s, m, TH, zh, f, sh, z.
5. b, th, r (up), m, d, j, r (up), s, n, sh, z, t, g.
6. p, g, h (down), f, w, ch, h (up), g, y, n, w, k, t.
7. sh, f, s, th, m, n, v, zh, TH, z, ng, l, r (down).
8. t, g, d, k, p, ch, b, j, h (down), h (up), w, y, r (up).

Exercise 4

1. pk, pd, pdl, bm, bml, bn.
2. tm, tml, tb, dm, dmr, ch m.
3. ch mn, jn, wk, wv, wd, wd TH.
4. g sh, g sh ng, kv, dp, dpl, dnd.
5. ln, ln ch, lnd, nt, ntm, nv.
6. nm, nml, ml, mld, l ng k, lk.

Exercise 5

1. Pa, palm, balm, farm, shah.
2. Pay, paid, pale, bale, bake.
3. Bee, tea, dee, gee, fee.
4. Paw, pawl, tall, chalk, thawed.
5. Dough, door, dome, shore, bore.
6. Chew, shoe, lieu, rue, woo.

Exercise 6

1. Pack, back, tap, cap, catch.
3. Deck, dell, debt, cheque, red.
3. Ill, bill, chill, kill, mill.

3

4. Dock, shod, rod, rock, mock.
5. Touch, Dutch, dumb, rung, lung.
6. Took, shook, book, look, push.

Exercise 7

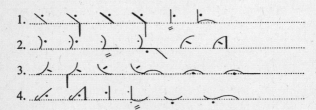

1.
2.
3.
4.

Exercise 9

1. Cap, catch, path, bath, pad, padlock, cash, cashier.
2. Tongue, chunk, rung, lunch, munch, hung, hope, hub.
3. Bill, billow, cheek, chick, reek, rick, meal, mill.
4. Arm, army, armour, ark, Archangel, arrow, arrear.
5. Row, rowed, roach, rogue, rope, mole.
6. Book, took, shook, look, loop, rude.

Exercise 10

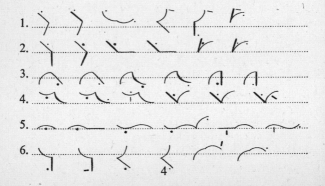

1.
2.
3.
4.
5.
6.

Exercise 11

1. They *should* ship *all the* coal *on* Monday, *the* tenth *of* May.
2. Ask *the* cashier *to* pay *all the* money into *the* bank at *two to*day.
3. Miller *and* Robey say they hope *to* get *all the* lead ready *to* catch *the* ship "Adelaide" *on the* fourth *of the* month.
4. *The* bill *of* lading *should* reach Canada *on the* fifth *of* March.
5. *Who*, among *all the* party, may move *the* vote?

Exercise 12

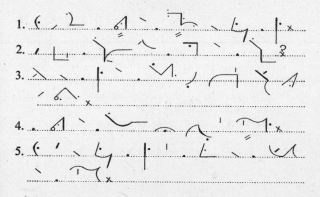

Exercise 13

1. Bare, berry, dare, dairy, fare, fairy.
2. Core, curry, repair, robbery, wrote, rotary.
3. Roam, roaming, room, roomy, ream, rim.
4. Rush, wrung, ruddy, rally, revenge, rosy.
5. Hope, happy, heavy, hang, hawk, hockey.

5

Exercise 14

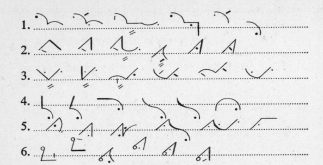

1.
2.
3.
4.
5.
6.

Exercise 15

1. Repair *of the* road *to the* ferry *should* make *a difference.*
2. *Which of the two, do* they say, *should put* up *the* fourth pillar?
3. They *had to* take *a different* route *to the* Heath.
4. They hope *to be* at *the* fair tomorrow, *and the* car *should be* at *the* door at *two.*
5. *It should* make *a difference to* Murray *and* Haigh.

Exercise 16

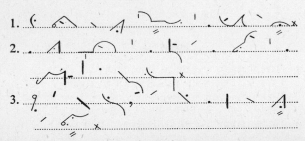

1.
2.
3.

6

4.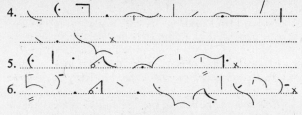

5.

6.

Exercise 17

1. Pie, pile, piracy, die, dial, dyke, shy, shire.
2. Boy, boiling, boiler, buoyant, buoyantly, toil, toiler.
3. Bough, vow, couch, outlaw, county, mouth, lounge, towel.
4. Pew, puny, due, endue, beauty, bureau, tube, tubing, duke, dupe.
5. Idle, idling, idler, icy, Irish, irony, ivy, ivory.
6. Oil, oiled, now, new, renewal, deny, denial, value, valued.
7. Wire, wiry, wore, worry, walk, Walker, week, weekly, wake, awake, aware.

Exercise 18

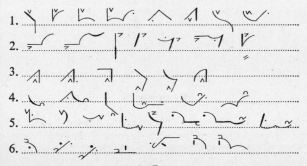

7

Exercise 19

1. *Do you* feel *it* right *to give the* boy so *much* money?
2. *Can you come to* Edinburgh *for the* fourth week *of* May?
3. I *have given the* cheque *to* my nephew.
4. He *should go and* see *the large* ship lying *beyond the* buoy.
5. *How can the* beauty *of the* isle fail *to* appeal *to the* duke?
6. *Do* they assume *the* china *to be* genuine?

Exercise 20

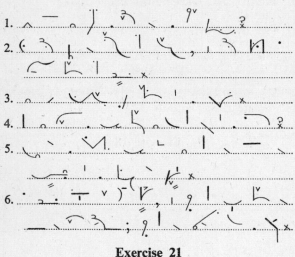

Exercise 21

1. I-may-*be* with-you on-Monday *the* fourth *of*-May.
2. If-*you*-will-*be* ready *when* I *come* I-*shall-be* happy *to*-take-*the* ride *with-you to-the* show.

8

3. I-*think-you*-will enjoy-*the* ride, *and you*-may take *a* fair share *of-the* game.
4. *How do-you*-like-*the* new book?
5. I-*think-you*-were right *to-come* away *when you*-were feeling weary.
6. I-*have-had a* talk *with* Webb *and* Duke, *who*-were both at-*the* party *on*-Monday.
7. I-saw Booth *today and* he-will-*be with* us at-*the* show.
8. If-*you-should*-know anybody *who-can* share *the* work *of-the* opera *with* us I-*shall-be* happy *to* know.
9. I-*have a* new camera *which* I *should* like *to* show *you when* I-see *you*.
10. I-*shall-be* happy *to* see *you* tomorrow if-*you-can* come.

Exercise 22

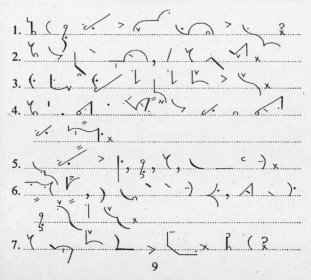

Exercise 23

1. Spice, spire, spikes, satire, sight, sightless.
2. Passage, passages, tasks, desks, absorbs, rasps, oxides.
3. Vessels, muscles, nasal, sense, senseless, senselessly.
4. Safe, savings, sews, news, nuisance, sings.
5. Lessens, lacing, Nelson, slaves, snores, soles.
6. Dusty, tasty, cask, excuse, razor, wiser.

Exercise 24

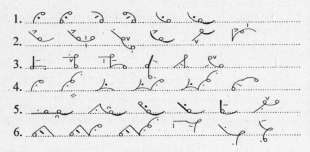

Exercise 25

Thank-you for-the notice *of-the* affair *on*-Saturday *the* sixth. I-*shall-be with-you* early, *and-if* I-may, I-will carry *you* back *to-the* city *to*-lunch. Unless *you have a* desire *to*-go *to-the* Royal Hotel, I *should* like *to*-take *you to-the usual* café *to*-lunch, *because the* meals *a*lways seem *to be* both dainty *and* cheap. I-*wish you*-were ready *for-the* visit *to* Sicily. These lovely days make us long *to be* away. I-*think-the* change *itself* would-be likely *to*-make *you* enjoy-*the* peace *of-the* village life *when-you* got back. *Those of* us *who have-had* such *a* change *of* scene know *this to be* likely. I-*shall-be* ready *to*-leave *as* soon *as you*, *and* it-is *for-you to* name *the* date.

Exercise 26

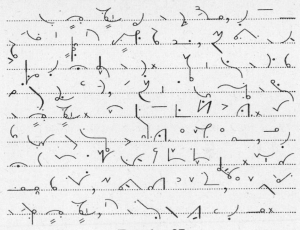

Exercise 27

1. Acids, asks, assize, assessing, assails, asleep, aslope.
2. Seed, seeks, sago, seems, sails, sleep, slope, sloth.
3. Peruse, pursue, days, daisy, rose, rosy, jealous, jealousy.
4. Sea, sea-sickness, ceasing, unceasing, science, society, sausage.
5. Pious, joyous, joyously, assiduous, zealous, zealously, Zulu.
6. Noise, noisy, sum, assume, sack, ask, tennis, Tennessee.

Exercise 28

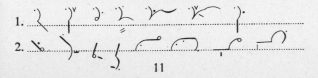

11

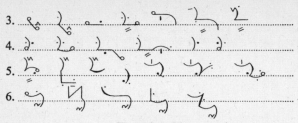

3.
4.
5.
6.

Exercise 29

I-am assuming *you*-will like *to* see-*the* details *of-the* sales *of-the* new books *on* Siam, *and*-I-am asking-*the* cashier *to-give-you* these up *to-this* week. If-*you would* like *to speak to-me on-the* business, or if-*you have special* reasons *for* supposing *you can* push *the* sales *of-the* books at-*this* time, I-*shall-be* happy *to* see *you*. I-*have myself* seen *to-the* dispatch *of all-the* review copies, *and-the* head *of-the* mailing room *has himself* seen *to-the* dispatch *of* copies *to* buyers by mail. *The* subject *with-which-the* books deal seems-*to be* popular now, *and*-I-*have-had several* visitors *to-the* showroom each day since *the* issue *of-the* volumes.

Exercise 30

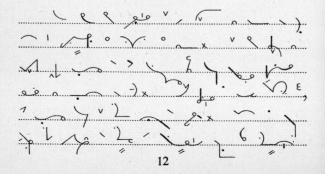

Exercise 31

1. Sweep, sweet, Swede, switch, swivel, Swiss, swish.
2. Paces, basis, doses, chases, cases, guesses, faces.
3. Poses, supposes, deposes, mixes, noses, laces.
4. Nieces, necessary, success, successful, exercise, exercised, excessive.
5. Emphasize, emphasized, emphasizing, census, insist, parenthesis, synopsis.
6. Policy, policies, jealousy, jealousies, mercy, mercies, legacy, legacies.
7. Possess, possesses, recess, recesses, abscess, abscesses, excess.

Exercise 32

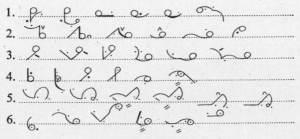

Exercise 33

I-*wish you to*-write *to-me as to-the* disposal *of-those* cases *of-yours* which I-*have-had* lying *in*-these offices *for a year* now. *You have-had* successive notices asking-

13

you to remove *them, but to* no purpose. *The* cases *themselves are* ugly, *and*-they *can* scarcely *be* said *to be* sweet-smelling. Besides *this, the* space *in*-these offices *is too* small *for*-my business, *and*-I-*have*-no room *to* spare *for*-these packages. *This-is an* unnecessary annoyance *and*-I insist *on-your* taking-*the* cases away by-*the* tenth *of*-July at-*the* outside.

Exercise 34

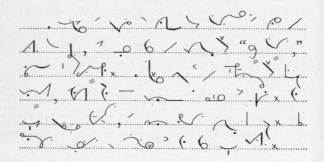

Exercise 35

1. Post, poster, taste, taster, chest, Chester, adjust, adjuster.
2. Fast, faster, mast, master, masterpiece, masters.
3. Opposed, supposed, deposed, exposed, accused, excused, mixed.
4. State, stately, stop, stoppage, sturdy, sturdily, story.
5. Steam, steamship, stale, stealthy, stair, staircase, store.
6. Testify, testifies, justify, justifies, suggest, suggesting, suggestive.
7. Mist, misty, honest, honesty, best, bestow, beset.

14

Exercise 36

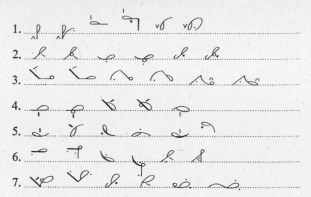

1.
2.
3.
4.
5.
6.
7.

Exercise 37

The first cost *of-the* new styles may-*be* heavy, *but it*-will soon *be* repaid by-*the* saving *in* waste *and* by-*the* immense sales *which*-will follow. Business must *be influenced* by-*the* fact *of-our having-the* best *and* cheapest *and* latest styles *to* show *to* customers, *and-we-think* they-will endorse *our* hopes. *We-are* seeking, also, *to influence the* big buyers *to* ask *to* see-*the* new designs, *and*-if-they *can-be* induced *to*-look at-*them we-think* business must follow.

Exercise 38

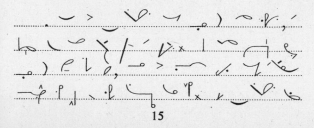

15

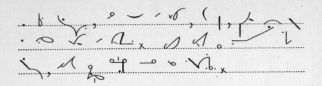

Revisionary Exercise (A)

16

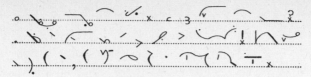

Exercise 39

1. Pay, pray, prayed, by, bright, brighter, tie, try, trial, cry, cried.
2. Crowd, grey, eager, eagerly, meagre, figure, tiger, cheaper, taper.
3. Pie, ply, apply, play, pledge, pledger, blame, blames, imply, reply, total.
4. Offer, offering, every, afraid, average, author, authors, either, tougher, differ, Jeffrey.
5. Shrew, shrewd, shriek, shrink, fissure, treasure, measure, leisure, calmer, manner.
6. Bunker, drinker, tinker, conquer, conquering, thinker.
7. Flow, flung, fled, fledge, Ethel, camel, official, hopeful, joyful, positively.

Exercise 40

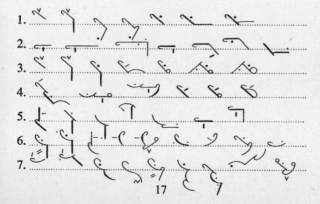

17

Exercise 41

Dear Clay,

If-you-are at liberty *on-*Friday *next*, I-*shall-be-*pleased if-*you-*will try *to-come in* and see *Dr.* Driver, *our principal member for-the* Borough. He-*is to-take-the chair* at-*the* club dinner *in* April, *and-*I *should* like-*you to* know *him*. *The number* at-*the* dinner may-*be larger this year, because of-the* increase *in-the number of-members in-the* local *and* neighbouring clubs *during-the* past *year*. I-*think-you ought-to-be* at-least *an* honorary *member of-our* club. *The* other *members would-be* happy *to-have-you with-them, and-*they *would cheer you* up, *and-in truth you-can* do *with-it. It-would-be* no trouble *to-me to* push *the* case *for-you* if-*you* care *to* apply.　　　　Faithfully *yours*,

PETER FLETCHER.

Exercise 42

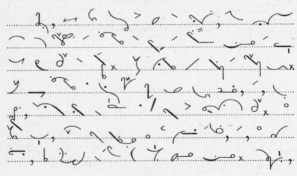

Exercise 43

1. Offer, offering, ever, every, ether, either, fry, fro, free, throw, through.
2. Frayed, frame, frail, frock, fresh, thread, throb, thrive, thrash, tether, driver, otherwise.

18

3. **Thirsty, Kaffir, lever, verb, verbal, river, ruffle, revel,** hovel, cavalry.
4. **Gravel, novel, naval, fly, flier, flow, floor, flap, fled,** fledge, flame.
5. **Flaming, flag, bevel, travel, traveller, muffle, muffler,** arrival, privilege.
6. **Parallel, parlour, dark, darkness, church, sharp,** sharply.
7. **Terminus, engineers, philosophy, tolerable, former,** Norfolk.
8. **Purchase, occur, nullify, fulfil, literature, lecture,** capture.

Exercise 44

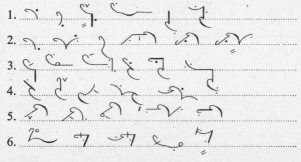

1.
2.
3.
4.
5.
6.

Exercise 45

Dear-Sir,

I-*believe you-are* proposing *to* buy some house property *in* Beverley. If-*this-is* so, I-*shall-be*-pleased *to-call and* show *you* details *of* Waverley House *and* Crowther Grange, *and* other desirable houses *which* I-*wish you would* look *over*. If-*you*-will *tell-me* just *what-you* desire, I-*think* I-*can* suit *you*. I-*shall*, *however*, leave *all* details *till* I-*see-you*. If-*it-is largely a* case *of*

19

low price, *as* I gather *it-is*, I-know I-*can* offer *you* value *equal to any*, *and-with* early *delivery of-the* premises, *in all*-cases. I specialize *in valuation* business, *and-this* brings *me in*to touch *with* just *the* right *people for-your* purpose.

Faithfully yours,

Exercise 46

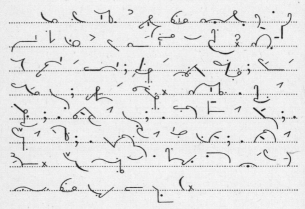

Exercise 47

1. Spree, supper, splice, supplies, stray, suitor, settle, screw, seeker, cyclists.
2. Sweeper, switcher, swagger, stupor, stagger, sweetly, steeple, stickle, saddle, sadly.
3. Cipher, severance, summer, sooner, civility, personal, swimmers, stifles.
4. Distress, excrescence, express, offspring, gossiper, gospel, mistress, mistrust.
5. Disgraced, disclosed, prescriber, obtrusively, tortoiseshell, peaceful, glassware, praiseworthy.

Exercise 48

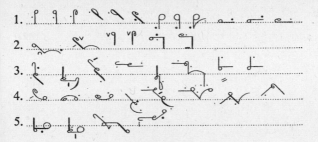

1.
2.
3.
4.
5.

Exercise 49

From what I-know *of* Cedric Spring he-*has* no claims *to* supreme cleverness. *It-would-be* safer *to* describe *him as a* spruce *young* fellow, *with a very* strong *belief in himself.* He-*is*, possibly, *a* bit masterful *in-his* manner; *but* he-*is-the more* likely *to* succeed *because of-his* liking *for* work. *Nor do* I-*think* he-*is in any* extreme sense *a pleasure* seeker. Far *from it.* I-am-*sure there-is-no-more* honourable fellow *in-the* city, *and it*-will *surprise me* if-*he* fails *to*-make *a* name *for-himself. As-he* lives *near me*, I travel *with him several* days *a* week, *and* I-must say he-*has a* plausible tongue, *which-should* assist *him in-his* business.

Exercise 50

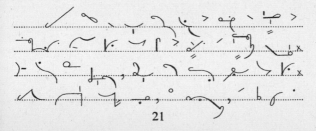

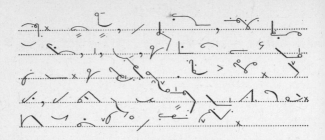

Exercise 51

1. Pun, bone, tone, done, chain, Jane, cane, gain, rain, wine, yawn.
2. Pawning, pawnshop, toning, chaining, caning, gaining, regaining, train, training.
3. Fine, refine, vain, ravine, then, shine, shone, ocean, mean, meaning.
4. Proof, brave, tough, trough, chafe, cave, gave, rough, wife, preserve, observe.
5. Proving, toughen, traffic, deafen, deafening, driving, divide, dividing.

Exercise 52

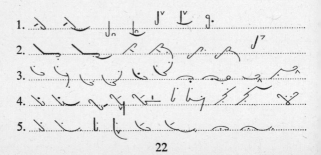

22

Exercise 53

It-may-*be difficult for-you* to follow *the general principles* upon-*which* foreign business *is* carried-*on*, *but* if-*you-are* to-win *your* way *in a* firm *which* does business *with-the Northern and Southern* States *of* America, *you*-will-*have* to-try. No business man, *and*, above *all*, no business man *whose principal* business *is with* foreigners, *can* possibly leave *this* branch *of* economics *from-his* training. If-*he should* refrain *because of a general* dislike *of-the* science, he-will *surely* suffer *in-the* long run. *The truth of-this has-been* shown *over and over* again *within* my-own circle, *and*-I *speak for-your advantage. The principles* may appear *difficult* to follow, *and*-if-*you* imagine *the* task *beyond you*, *it*-will prove so. *But be* brave; face *the* plain *truth*; *and you*-will lighten *the* work *and* succeed, *as you*-will deserve to succeed.

Exercise 54

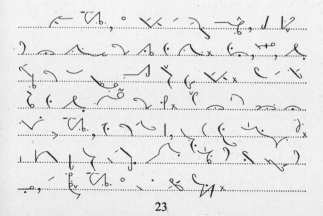

23

Exercise 55

1. Pounce, pounces, pounced, bounce, bounces, bounced, ten, tense, retains, tenses.
2. Dance, dances, danced, chance, chances, chanced, Jane, Jane's, rejoin, rejoins.
3. Cleanse, cleanses, cleansed, glance, glances, glanced, reign, reigns, wine, wines.
4. Learn, learns, expense, expenses, appearance, appearances, assurance, assurances.
5. Refine, refines, even, evens, Evans, assign, assigns, essence, essences, announce, silence.
6. Puff, puffs, prove, proves, reproves, deserve, deserves, behave, behaves, swerve, swerves, transit, Stevenson, densely.

Exercise 56

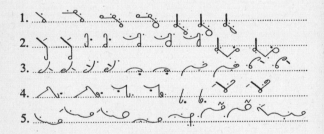

Exercise 57

The Fens, *a* stretch *of* marsh along-*the* shores *of-the* Wash, used *to-be-the* scene *of*-many *a* chance affray *and* many *a* set battle *owing to-the* inroads *of-the* Saxons *and* Danes *on-the* domains *of-the* natives. *It*-seems *to-have-been a* vast primeval forest at-*the*-time *of-the* Romans, *who*, *with their usual* vigilance, saw *a* means *of* saving *this* expanse *from-the* ravages *of-the* waves by *a* clearance *of-the* trees *and-the* raising *of* banks. King John, *of whose* violence against *the* barons *there-is but* one *opinion, nearly* lost *his* life *in* one *of-the* treacherous channels *of-the* Wash. *Those-who-have* read Kingsley's romance *of-the* endurance *and* stout resistance *of-the* Saxons *in-the* Isle *of* Ely, must *have-been* struck by-*the* graphic details *of-the* rough roads *of-those* days, *and* even now they-*are* none *too* easy *for* transit. Times out-*of number, the* waves *of-the*-sea carried away property, causing havoc *and* distress *to-the* farmers.

Exercise 58

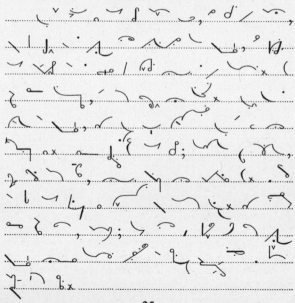

Exercise 59

1. Fusion, infusion, vision, provisions, revision, sessions, mission, submission, admission.
2. Nation, tension, attention, examinations, mention, manipulation.
3. Oppression, depression, expressions, liberation, station, visitation, hesitation, illustration, section, transactions.
4. Fiction, suffocation, navigation, location, dislocation, selection, legation.
5. Passion, occupation, caution, precaution, application, auction, erection, rations, exploration.
6. Petition, partition, repetition, dictation, flotation, addition, magician.

Exercise 60

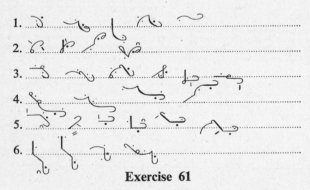

Exercise 61

1. Opposition, supposition, suppositions, exposition, disposition, decision, indecision, physician, physicians, cessation.
2. Accession, succession, annexation, taxation, authorization, sensation, sensations, sensational.

3. Revision, revisionary, nation, nations, national, nationality, diction, dictionary.
4. Education, educational, action, actions, actionable, tuition, situation, fluctuation, superannuation.

Exercise 62

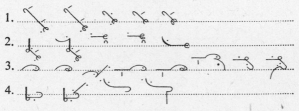

Exercise 63

In 1858 *was* set up *a* Royal Commission *on* popular education *in all-the* nation. *The* commissioners, at *their* discretion, were *to* arrange examinations; *to* obtain *information from* every direction, *to-the* exclusion *of* none; *to-call-*upon physicians, musicians *and* educationalists *of-*every class; *to-*take depositions *when* necessary; *and,* briefly, *to-*review *the general* situation, so-*as-to* secure *satisfaction, beyond all mere generalization, and* show if *there-had-been* progression or retrogression. *The* commissioners' work *was* sensational *in-the* facts brought out. *There-was* ample *justification for-the* commission, *and-the* adoption *of-the* commissioners' advice *was* followed by *an* alteration *in-the general* scheme *of* national education.

Exercise 64

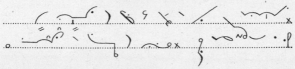

27

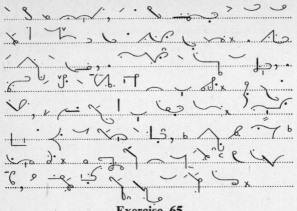

Exercise 65

1. Happy, happiness, hobby, hid, hidden, hatch, Hodge, heavy, heath.
2. Hash, heather, haze, haste, hustle, hone, hive, heckle, Hooker.
3. Behave, adhere, adhered, adhesion, boathouse, *over*hang, unheeding.
4. Hue, hewer, high, highroad, hoax, hoaxing, cohesion, mohair, *any*how.
5. Hum, humming, hill, hair, harm, mishap, apprehend.

Exercise 66

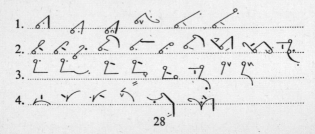

28

Exercise 67

Dear-Sir,

I-am-*surprised to*-hear *of Mr*. Hugh Hamer's opposition *to-the* highly reasonable views taken by Professor Hawkins *on-the* syllabus *in* history. Professor Hawkins, I-*believe*, does *his* best, *in-all-circumstances*, *to* help *his* pupils *and to* adhere *to-the* scheme *of* history lessons *which* deals *with-the* extension *of* commerce *and-with all* forms *of* man's activity. He-*is* heedful *of* every-*circumstance which*-may affect *the* coherence *of* history *and-the* historic *belief* expressed *in-the* phrase "Commerce follows *the* flag." *There-can-be* no misapprehension *of-his* meaning, *and*-none *but a* blockhead *would-be* likely *to* misapprehend *him*. He shows *how-the* upheaval *of* war, *though* harmful *to* humanity *in* other ways, may help *a* nation's commerce. I humbly hope *Mr*. Hamer may behave reasonably *and* cease *to* harass Professor Hawkins *in-his* historical course.   *Yours*-truly,

Exercise 68

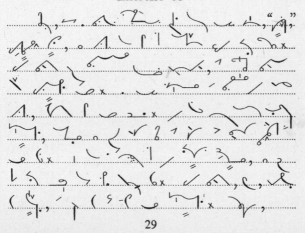

29

Exercise 69

1. Arab, Arabic, ark, arm, aroma, arrive, arrival, arrange.
2. Rope, repair, refine, refining, refuse, refusing.
3. Bar, Barry, injure, injury, floor, flurry, customer, customary.
4. Artist, artistic, arrayed, urge, rage, remain, remaining.
5. Trespasser, pasture, preparation, rear, hurry, recover, recovery, professor, supervisor, grocer, successor.
6. Burn, burns, return, adjourn, learn, portion, extortion, charge, verify, pardon, sparkle.
7. Tire, tiresome, secure, securely, similar, similarly, thorough, thoroughfare, Cork, Carrick.

Exercise 70

Exercise 71

To secure-*the* best *from himself and to-give* right service *to* others, both-*the* clerical worker *and-the* manual labourer must *have* fresh air *and* healthy rooms *to*-live *in*, bright airy rooms *into which-the* sun's rays may pour *and-the* breezes blow *when* desirable. Dark rooms retain germs *of* disease *and* either reduce *the* worker's life or weaken *his* physical strength, so-*as-to*-

30

make *him* unable *to-do* severe work either *of*-brain or muscle. *A* robust man may carry *on for a* time *in* dreary rooms, *but* eventually such places must cause injury *to-him and* bring *on* loss *of* force *and* energy. He-will arise *in-the*-early morn dull *and* weary *from-the* outset, *in* place *of* rising merry *and* bright, *and* ready *for anything in-the* day's work. *In-our-opinion* the brighter *the* rooms *we* live *and* work *in*, *the* better *our* work *is* likely *to be*.

Exercise 72

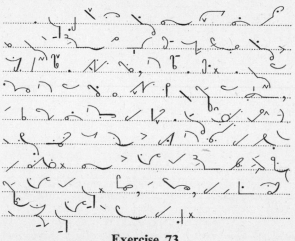

Exercise 73

1. Losses, swells, laws, elation, Alpine, lupin, lucid, local, illustration, lever.
2. Alcove, legation, align, lancet, loosen, Allington, appal, billow, towel, thrill.
3. Vole, volley, choral, gorilla, kneel, kingly, strongly, canals, kennel.

31

4. Fossils, nervously, chancel, resolve, delta, belfry, gallop, Philip.
5. Unlock, lock, films, mailing, kneeling, Nelson, scaling, felicity, aimlessly.
6. Brush, trash, blush, nutritious, spacious, sugar, chivalry.

Exercise 74

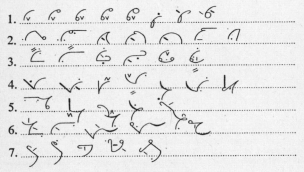

Exercise 75

A life *of* leisure *is a* life *of-pleasure.* Needless *to* say *this-is a* fallacy, *but,* false *as-it-is, it-is* fairly widely spread. Many foolish fellows bewail *their* lack *of-*means *to-*choose either *to-*loll or *to-*labour, just *as-*they like. They look jealously *on-those-who* appear *to-have nothing* else *to-do but* eat *and* drink *and-*enjoy *a* merry life, *when-the* poor man toils ceaselessly *for* food *and* lodging *for himself and-*family. *But in* simple *truth, there-is-*no*-more* awful life than-*the* lazy, useless life *of-the* idle man, *and it-is* also true *to* say *there-are* exceedingly few rich men nowadays liable *to-the* charge *of* laziness, *because-*they know-*the* busy life *is-the* happy one. Happiness *is an* elusive *thing, and-more* rich men than poor fail *to-*grasp *it.*

Exercise 76

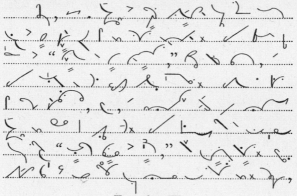

Exercise 77

1. Quick, quicker, quest, request, requisition, quire, enquire, squire.
2. Sanguine, linguist, well, weld, wealthy, well-known, unwell, while, meanwhile.
3. Ruler, dweller, fuller, chancellor, bearer, restorer, explorer, admirer.
4. Plump, Bombay, embarrass, impartial, lumber, dampen, where, everywhere.
5. Impression, ample, error, colour, popular, scullery.

Exercise 78

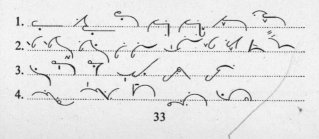

33

Exercise 79

We-shall require consular invoices *for-the* four cases *of* liquid glue, *and-for-the* square bottles *of* hair restorer *which we-are* to ship *to* Guatemala by-*the* "Welsh Rose," sailing *next* Friday. Please ask *Mr.* Wheeler or *Mr.* Weldon *to* see *to-this.* Meanwhile, *as we-are-the* insurers, see *to-the* policy *as-soon-as*-possible. If-*the* wharfinger *calls,* I-*wish* to see *him as to-the* disposal *of-those* bales *from* Bombay by-*the* "Emperor," now lying *in-the* Empress Dock. *It-is important to* know *whether it-is* possible or *impossible to*-make *delivery of*-these bales *to* Messrs. Ambrose & Kimber *this* week. I-am relying implicitly upon *you to*-deal quickly *with-the* mails *for-the* Southampton boat *tomorrow.*

Exercise 80

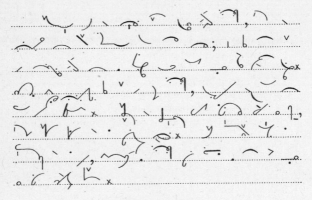

Exercise 81

If I-*can* spare *the* necessary time, I-*shall go to-the* head office *tomorrow.* I-*shall-do* my best *to* induce *the* authorities *to*-raise *the* rate at-*which we-are* to insure

34

Messrs. Morris & Moore's four bales *of* rags. *The* rate *should-be* higher, *because of-the* risk *of* fire *and* damage *to-the* rest *of-the* cargo. I-*shall-be* sorry *to*-receive *a* refusal, *as-the* business *is* scarcely worth-*the* worry *and* risk unless *we* secure *a* fair rate. *We-have-had* numerous instances *of* loss *on* similar policies *in-the* past. I-*think-we should-have a* due sense *of-the* grave loss *and* injury *which*-may follow *a* refusal *to*-raise *the* rates *on*-these risky packages. Everyone knows *how* easily oily rags take fire.

Exercise 82

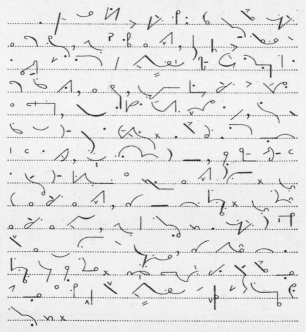

Revisionary Exercise (B)

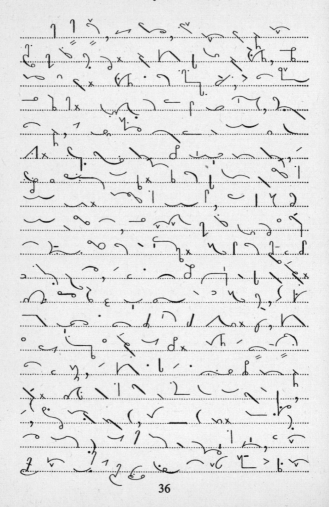

Exercise 83

1. Apt, pat, soft, spot, spots, pleat, pleats, fret, frets, fleet, proud, white, halt, silt.
2. Aged, jade, sobbed, died, aided, avoid, oozed, braid, braids, glowed, viewed, vowed, glades, grades.
3. Print, prints, pound, pounds, blunt, blunts, grant, grants, quaint, friends, fronts, affronts, anoints, rafts.
4. Disappoints, extends, residents, inclined, awakened, currents, doubled, seated, stated, rifled.
5. Secret, sacred, seated, sedate, effort, afraid, dread, adroit, regret, mental, hotel.
6. Pat, Patty, abode, body, chat, chatty, dead, dado, omit, motto, Lot, Lotty, Lotty's.

Exercise 84

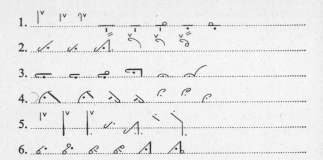

1.
2.
3.
4.
5.
6.

Exercise 85

Truth has-been divided *in*to three kinds: *truth* about *things*; *truth of*-thought about *things*; *and truth in-the* accurate expression *of*-thought about *things*. *According to* ancient authorities, *truth could-be* said *to be a* correspondence between thought *and thing*. *It*-seems perfectly easy *for any*one *to-think* accurately about *a thing with-which* he-*is quite* well acquainted. *But-the* case *is*-not *quite* so simple *as-that, and-there-is, without* doubt, *a great*-deal *to be* said before *it-can-be called* simple. Suppose *an* unfortunate accident occurred *in a* London street, *and-that* six *people* witnessed *the* accident, *and*-were asked *to*-relate exactly *what had* happened. *It-is quite* certain *that-we should* receive *different* accounts *from* each *of-them. The* result *would*-not-*be a* correspondence between thought *and-the thing* thought about; *and so-the* statements *would*-not-*be* true. *It-is to be* regretted *that* limited space prevents *a more* extended argument, *though we could* extend *it* if-*we cared to-do* so.

Exercise 86

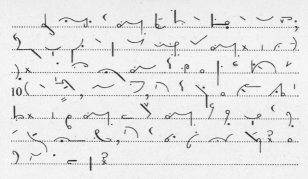

Exercise 87

1. Aimed, mud, seemed, steamed, bloomed, timed, timid, trimmed, streamed, claimed, flamed.
2. End, annoyed, signed, stunned, poisoned, thousand, listened, reasoned, old, piled, boiled.
3. Toiled, skilled, failed, smiled, tired, retired, dared, shared, insured, wired, inferred.
4. Delayed, solid, worried, thronged, stampede, whimpered, angered, drunkard.
5. Pilot, bolts, hamlet, relates, support, answered, judged, select, animate.
6. Traded, trotted, edited, dictated, doubted, detained, tightened, plant, planted, drift, drifted, acquaint, acquainted.

Exercise 88

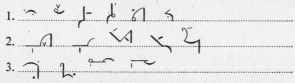

4.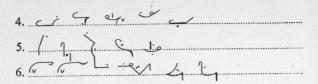

5.

6.

Exercise 89

If-*the* little stones *which-you have* rolled *from under your* feet were able-*to speak*, they-*would* relate *to-you a great* story, *the* story *of-this* old world *of-ours as-it-was* thousands *of-years*-ago. They *cannot, however, and-the* story will-not-*be told* by-*them*. *But* let us suppose *that*-one *particular* pebble *could* talk, *and-that-it* seized *the opportunity to-do* so. *It-would tell-you, and-the* other *gentlemen of-your* party, *of* changes *in* climate, *great* mad upheavals, *when-the* mighty ocean turned *to* dry land, *and-the* highest hills *and-the* hard rocky mountains tottered *and*-fell *towards-the* sea *and* became, indeed, *the* sea bottom. If-*we* listened, *as a child* might listen, *to-the* story *told* by-*the* pebble, *we* might learn *of-the* movements *which-are*, even now, tending *to*-turn parts *of-the* earth *in*to *more* habitable places, *and* other parts *in*to desolate wastes.

Exercise 90

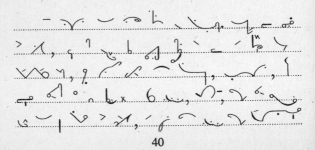

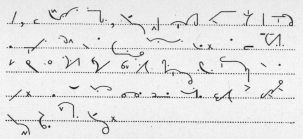

Exercise 91

1. Fitter, voter, enter, sorter, avoider, thunder, asunder, finder, founder.
2. Another, grandmother, grandfather, eccentric, centralize.
3. Potter, plotter, spotter, doubter, auditor, painter, rounder, elector, embroider, protractor.
4. Lighter, loiters, slander, moulder, ringleader, breechloader, leader, lather.
5. Sombre, timber, rinker, imponderous, slumber, slumbered.
6. Malinger, malingered, adventurous, pictures, fractures.
7. Enter, entered, wonder, wondered, gender, gentry, inventor, inventory, tenders.

Exercise 92

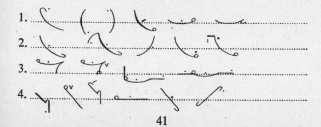

5.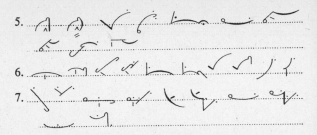

6.

7.

Exercise 93

Chambers *of*-Commerce *are to be*-found *in-the* chief centres *of-the*-country. They take *in-hand* the collection *of information for* both importers *and* exporters, *and*-they gather *in-their* files *wonderful* facts *and* figures dealing-*with* matters *of importance* to-their members. *There-are* usually *different* sections, *under different* chair men, *for different trades*, such-*as-the* leather *trade*, *and*-these sections naturally endeavour *to* centralize their efforts *on-the particular* business *in-which-their members are* engaged. *The* chambers keep *a* watchful eye upon legislators, so-*as-to* enter *an* early protest against *any* legislation likely *to* hinder international *trade*. One chamber took-*the rather* un*usual* course *of* acting *as* trustees *for* debenture holders *of*-property *in a* foreign country. *The* present *writer is*-not aware *of* another-instance *of-this wonderfully* useful service by *a* Chamber *of*-Commerce.

Exercise 94

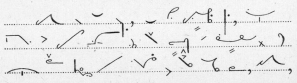

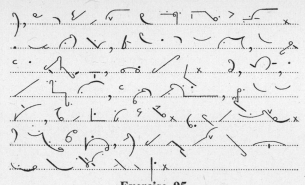

Exercise 95

1. Lay, layer, payer, player, gaiety, gayest, aeronaut.
2. Theatre, theory, theoretical, re-invest, re-engage, re-enter.
3. Amiable, marrying, carrying, agreeable, ideal, idealist.
4. Borrow, borrower, grow, grower, low, lower, lowest.
5. Brew, brewer, brewery, flue, fluent, blue, bluish.
6. Miscellaneous, mysterious, insidious, victorious, furiously.

Exercise 96

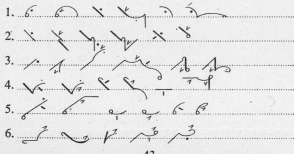

Exercise 97

The various rooms *in-the* British Museum *are the* resort *of-the* theologian, *the* geologist, *the* historian, *and-the* scholar *in* every department *of* science *and* art. *There-are* to be-found relics *of-the* Assyrians, *the* Babylonians, *and* other ancient nations long-since passed away. *Wonderful* specimens *of* beautiful Indian *and* other oriental arts *and-*crafts, miscellaneous ornaments ingeniously carved, *and* showing-*the most* delicate work *and-the* liveliest imagination *of-the* artist, *are to be* seen *in-the* Museum. No-wonder *that-it* exercises *a great* attraction *for-the* visitor *to-*London.

Exercise 98

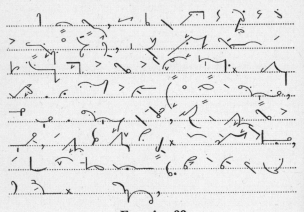

Exercise 99

1. Memoir, reservoir, hardware, frequent, frequently, subsequent, subsequently.
2. Twelve, twelfth, farewell, overwhelming, Brunswick, herewith, sandwich.

3. Tweedle, twig, Cornwall, limewater, misquote, misquoted, misquotation, driftwood.
4. War, warlike, warmhearted, warfare, warmer, warp, warranty.

Exercise 100

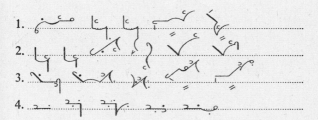

Exercise 101

On Wednesday last, *in-the* Memorial Hall, Worksop, *Mr.* Walter Wilde, *of* Wakefield, *delivered an* extremely fascinating lecture *on-the* Empire. He referred *to-the* enormous size *of-the* dominions, *to-the* millions *of-people of* various races living *in-them, and to-the* bewildering variety *of* animal life *to be*-found *in-the* area included *in-the* Empire. He deplored-*the* frequent wars, *which had* weakened British South-Africa *in-the* past, *and* expressed *his belief that-the* future *would tell a very different* story. *Mr.* Wilde spoke *in* warm appreciation *of-the* ever-growing love between-*the* dominions *and-the* mother-country, *and* declared *that* genuine affection *was-the* best possible bond *of* union between us. Subsequent speakers included Messrs. Hardwick, Shadwell *and* Wagstaffe, *and-the* audience accorded *a* warm expression *of thanks to Mr.* Wilde *for-his* lecture.

Exercise 102

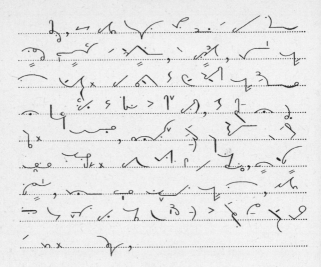

Exercise 103

1. Compassion, committee, contain, contained, congenial, confession, conversation, concession, conceal, concealed.
2. Discontinue, discontinued, recognize, recognition, recommendation, commerce, commotion.
3. Accompanist, accomplish, accommodate, introduced, introspect.
4. Magnanimous, magnificent, magnitude, translate, translation, transport, self-denial, self-reliance.
5. Self-confident, self-contained, instruct, instructed, inscroll, inhale, inhabitant, inseparable.
6. Inhumanity, immoderate, innumerable, unnoticed, irrelevant, *under*rate, *al*ready.

Exercise 104

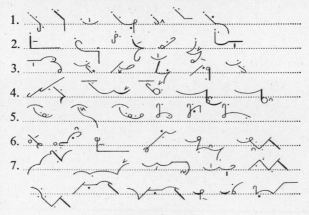

1.
2.
3.
4.
5.
6.
7.

Exercise 105

The almost innumerable terms connected *with* business *should-be under*stood by-*all who* engage *in trade*. They-*are* introduced *in*to practically every transaction, *and* he *would-be* considered incompetent *who* did-not *under*stand *them. The* mastery *of*-these terms *is*-not *a* task *of*-such magnitude *as to* disconcert *any*one *of* reasonable self-reliance *and* self-control. No enterprising man need entertain *a* moment's doubt *as to-his* ability *to*-learn these *significant* terms. *The* transmission *of* goods *to a* commission agent or other consignee involves *the* preparation *of* documents *which*-will ensure-*the* transfer *of-the* goods *to-him without* unnecessary delay. *The* arrangement *of* consular invoices *and* other forms properly *inscribed and* attested must *be* recognized *as a* common matter *of* daily routine, *and a* man *would* feel uncomfortable if-*he*-were ignorant *of*-these-*things.*

47

Exercise 106

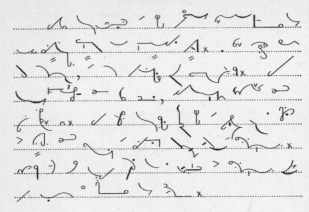

Exercise 107

1. Paying, spying, stating, chewing, stitching, hiring, robbing, dying, edging, breaking, laughing.
2. Soothing, sighing, showing, knowing, laying, failing, rowing, muffling, offering.
3. Pouncing, entrancing, chancing, scoffing, leaning, shining, pacing, paining, paving, joining.
4. Plotting, abiding, promoting, folding, smattering, painting, skating, *believ*ing, *cheer*ing, *near*ing.
5. Adoring, adoringly, sparing, sparingly, sweepings, searchings, scoffings, failings, paintings.
6. Possibility, brutality, suitability, legibility, minority, legality, mythological, etymological.
7. Achievement, pavement, refinement, consignment, monumental, regimental, experimental.
8. Absolutely, politely, nicely, urgently, attractively, possibly, horsemanship, stewardship, editorship.
9. Heedfulness, heedlessness, lawfulness, lawlessness, forward, wayward, dockyard, backyard, *there*after.

Exercise 108

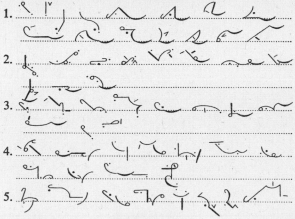

1.

2.

3.

4.

5.

Exercise 109

Herewith *we-have-pleasure* in forwarding *to-you*
several mining market cuttings *from this* morning's
papers, *and-we* hope *to* add *thereto within a* day or-*two*.
The old mines *have-been* strongly supported, *in* consequence *of-the* announcement *of-the* success *of* recent
crushing operations, *and*, *as-the* labour costs *are* likely
to be reduced *short*ly, *there-is*-no reason *why-the*
experiments *should*-not-*be* carried further. *You*-will
recollect *that-we* warned *you* against *your* extreme
hopefulness regarding-*the* possibility *of*-profit *from-the*
new workings; *but-you*-were sanguine *to-the* point *of*
recklessness. Irregularities *in-the* directorship *have*
come *to*-light, *and*, unfortunately, *our* pronouncement
as-to-the mineralogical conditions *has-been* amply
justified. *We-shall* send-*you a* supplemental report later,
and-will keep *you* constantly advised *of any* changes
in-the situation.

49

Exercise 110

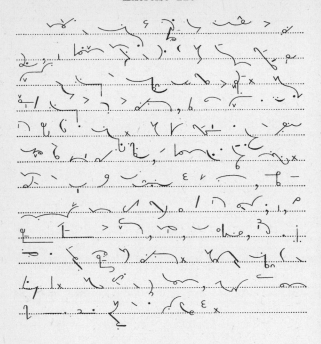

Revisionary Exercise (C)

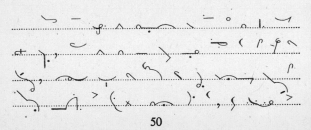

51

Exercise 111

1. Pumped, plumped, tramped, damped, jumped, encamped, exempt.
2. Presumption, resumption, exemption, assumption, redemption, temptation, extinction.
3. Function, sanction, anxious, anxiety, anguish, languish, sanctuary.
4. Pessimist, pessimistic, optimist, optimistic, post, postage, postpone.
5. Punctual, punctuate, compunction, strong, strongest, distinct, distinctly.
6. Post-free, postscript, postage-stamp, substitute, substitution, waistcoat, wasteful.
7. Mistake, mistaken, *most*ly, blast, blast-furnace, testimony, testimonial.

Exercise 112

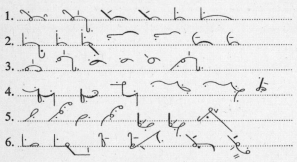

Exercise 113

Dear-Sir:

Thank-you for-your prompt-reply *to*-my-letter regarding-*the* syllabus *of-the Southern* Institute. I-am anxious *that* my nephew *should* join *on-the* resumption *of-the* classes. He-*was to-have* begun last session, *but-*

52

was obliged *to* postpone *the* matter through sudden illness, *which* caused us considerable anxiety. Unless I-am mistaken, I-*have-had-the pleasure of*-meeting Professor Lawson, *the principal of-the* Institute, *and*-I-*shall call*-upon *him next*-week *to* arrange about textbooks, *and to* obtain *his* sanction *to-the* course *which* I-*wish* my nephew *to*-take. *Thank-you*, also, *for-the* invitation *to-the* opening ceremony. I-*shall* certainly *be*-present at-*the* function if-*it-is* at-*all* possible. *The* programme *is very* tempting, *and*-I presume I-*may* bring *a* friend. If I-am-not mistaken *on-this*-point, perhaps *you*-will kindly send *a* postcard *to-that* effect.

         Yours-truly,

Exercise 114

Exercise 115

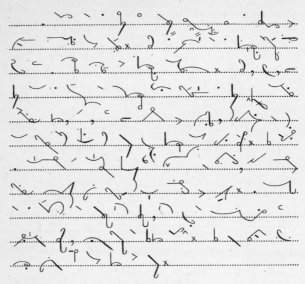

Exercise 116

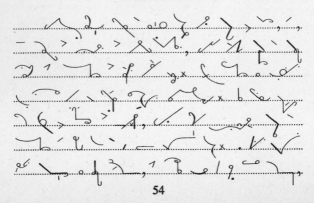

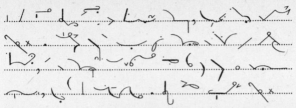

Exercise 117

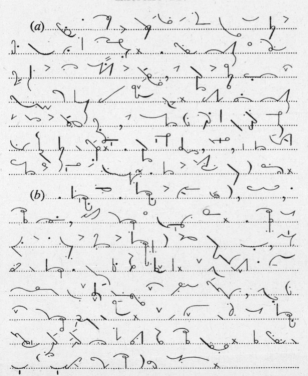

(a)

(b)

(c)

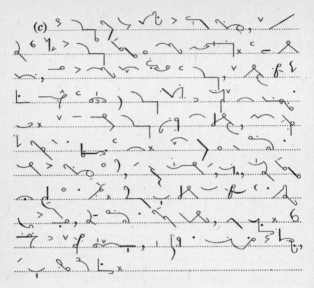

Exercise 118

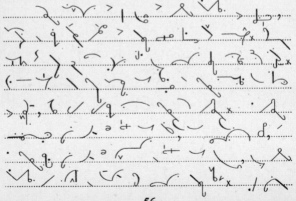

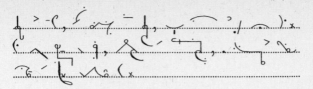

Exercise 119

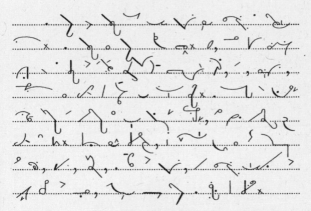

Exercise 120

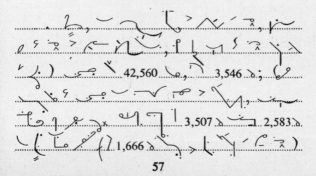

42,560   3,546

3,507   2,583

1,666

3,714 2,746

15

50 16,712

5 449

230,473

394

1s. 1d., 1s. 4·35d.

1s. 1·80d. 8·92d.,

4·02d., 1½d.

8,843 12

Exercise 121

If-you wish to-write at a high-rate, you-must read and master the rules so-as-to follow them fully, and-be-able-to apply them on all | occasions. I-feel that-you-cannot fail to fall into-the true and right way if-you-will only try. The race is to-the sure and-not to-the | strong. Do-not tarry by-the way. Remember-the fable of-the feeble tortoise that outstripped the hare. Master one thing at a time, and you-are sure to-win. | Set apart for study a small portion of-each day. Have patience; "Rome was-not built in a day." High hills grow less as we ascend them. That-which-is | lightly got is little valued. If-you would get gold, you-must dig deeply: it-is-not got on-the surface. Neither can you enter on-the possession of-learning | without some trouble. If-you would obtain a high position, you-must-not-be beaten by what-is difficult. Let your-letters be neat and light; a large and heavy | style wastes time. (183)

Exercise 122

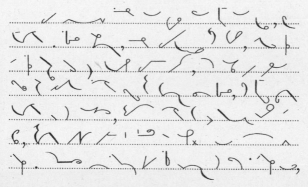

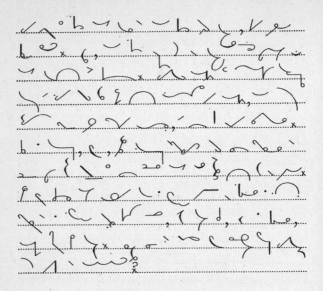

Exercise 123

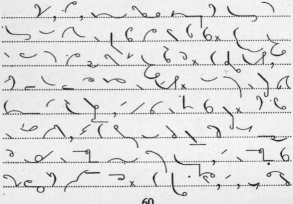

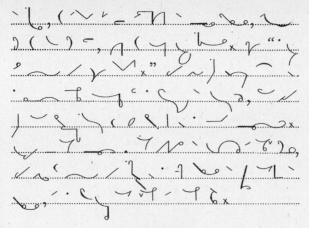

Exercise 124

A *preliminary* meeting was held in-our Masonic hall last Saturday to consider-the preservation of-the Park Estate for-the use of-the general *public*. Several *peculiar circumstances* have | *prejudiced* the consideration of-the-matter in-the past, and-the *peculiarity* of-the case when *published* in-the newspaper arrested-the attention of-many local celebrities who saw that | action was-necessary if-the reputation of-the town was to-be upheld. The Estate contains some very old ruins, in-the *perpendicular* style of *architecture*, and its history is | somewhat hidden in obscurity; but-the buildings are in-such a state of dilapidation that-it-is-now deemed wise to-protect them from further decay. It-is-said that | if-the prerogative of a local lord were exercised, in-all-*probability* none of-the land would-be available for-the use of-the people; but, as-this-is very im*probable*, | we-need-not enter upon a debatable topic which-might cause us to show any but charitable feelings. At-the meeting the chair was-taken by a *publisher* who *practises* | much real charity and who-has *distinguished* himself on-the local bench, a tribunal of-which we-are proud. On-the platform were Mr. Arthur Johnson who-has *performed* signal services | for-his town; Mr. James Smith, the applicability of whose im*practicable* and *republican* theories is of little account in-the *performance* of-our daily duties; | and Dr. Rawson, a very *proficient* master in-the-art of logic, and-one who-has a very wide *practice* among some of-the best families of-the district. (269)

Exercise 125

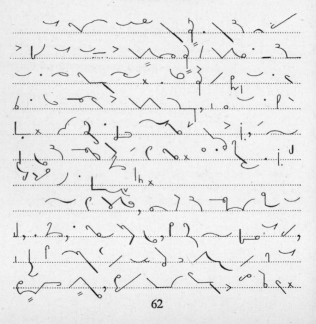

Exercise 126

The chairman said an *advertisement* had·been inserted in-the local-press inviting-the residents to-give *substantial subscriptions* to a central fund, and-the amount *subscribed* being out-of | all-*proportion* to expectations, there-was-now no fear of a *deficiency*, and-there-would-be no difficulty in *discharg*ing all initial expenses. Among-the observations made by-the speakers | those of Dr. Rawson were-the most *practicable*, and-we hope they-will-have a wide *publication*. He gave a *description* of a scheme somewhat different from ours and led | the audience to-follow its applicability to-the-present-case. Of-course, Mr. Smith, who-is very far from being *deficient* in eloquence and who-is a *practised* speaker, had | some wild statements to-make, and spoke of-the evils of-the dis*proportion* in-which-the enjoyments of-life are distributed. His speeches are very un*substantial,* but as a *performer* | of-the ludicrous it-would-be difficult to-find his equal either in-this-country or in-any *republic*. When-the next edition of-the local paper is *published* I- | will-forward you a copy and you-will-be-able-to realize how unflattering he-is in-his remarks about what-he calls-the dis*proportionate* distribution of wealth. (208)

Exercise 127

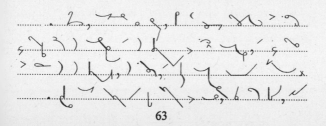

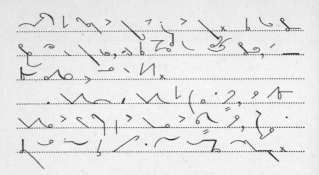

Exercise 128

He who wishes to-become a fluent speaker must first of all be *capable* of-making a speech; but it-is a somewhat sad fact that some people are naturally | in*capable* of-expressing their thoughts verbally. It-is-no abuse of language, however, to state that even nature may-be overcome, and-the taciturn person may acquire such fluency as- | to surprise his friends by his eloquence. It-is-only necessary to-recall-the *character* of Demosthenes, and how he developed the *characteristics* of a great orator to-prove | that-this-is so. It-is *especially* essential that *familiarization* with details of-the subject be acquired beforehand, otherwise a *mortgage* is placed on-the chances of-success by an | in*sufficiency* of facts, when a *sufficiency* would *probably* mean unqualified success. With-the precision of a *mathematician* he-should marshal his facts, *familiarize* himself with apt illustrations to *establish* them, | and keep in-view the *immediate* purpose of-his speech. Then-there-are certain gestures which-can-be suited to-circumstances with *mathematical* accuracy, but-these should-be as far | removed as-possible from merely *mechanical* action, if-the *maximum* results are to-be attained. Some fail to-*govern* themselves in-this-matter, and-thus *extinguish*-the possibility of being | effective. Further, a homely and *familiar* style should-be cultivated and adopted as occasion requires. The *efficient* cultivation of-the voice should receive *especial* attention. Unfortunately it-is too often | ignored or treated with but in*sufficient* consideration by-those-who do-not recognize its *expediency*. (255)

Exercise 129

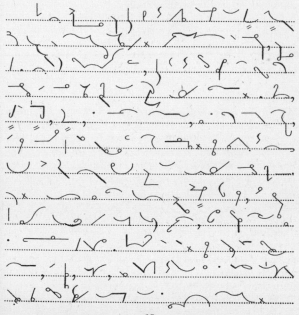

65

Exercise 130

Ministers of-the crown have various duties to *perform* on behalf of-their *government*. One is at-the Exchequer controlling-the *financial* business of-the-country, and looking into-matters | of *expenditure*; and-in-this work he-has often to-meet criticism from-the wealthy classes, from leaders of-commerce, and-from *manufacturers* because-he seeks to tax-the commodities | they *manufacture* or export. It-is in-the-months of *January, February,* and March that-he begins to-think of-his Budget for-the coming *financial* year. Another is *exchang*ing | views with foreign powers, and it-is-necessary that-he maintains an *imperturbable* manner under all-circumstances, and displays a broad spirit in-his views. A third is maintaining-the | impregnable state of-our coasts, or considering-the in*efficiency* of-our navy, which-is very *expensive,* and-formulating plans for making it more *efficient.* A fourth has to-deal-with- | the treatment of-prisoners who-are confined for offences of various kinds, and-though-he-may-be a kindly man, he-must-not-be swayed by false motives in-the | *discharge* of-his duties. A fifth is concerned with-the health of *metropolitan* and other areas throughout-the land. In addition to-all-this, such ministers are *cross-examined* in | Parliament, and-the result of-such *cross-examination* depends very largely on-the personal *magnetism* of-the holder of-the office. (231)

Exercise 131

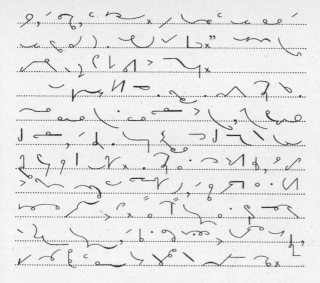

Exercise 132

During-the winter months the committee of-our institute *organize* a number of lectures, at each of-which there-is as chairman a well-known *representative* of local industries. Some | of-the committee are in-favour of-having subjects which allow only of-one style of-treatment. Our late secretary resigned because-he thought that-the committee *neglected* good opportunities | of enlightening-the *public* on-some debatable topics which-were discoursed upon by *irresponsible individuals*, somewhat ill-*informed*, and who-were *interested* in-the propagation of-certain principles without any | regard for-the *sensibilities* of others. We-regret that-he-should-have thus *relinquished* duties which he had *performed* in a most dis*interested*

manner, and-we certainly think that-such | topics
will-have-to-be *incorporated* in-our programme, or
we-shall-be guilty of a serious *negligence*, and lose a
connection which-may-be *irrecoverable*.   (146)

Exercise 133

In *November* last we-had a lecture on *electricity*,
and-the-chairman, in a very *interest*ing speech, said he
remembered-the time when people were afraid of-
travelling by *electric* | train or tram, and regarded an
investment in *electrical* undertakings as very unwise
indeed. He had some anecdotes to-tell of-the life of-the
lecturer, who formerly *represented* | his native town in
Parliament, but owing to being so *irregular* in-his
attendance at Westminster, he had to-resign his seat,
although a man was-never better qualified for- | the
work. Several-times he had complained of-the want of
independence of-members, showed much indignation
at-the humiliating position in-which he-was often placed,
and looked upon- | the routine work of-Parliament as
very un*interesting*. Among other things, one of-which-
was a story of-his escapades when a boy, the chairman
mentioned that in-his youth the | lecturer was very
regular in-his attendance at-the local technical school,
and gained several *certificates* for science subjects.
On-the *representation* of-his tutor, a clever man, who-
was | *responsible* for-the *organization* of a large *electrical*
company, the *govern*ing director of-which-was a
member of-the Automobile Club, the lecturer specialized
in *electricity*, and-now he-was | one of-the foremost
lecturers of-the day, and considered a first-class
organizer of *electrical* exhibitions.   (227)

Exercise 134

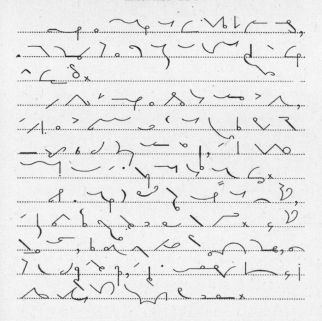

Exercise 135

The lecturer said *electricity* is in evidence everywhere, and today it-is an *indispensable* factor in-the life of a progressive people. Despite-the constant and *enthusiastic* efforts of electricians, | the exact nature of *electricity* is unknown. Among-the *reforms* for-which science is *responsible*, none has-been more singularly beneficial to-the race than-the application of *electricity* to- | the needs of-mankind. The *reformer* is-now turning his attention to domestic duties which-are undergoing a revolution in-the hands of-the *electrical* engineer.

Certainly the reformation is | very slow, and it-is very unfortunate that housewives in-this-country should show some opposition to-methods of *electric* cooking. Of *electric* cookers he-could-not speak too *enthusiastically*; | they-do-not fluctuate in temperature; the result obtained *yesterday* will-be obtained today, if-the-same conditions are imposed. He spoke of-the *sensibility* of *electric* waves in-the- | air, and of-the various methods of-producing *electricity*, which-were far from being *uniform*, and gave a wonderful account of-the generating of *electricity* by-the force of water. | All-were *unanimous* in-their praise of-the lecture. (189)

Exercise 136

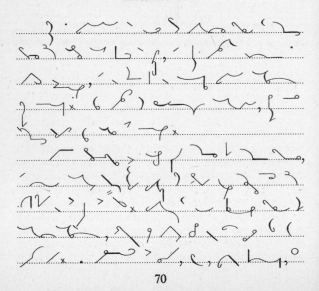

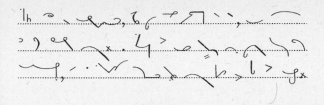

Exercise 137

In-this age when-we hear such un*sympathetic* remarks about-the decadence of sport, it-is very-*satisfactory* to-find so-many *Englishmen* taking a fairly *sympathetic interest* in-the | *University* Boat Race, the premier *English* sporting event, and it-is *questionable* whether any other event in-the pastimes of-the world touches so *universal*ly the great heart of-the | public in-*England* and abroad. All-classes of society take a very keen *interest* in-the race before-the day of-the event, and it-is-this *universality* that un*questionably* | shows that-the race is associated with *nothing* objectionable. The same cannot-be-said of-some-other forms of sport which contain the *minimum* of sport really, but-the *maximum* | of elements which-are undesirable. An *investigation* would frequently prove the utter *falsification* of-the meaning of-the-word sport. If-the newspaper is an index of *public interest*, then | surely all must *acknowledge* that-the training of-the two crews is a matter of *interest* to *Englishmen* throughout-the *universe*. At-this-time men discuss with *knowledge* the merits | or demerits of various forms of diet, and-with an *intelligence* which all *intelligent* people should accept as an *acknowledg*ment of-the extreme *interest* taken in-the various doctrines advocated | by food *reformers*. (213)

Exercise 138

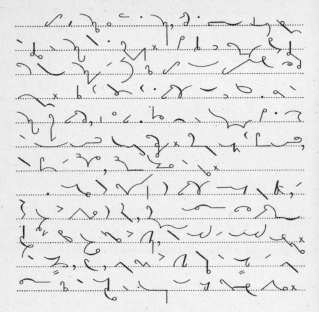

Exercise 139

The day of-the *University* Boat Race is-the first
out-door spring holiday, and-though-the weather
may-be un*satisfactory*, the crowd on-the river and
tow-path is an immense | and motley one. Here
we-have-the *Parliamentary* hand, the *insurance* broker,
the compiler of *prospectuses* and *amalgamation* schemes,
the *arbitrator* engaged in *arbitration* cases, members
of-the *legislature* who- | have turned their backs on
legislative matters for a short-time, the *administrator*
and-the *administratrix*; there we-have ladies in-the

72

height of fashion full of *enthusiasm* for-the | success
of-their favourites; the mischievous errand boys with
their baskets over-their shoulders, whose mischief is
excusable for-once; indeed, all-sorts and conditions of
influential and un*influential* persons, | each of-whom has
probably decided his or her choice in a most *arbitrary*
manner. The newspaper reporter is there with-his
pencil and book jotting down any matters of- | moment
in-the *characters* which delight the hearts of all
Pitmanites. The result of-the race is sent by *telegraphic*
communication, both *telegram* and cable, to all parts
of-the | globe. Undoubtedly people think more of-the-
manner of winning than of-the prize at stake, and-thus
the boat race exemplifies the saying of-the-most lovable
of all | Scotsmen, Robert Louis Stevenson, who wrote:
"Our business in-this world is-not to succeed, but to
continue to fail in good spirits." Here we-have a
splendid motto to- | remember in-our everyday life and
in-our pastimes.   (249)

Exercise 140

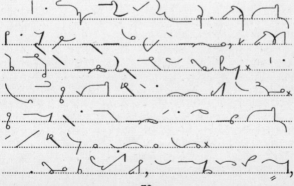

73

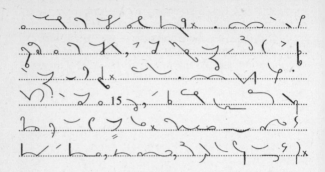

Exercise 141

The introduction of new methods of locomotion has considerably widened the field of-the newspaper, and added further variety to-the editor's duties. Among-the most popular modes of-travelling | is that of-motoring, the development of-which has-been very *remarkable* indeed. Newspapers have consequently *enlarged* the scope of-their contents, and given *circumstantial* accounts of *anything* and *everything* | of-importance associated with motors and motoring. There-are also periodicals devoted *altogether* to-the *interests* of motorists. *Interested* parties *organize* motor shows at which *everything* in-the way of | accessories, from *incandescent* lights, to-the most insignificant, but *nevertheless* necessary, parts are exhibited, each and everyone claiming to-have certain distinctive features. The multiplicity of-motors, both *public* and- | private, is a source of *danger* to-the general *public*, for some motorists are *unprincipled* enough to be reckless in-their driving. Such unlawful acts give offence, and | cause great alarm and *inconvenience* to-those passing along our streets. Therefore, it-is urgent that-those in author-

74

ity should seek an *enlarge*ment of-their powers to-check excessive speed | *whenever* motors travel through-the busy thoroughfares of-our cities and towns, and to inflict severer punishments on all who transgress or attempt to transgress the letter of-the law. | (210)

Exercise 142

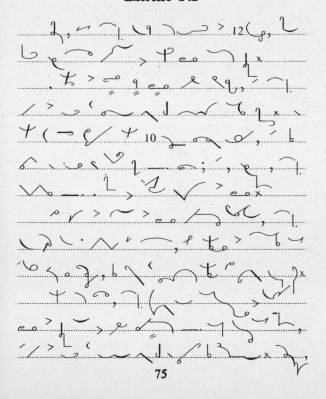

Exercise 143

Some say motorists should show more consideration, and give attention to-matters which concern the life and death of-the frequenters of-our roads. Though-the *difficulties* are great they- | are-not *irremovable*, and motorists themselves can-do a great-deal to-make-them *removable*. Often, too, we hear complaints by *denominational* bodies that weekend motoring is injurious to- | the cause of religion in general, and-there-would-be a general rejoicing among-the churches if *something* could-be done to convince people of-their folly in spending their | weekends motoring along-the countryside. In-our remarks *respect*ing the onward march of civilization, it-is well to consider all things *together*, and what brings *misfortune* to-the few | may carry with-it great blessings for-the-majority of-mankind. *Notwithstanding* this, however, there does appear to be a wanton heedlessness of-those things which-were very real and | dear to-the hearts of-our forefathers.

(157)

Exercise 144

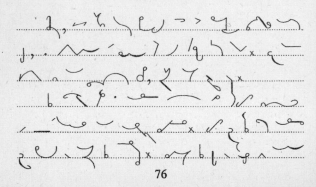

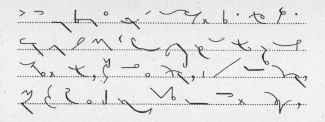

Exercise 145

I-am-very-glad to inform-you that our business has turned out very-satisfactorily indeed during-the past year, notwithstanding-that much has militated against our progress. Before dealing- | with-the figures in-the accounts, I-think-it-is-necessary for-me to-recall to-your-minds what I said at our last meeting. You-will-probably remember these- | words: "On-this-occasion we-have to-meet an adverse balance, and it-is deemed necessary to-take immediate steps to-improve our position. At-the beginning of-the year | we brought-forward a substantial amount, and-now we-are faced with a deficit. I-am-persuaded, however, that-we-could-not have-done better owing to-the peculiar-circumstances which- | were in operation during-the year." Those-who-were present at-the meeting in-all-probability remember-the statement on-this-matter in-the report. It-was felt that by- | some-means we-must regain our position, and-therefore every-circumstance likely to-have affected the profitable working of-the company was considered, and-the result reflects great-credit on | all-those-who-are concerned in-the re-organization, and-I-think-that-you-are satisfied in-this-respect.   (198)

Exercise 146

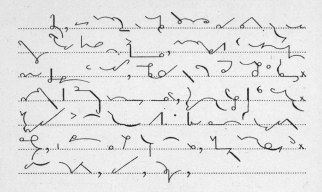

Exercise 147

Turning to-the accounts for-the-year now under review, I-think-you-will-agree-with me that-we-have-done exceedingly well. On-the credit-side of-the trading | account you-will-find that-the business done shows an increase of £20,000. On-the-other-side we show an increase of working expenses, but-the increase is- | not heavy, and-furnishes us with an example of-the fact that-the better-the business we-do, the lower is-the ratio of-expenses. On-the assets side of- | the balance-sheet the property account item is-the same-as before, while-the cash shows an increase of £1,200. On-the liabilities side of-the | balance-sheet the cost of renovation has-been charged to-the reserve account, and-I-think-you-will quite-agree-with-this. Our dividends for-the past five years have | averaged 10 per-cent per-annum. Early in-the coming year there-will-be a special meeting to discuss-the-matter of further developments, and-I-take-the-liberty of | urging all to

be present. In-the-meantime I-trust we-shall continue
to-prosper so-that-we-may-have a substantial increase
in-our-profits.   (206)

Exercise 148

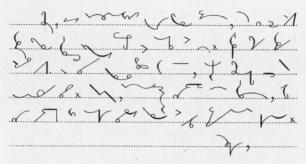

Exercise 149

It-is-said that civilization has deprived man of-his
love of nature, and it-is-only-necessary to observe-the
small-proportion of-city dwellers who delight in-the |
out-of-doors life to-find confirmation of-this-statement.
This-has-been spoken of many-times, and as-we-think,
and as-we-shall maintain, it-is very unfortunate | that-
such a state-of-affairs exists. Nature is ever striving
after perfection; and-this-is-the one great lesson of-life
we-have to-learn, that-the greatest happiness | is-to-be-
found in-the pursuit of-perfection, for, as Stevenson
says, it-is more blessed to-travel than to arrive. All
lovers of nature should read Stevenson's account | of a
leisurely journey through-the north-east of-France by
canoe and on foot. He-was a lover of nature. Being in
perfect agreement with him, and wishing to | emulate
his example, we spent a holiday afloat in France last
summer.   (162)

Exercise 150

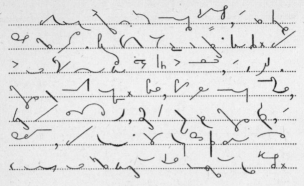

Exercise 151

Three of-us had arranged to-make-the trip. All
of-us are members of-the-same political-association,
while two are also prominently connected with a
medical-association, and- | the third with a traders-
association. On a Wednesday-evening we left-the shores
of England for France. Arriving in Paris, we hired a
flat-bottomed Norwegian boat, somewhat smaller- |
than we-had intended, and-from this-city we rowed
ourselves down to Nantes, leaving Paris on a Thursday-
afternoon. We-went by-the Seine, along two canals,
and down- | the Loire, a distance of-over three hundred
miles, which occupied a joyous month, out-of which
we spent more-than half-the time on-the water. We-had
a | very large umbrella that protected us absolutely
from sun and showers, and-in-the locker of-the boat
there-were appliances for-the-preparation of-simple
meals. As-well-as- | can-be remembered, we-went
through about forty locks; we stayed at thirty inns,
and our expenses worked out to a total of twenty francs
a day for dinner, bed, | and early breakfast.   (183)

Exercise 152

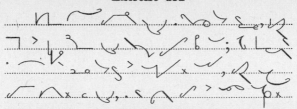

Exercise 153

The weather was glorious during-the whole trip, and our picnic lunches under-the-trees, though of-the very-simplest character, were most enjoyable. Looking back upon-the time, it- | appears we-were in-such excellent spirits that what we ate was of-little consequence. We gloried in-the fact that-we-were in-the real France of-the real | French, and-were enjoying nature among new and strange surroundings. We-have-been-informed that-we-did-not take-the best route, and-therefore as-soon-as-we-can we- | shall take-the opportunity of carrying into-effect the suggested alternative. Let-us urge those-who-have-not experienced such a holiday to-try it by-all-means as-soon- | as-they can, since it-seems to-us that in-these-days of advanced civilization it-is-necessary that-we seek communion with nature whenever we-can, and especially at | holiday times.

(152)

Exercise 154

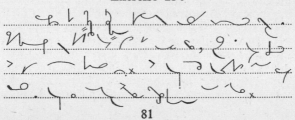

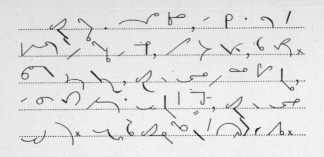

Exercise 155

From-time-to-time we-have-discussed the question of-the influence of-the-press, and you-cannot deny that on all occasions I-have-been able-to-make out | a fairly strong case for-the justification of-the statement that journalists on-the whole work for-the cause of-progress; and-if-you-should-not-be willing to allow | this, they-would-be unduly condemned for-that for-which they-were-not altogether responsible. You-will recollect that some-time-ago, I-cannot-say-the exact date, you stated | that-you-were-not satisfied that-the influence of-the-press was for good. I-would-not reopen this-question so soon again if-it-were-not for-the speech | of-one-of-our leading orators the other-day, which impels me to-write a few-words respecting it. He-was-the principal guest at-the annual dinner of-the | local Press Club, and-I-have-carefully perused more-than one report of-the speech in-the several newspapers in-which-it-has-appeared. He said he-was getting on | in life, and for-some-time past had withdrawn from public-life, and hoped that-he had done with public speaking. The great terror of-every public speaker in-his- | time was-the reporter; but to-some-extent, and to what-extent is apparent from a study of newspapers, pressmen had ceased to-report the speeches to-which-it-was | understood the whole community were looking-forward with breathless interest. (250)

Exercise 156

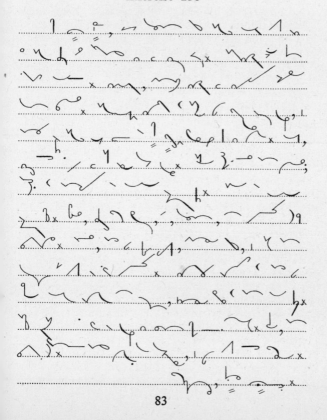

Exercise 157

At-any-rate, the speaker continued, the reporter was no-longer the terror of public speakers, and-now only reported the speeches of-the great lions of-the front bench. | He believed that-the-press did work for-the cause of-progress, but at-the-same-time he warned his hearers of-their influence in-the cause of peace, and | implored them to hesitate before they-did anything to-bring-about-the horrors of war. It-is on-this-question of war, he went on to say, that-you-are-not at- | one with me. You-must-not-be vexed if I-venture to-repeat that I-cannot-see why you-should condemn at-all-times, and-under-all-circumstances the influence | of-the-press in-this-matter, as-if-it-were-the duty of-the journalist, in-so-many-words, to denounce all wars and cry for peace on-every occasion. | A notable writer says war is sacred, and-there-can surely be no-doubt that-it-is absolutely-necessary to use force for-the suppression of tyranny and wrong-doing. | I-may-not-be-able-to see-you for a long-time to-come, so I-hope-you-will-not fail to-write me on-this-subject. Doubtless you-will- | be-able-to find some objections to-my-statements; still I-am-able-to-think that-you-will modify your views in-the-early future. If-it-be-not too- | much trouble to-you, will-you-kindly post to-me the copies of-the pamphlets I-lent you some-time-ago, and although you-may-not have read all of- | them, perhaps you-will give me your opinion on-those you have perused. We should exhibit charity in-our-words at-all-times, and-in-this spirit I-trust we- | shall always express our thoughts when writing to-each-other on controversial topics. (313)

Exercise 158

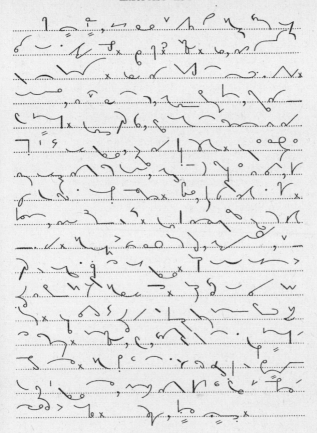

Exercise 159

I-wish-there-were more people who-would remember-
the saying that to understand everything is-to forgive

85

everything; in-other-words, whenever-there-is cause to criticize-the actions | of-others, we should try to-get at-the real motive of-the actions, and-then we should-be more charitable towards such persons. I-know-there-will-be some | who-will object to-this view; but my-dear-friends, if-there-is-to-be a larger-hearted sympathy abroad, I-am-sure-there-is no other-way of attaining | it than that I-am advocating, and no other-way in-which-there-is anything like so-much chance of-success. How-can-there-be true brotherly feeling in-our | hearts if-we condemn others before-there-is an opportunity of understanding-their motives, and-if-we pass upon-their actions a hasty judgement? In-order-that there-may-be | an advance in-this-matter people will-have to-look above-their own desires of-making-their-way in life at-all-costs, and-instead, think of increasing-their-value | to-mankind in-general. (184)

Exercise 160

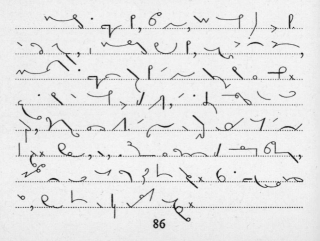

Exercise 161

As Bulwer Lytton says, if-we serve mankind we serve ourselves. I-believe-there-will-be some who-will say they-will-think about it, and pending-their-decision I- | would urge them to-reflect that men are naturally inclined to doubt-the truth of-such statements. Then-there-are others who hesitate in-some-other-respects; perhaps, in-order- | to count on-the material advantages or disadvantages of-such a course. For-their-own sake, I-would ask-them to change their view of-life, and-they-are sure | to benefit more-than-their worldly thoughts could possibly have suggested. The wise-men of-the past have assured us that in-their-opinion the best course of-life | is that-which suppresses the selfishness inherent in-man, and-I-think-there-will-be many who, from-their experience, will support them in-their-statement. Whether I address you | as my-dear-sir, my-dear-madam, or my-dear-fellow-citizen, let-me ask-you to ponder over-this-matter and to-remember that in-the beautiful-words of | Adelaide Procter, "Glorious it-is to-wear a crown of a deserved and pure success"; and-though-there-is much that may baffle you in-order-to carry out this | high ideal, it-is as true today as ever it-was that without sympathy nothing is understood. (227)

Exercise 162

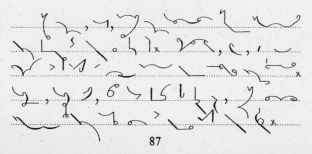

87

If anyone says he does-not-need-the sympathy of-his-fellows, he-is-not true to-himself or to humanity, for-the whole structure of society rests upon sympathy | among individuals towards-one-another. If-it-were-not so, then society as-it exists today would-be impossible. The strongest of-us imperatively requires sympathy, for-some-time or-other | our natures are certain to-call for-it, and-if-it-is refused, that-which-is best in-us becomes warped. History and literature furnish us with many examples of- | this. An unsympathetic nature is like-the biting Arctic winds, but a sympathetic disposition is like-the balmy breezes of-the south, and-the more expansive our sympathies the more | nearly do we approach towards-the ideal "of a deserved and pure success." (133)

Exercise 164

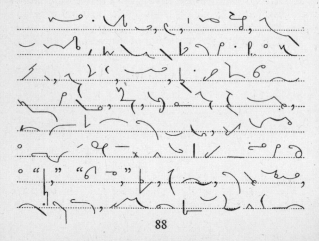

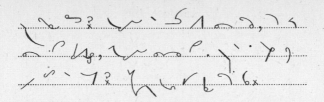

Exercise 165

Money has-been defined to-be desire capitalized, and-as-far-as I-am-concerned, I-am-content to accept this-definition. I-have-thought of-it in-all-ways, | and-I-have-concluded, after-consideration of-every-circumstance connected with-the-subject, that-the definition is satisfactory. I-am-confident that if-you-will-think of-the-matter you- | will, as a necessary-consequence, come to-the-same-conclusion. In a genuine inquiry, the conclusion is-not arrived at without some-con-sideration of opposite views. In-fact, those-views | must-be-considered if-we-are to-come to a satisfactory-conclusion. Having-regard, therefore, to-the interesting nature of-the question before-us, it-will-be agreed that-it | deserves to-be fully-considered and must-be looked at from-every standpoint. It demands that everything that can-be-said about it shall-be-considered, and-that anything which- | may, in-any-way, help-us to an opinion shall-be-taken-into-consideration, in-point-of-fact, must-be taken-into-consideration. Limited space, however, forbids my enlarging upon- | the question in-the-manner I-would like, so-that I-must-be content to-leave out some-considerations, of-which a great-deal might be-said, and respecting which | there might, perhaps, be a disagreement. I-shall consider this-question more fully in-another-place. (226)

Exercise 166

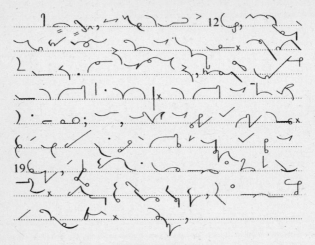

Exercise 167

Let-us-consider a few points, and-I-shall-be content to-leave-the further-consideration of-the question to-the reader. A great writer, speaking on-this-subject of- | money, points out that in-view of a future exchange money is, as-it-were, our security. For, he-says, it-is-necessary that-he who brings it should-be- | able-to get "what-he wants." If-the reader will-take-into-consideration the full meaning of-the-last sentence, he-will-see that "what-he wants" is but another- | way of saying "what-he desires." Again, another authority declares that coined money is a kind of bill or order payable at-the will of-the bearer. In-like-manner | still another writer states that a coin must-be-considered as a bill upon all-the tradesmen in-the neighbourhood. That-is, if I-have-received a coin for-services | rendered tosomebody else, I-can-have, in return, anything I-desire which-is equal in-value to-it. A fourth authority says money is a warrant which-gives-the | bearer the right to-draw from society when-he desires services according-to-the value of-the-coin. Similar questions on-the nature of-money have-been answered by various | other writers in-the-same-manner, so-that I-have-concluded that-the definition referred to is tolerably accurate, and it-cannot-be-said that I-have come to an | unsatisfactory-conclusion, and-I-hope-you-are-satisfied. Nowadays most of-the transactions of-commercial and-industrial-life are carried-out as-far-as-possible by-means-of various forms | of paper-money, the most-important of-which in-this-country is-the cheque currency with-which our banking system provides us. (292)

Exercise 168

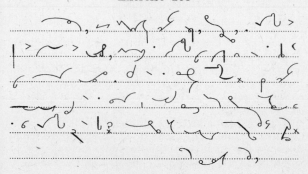

Exercise 169

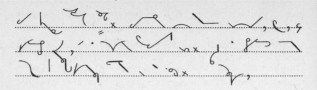

Exercise 170

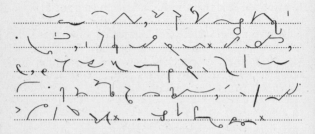

Exercise 171

You-will-be-glad-to-hear that under-the-circum-stances I-was-able-to attend the lecture, and-though as-a-rule I-do-not care for-such meetings, I- | enjoyed it very-much indeed. Having-regard-to-the subject I-think-there ought-to-have-been a much larger audience, but-some who ought-to-have-known about it | pleaded ignorance in justification of-their absence. With-regard-to-the lecture itself I-have-pleasure in giving you a summary of-the chief points. In days gone by, according- | to-the lecturer, it-appears-to-have-been-the rule rather-than-the exception to walk as-much-as-possible, and-only to-ride when it-was absolutely-necessary, notwithstanding- | the-fact that longer hours were worked then than-now. At-the-present-day, however, all-over-the-world there-is an ever-growing tendency, on-the-one-hand to- | ignore to-a-great-extent

92

the value of walking, and-on-the-other-hand to-travel on all occasions by vehicles of-one-kind or another. Unfortunately, as-the speaker | truly observed, city life of today necessitates the use of rapid means of locomotion, but-there-is-no reason why people should, as-a-matter-of-course, spend their | leisurely weekend, or-their annual holiday, scouring the countryside in a motor, or rushing across great stretches of-country in a train. (233)

Exercise 172

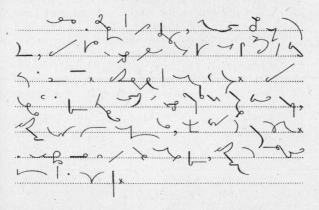

Exercise 173

In continuation of-his address on-the benefits of walking exercise, "Let-us-consider-the-matter for-a-moment," said-the lecturer, "and try to estimate the advantages of walking | and walking-tours. The roads of-every country in Europe, except those of Sweden, Russia, Greece and Turkey, are familiar to-me. I-have

walked through France from north to- | south, and
nearly from east to-west. I-have walked through a
large-part of-Germany, and-have crossed the Alps on
foot by three different passes. I-know-the | roads of
Italy from-the frontier to Rome. I-have-been across
pathless Bohemia, and through Hungary and-the
Austrian Tyrol. I-can, therefore, speak on-the-subject
of walking | with some authority, and-from-first-to-last
my expression-of-opinion should-be of-great value.
In-the-first-place, a walking-tour has great educational
advantages. It teaches | us-the physical features of a
country in-such-a-manner-as no other-way can. The
level of-the-country, the position of-the towns, the flow
of-rivers, | and-the nature of-the soil are made real
to-us. The average Englishman, whose idea of a lake
is Windermere, of a mountain, Snowdon, and of a river,
the | Thames, would open his eyes if-he found himself
by-the side of Lake Constance, or if-he crossed the Alps
and Pyrenees, and followed-the seven hundred miles
of- | the Rhine. In-the-second-place, the wanderings
of a man on foot with-his eyes open and brought face-
to-face with-the peoples of other nations, narrow down |
his prejudices."   (272)

Exercise 174

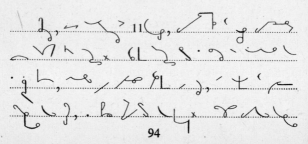

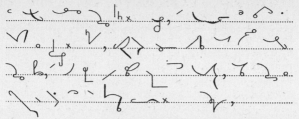

Exercise 175

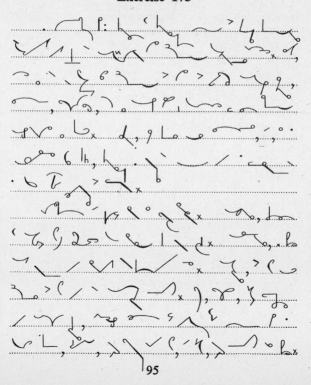

Exercise 176

In-conclusion, the lecturer said "When first I-went to Portugal I shared all-the indignation of-my country-men at-the easy-going habits of-the people of-the peninsula. | But in-the short-space-of-time it took me to-reach my hotel from-the landing stage, I determined never to say another-word against them on-the-matter, | for-the enervating heat took all-the energy out-of me. In-the-third-place, the traveller learns at first-hand the true character of-the people among whom he | finds himself, and-the facts of-life are impressed upon him in-a-way the pages of a book could never effect. In-the-next-place, and-in-the-last- | place, there-are-the physical benefits to be derived from walking. Too-much food and too-little exercise is-the root of-most of-our bodily ills; and-if-we- | would indulge more freely in walking, and-think less of-our ease and-the-trouble of walking, our lives would undoubtedly be free from-many of-the aches and pains | of-which-we-are-now so ready to complain." (189)

Exercise 177

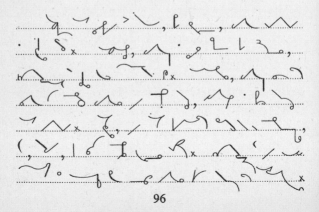

96

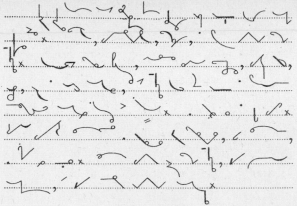

Exercise 178

At-the-present-time great attention is paid to-the
exploration of-the North-and-South Poles of-the earth
by explorers of all nations. Some of-the names made |
famous in-connection-with polar exploration are
Nansen, a Norwegian doctor, who sailed in-the "Fram"
and succeeded in getting very near to-the North Pole;
Lieutenant Peary, a daring | American who-was-the
first to-reach the North Pole; Amundsen, who ac-
companied Nansen in-the "Fram," and who-was-the
first to discover-the South Pole; and Scott, who | un-
fortunately lost his life while returning after having
reached the South Pole. Among-them they-have
added much to geographical knowledge, and-in-a-great-
measure investigators at-the-present- | day know as-
much about these in-point-of-fact as-is likely to-prove
of scientific value. But sooner-or-later sentiment
rather-than science will-be gratified by- | the discovery
and publication all-over-the-world of-every secret
of-these untrodden regions.   (165)

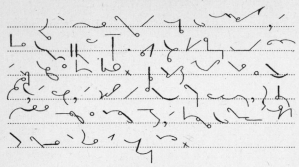

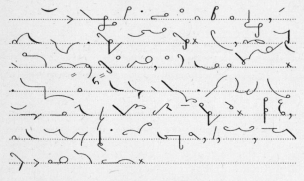

Exercise 181

All-parts-of-the-world are becoming, in-fact, more-and-more well-known, so-that-we-shall soon regard it as-a-matter-of-course that blanks on-our | maps will grow less-and-less, till in a short-space-of-time they-will disappear altogether. Some may exclaim, "Do-you-mean-to-say that at-the-present-time | we-may, as-a-matter-of-fact, look to-the time when discoveries will no-longer add to-our knowledge of-the geography of-the-world, in-which, from-first- | to-last, we-have-been so-much interested? We-shall-be-glad-to-hear when-such may-be looked for." In-reply, attention may-be-called to-the facts-of- | the-case, and by-way-of-illustration, Africa may-be pointed to. For-many-years past explorers have plunged deeper-and-deeper into-the hidden recessesof-the African continent, | and, whether right-or-wrong, they subjugated the savage inhabitants in a more-or-less complete fashion. Africa was then divided among-the European Powers, and exploration was carried out | to-a-great-extent in-the-last-years of-the nineteenth-century, so-that-we-are-able-to-make a very complete map of-the whole continent.　　(207)

Exercise 182

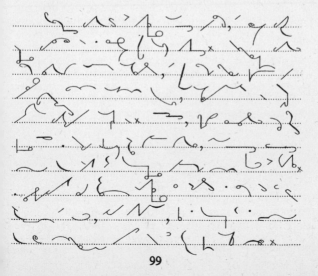

Exercise 183

When-we ask what-is-the-matter complained of, and inquire into it, it-must-be borne-in-mind that-it-is-not worse than what savage tribes practise among- | themselves, or towards-one-another; though, by-the-way, we-do-not for-a-moment defend wanton barbarity on-the-part-of civilized man towards savages who for-the-first- | time come under-his control. Unhappily, this-is always more-or-less an incident of-the contact of civilized and savage man. If-we-cannot-see all-the-way to | a better state-of-things, we-may at-least anticipate some of-the advantages which civilization should in-the end be-able-to bestow, on-the-one-hand on-the- | native population, and-on-the-other-hand, or on-the-other-side, on itself. In-the-first-place, or in-the-first-instance, exploration affords a healthy subject of interest | for-the more adventurous spirits of all nations, and adds additional chapters of interest to-the story of-the-world. In-the-second-place, new markets are opened for commerce, | and new fields for-the exercise of ability. In-the-third-place, regions are opened-up which-may-be of-much value as an outlet for-the overgrown population of | other regions. In-the-next-place, or in-the-last-place, colonization is a hopeful part of-that onward march of-humanity, in-which all-have-the deepest interest.   (239)

Exercise 184

The various political-parties in-this-country are represented in almost every district by local-clubs, where party-questions are discussed, and-all-matters affecting the welfare of-the different- | parties receive consider-able-attention. Well-known leaders visit-the districts periodically and deliver important speeches on-such questions as party-government, party-organization, the relative strength of-the several parliamentary- | parties, etc. The rivalry between-the political-parties serves to-maintain a high standard of excellence among-them all.

Our Professor-of-Commerce is giving a garden-party in-a- | month's-time, and several well-known people are expected to be-present. There-will-be Professor-Morgan, our Professor-of-Chemistry, Professor-Jackson, our Professor-of-Music, a famous Chancery- | Judge, Colonel-Jackson and Colonel-Anderson, prominent members of-the Conservative-party, and Major-Jones, the prospective candidate of-the Liberal-party.

(142)

Exercise 185

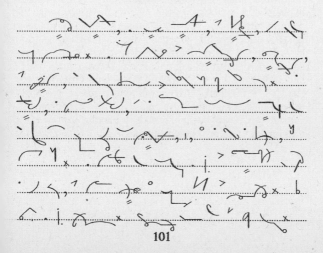

Exercise 186

The Bank-of-England was founded in 1694, and it-is-the most-important national-bank in-the-world. It issues bank-bills, drawn on itself | for any amount between £10 and £1,000, and its directors fix-the "bank-rate." To encourage persons of limited means to-save, there-are savings-banks and | penny-banks. Bankruptcy disqualifies-the bankrupt from membership of a Town-Council, Sanitary-Authority, Education-Authority, or vestry. These disqualifications may cease if-the bankrupt can prove that-his bankruptcy | was due to misfortune.

The embankment known as-the Thames-Embankment is, next to-some sea-embankments, the finest in-the-world. I should like to-call-attention-to-the- | fact that special-attention must now be given by book-keepers to-the-system which enables-the merchant to ascertain whether, say, the silk-department, the shipping-department, or-the | foreign-department of-his business is making a profit or a loss. A large-number of excellent positions in-the electrical-department, the paving-department, or-the cleansing-department of- | our corporations are open to-those-who-have a good knowledge of book-keeping. My-attention-has-been-called to a youth who-gave special-attention to book-keeping when | at-school, and who-is-now reaping the reward of-his zeal. Advertisements appear regularly in-the "Accountant's-Journal," the "Journal-of-Commerce," and other weekly-journals for persons qualified | to act as book-keepers. (245)

Exercise 187

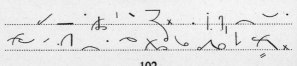

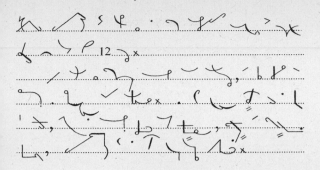

Exercise 188

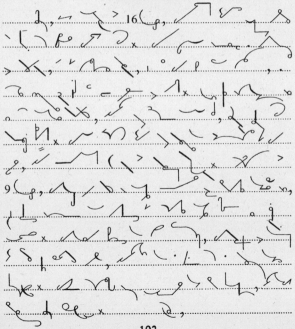

103

Exercise 189

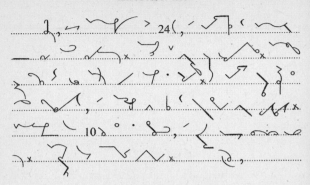

Exercise 190

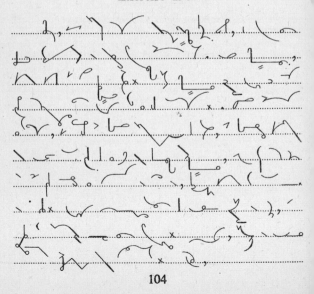

Exercise 191

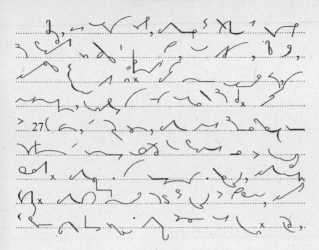

Exercise 192

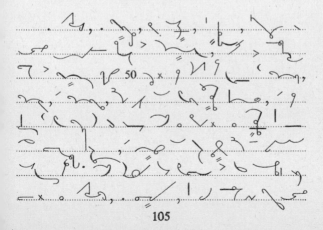

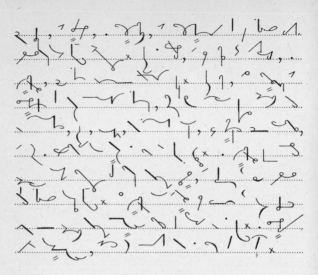

Exercise 193

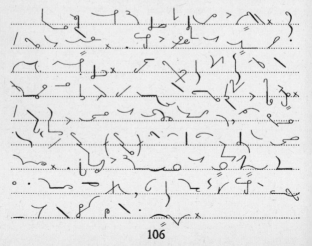

Exercise 194

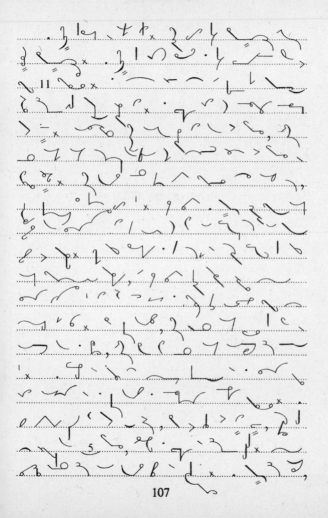

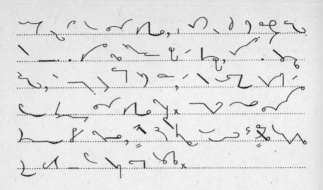

Exercise 195

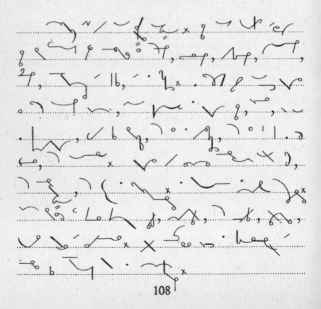

Exercise 196

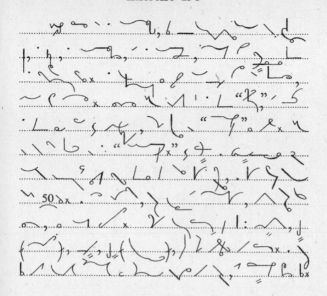

Exercise 197

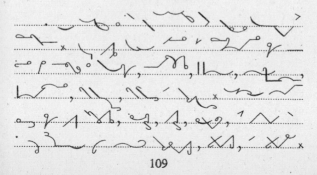

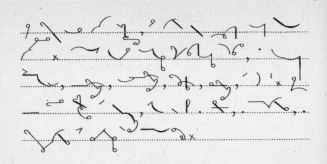

Exercise 198

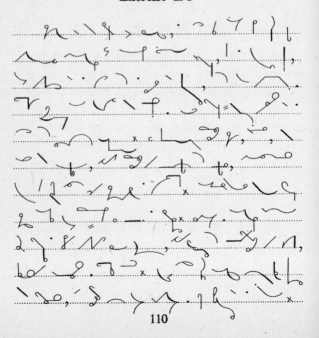

Exercise 199

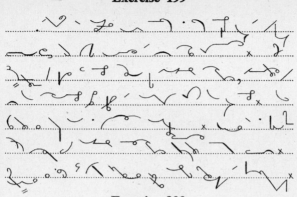

Exercise 200

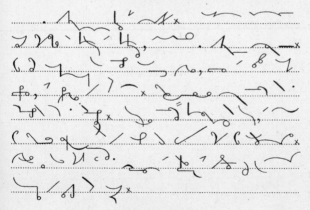

Exercise 201

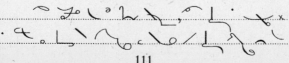

111

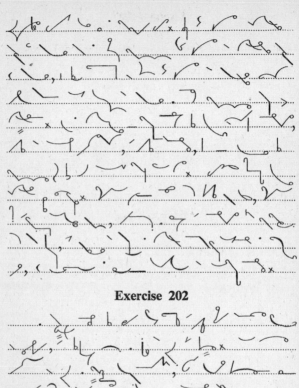

Exercise 202

112

Exercise 203

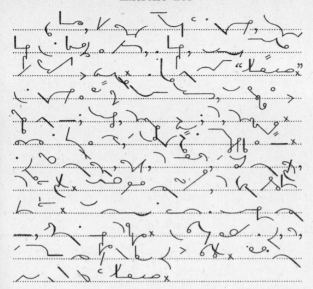

Exercise 204

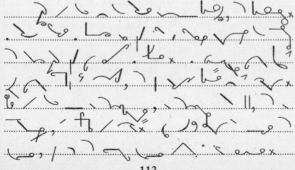

Exercise 205

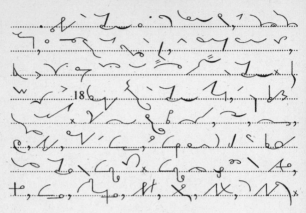

Exercise 206

Exercise 207

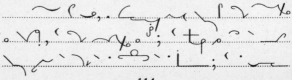

114

Exercise 208

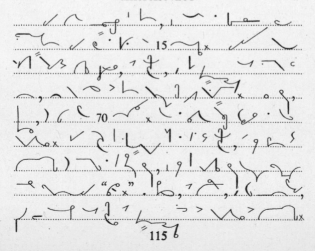

Exercise 209

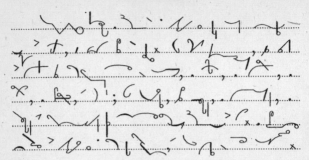

Exercise 210

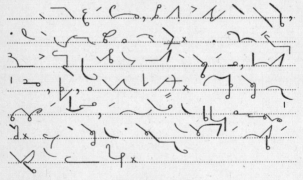

Exercise 211

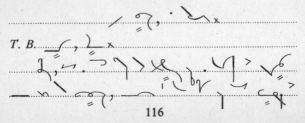

T. B.

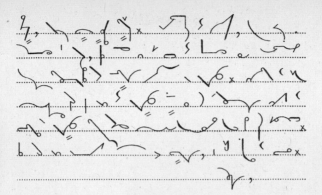

Exercise 212

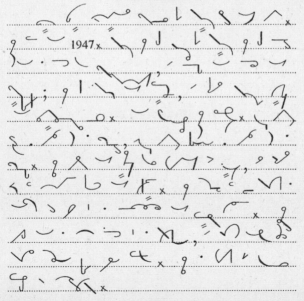

1947

Exercise 213

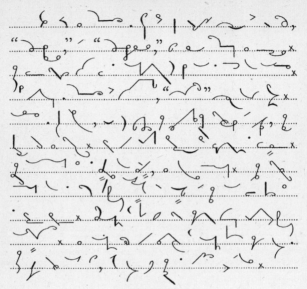

Exercise 214

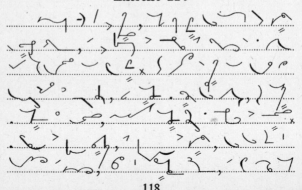

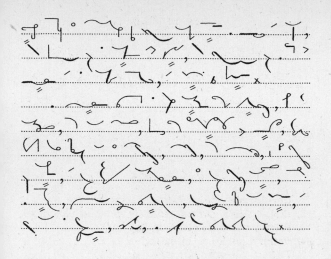

Exercise 215

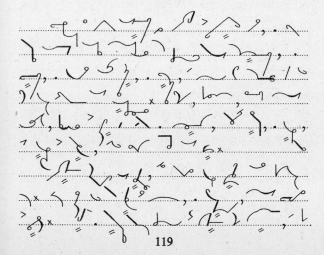

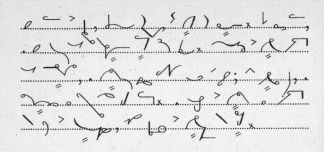

Exercise 216

1. Compatible, compatibility, incompatibility.
2. Pity, pitiable, pitiless, pitilessly, piteous, piteously.
3. Petrify, petrified, petrifaction.
4. Putrefy, putrefied, putrefaction.
5. Patron, patrons, patroness, patronage.
6. Passion, passionate, impassioned.
7. Patient, patience, patiently, impatience, impatient, impatiently.
8. Poor, poorness, poorer, poorest.
9. Pure, purer, purest, purity, purify, purification, impure.
10. Purpose, purposed, purposeful, purposes, purposing.
11. Perhaps.
12. Propose, proposed, proposition, proposal, proposer.
13. Prepare, prepared, preparation, preparatory.
14. Proper, properly, improper, improperly.
15. Property.
16. Propriety, impropriety.
17. Appropriate, appropriated, appropriation, appropriator.
18. Protect, protected, protection, protectionist, protector, protective.

19. Product, *production*, *productive*, *productivity*.
20. Compare, compared, comparison, comparative, comparatively, comparable, incomparable.

Exercise 217

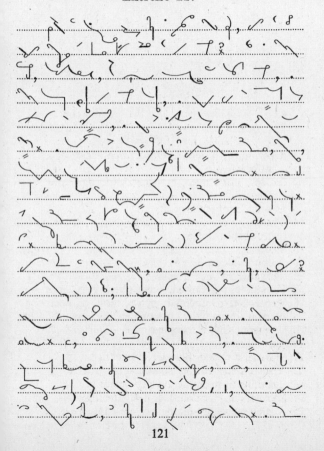

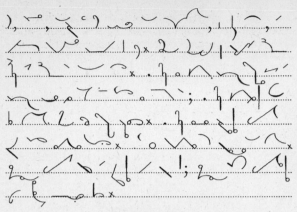

Exercise 218

1. Operate, operated, operator, operation, operative, inoperative.
2. Porter, porterage, importer, exporter, importing, exporting.
3. Proffer, proffered, profferer.
4. Prefer, preferred, preference, preferential, preferable.
5. Provide, provided, providence, provider, improvidence.
6. Pervade, pervaded, pervasive, pervasion.
7. Persecute, persecuted, persecution, persecutor.
8. Prosecute, prosecuted, prosecution, prosecutor.
9. Person, personate, personated, personation, impersonation, impersonator.
10. Parson, parsonage.
11. Pursue, pursued, pursuer, pursuant.
12. Perish, perished, perishable, imperishable.
13. Prominent, prominence, prominently.
14. Permanent, permanence, permanently.
15. Pre-eminent, pre-eminence, pre-eminently.

16. Prince, princely, princes, princess, princesses.
17. Beauty, beautiful, beautify.
18. Bribe, briber, bribery.
19. Birth, birthday, birthmark, birthright.
20. Bury, buried, burial, burying.

Exercise 219

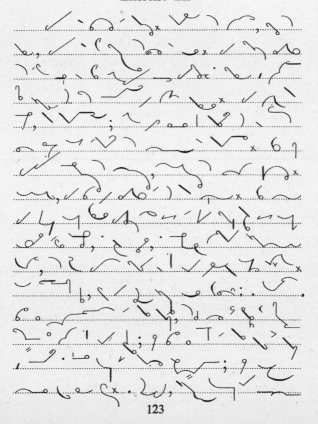

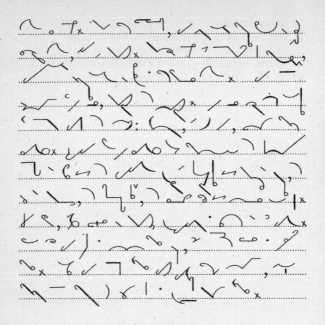

Exercise 220

1. Abundant, abundance, abundantly, superabund-
ance.
2. Abandon, abandoned, abandoner, abandonment.
3. Tuition, tutor, tutorial, tutelage.
4. Temporal, temporary, temporarily, temporize.
5. Temper, temperate, tempered, temperance.
6. Attend, attended, attendant, attentive, attentively,
attention.
7. Continue, continued, continuant, continuation,
continuance.
8. Continent, continental.
9. Travel, travelled, travelling, traveller.

10. Trivial, triviality.
11. Iterate, iteration, reiteration, reiterated, reiterating.
12. Debt, debtor, indebted, indebtedness.
13. Doubt, doubted, doubter, doubtful, doubtfulness.
14. Audit, auditor, audited, auditorium.
15. Edit, edited, editor, editorial, editorship.
16. Detriment, detrimental.
17. Determine, determined, determination, indeterminate.
18. Differ, differed, differential, differentiate, indifferent.
19. Defer, deferred, deferring, deference, deferential.
20. Adverse, adversity, adversely.

Exercise 221

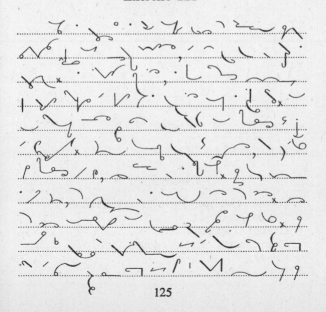

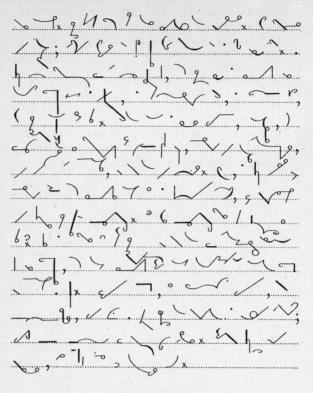

Exercise 222

1. Diverse, diversity, diversify, diversification.
2. Decease, deceased.
3. Disease, diseased.
4. Dear, dearer, dearest, dearly, endeared, endearment.
5. Agent, agency.

6. Act, actual, actually, active, actively, actuate, actor.
7. Cause, caused, causation, causality.
8. Access, accession, accessible, accessibility, inaccessible.
9. Excise, excised, excisable.
10. Exercise, exercised, exerciser, exercising.
11. Cultivate, cultivated, cultivation, cultivator.
12. Column, columnar.
13. Culminate, culminated, culmination.
14. Calumny, calumniate, calumniation, calumniator.
15. Create, created, creation, creator, creative, creature.
16. Carry, carried, carrying, carriage.
17. Credence, credential, credible, credibility, credulous, credulity.
18. Credit, credited, creditor, discredit.
19. Accord, accorded, accordance, accordingly.
20. Guide, guider, guidance, guiding, guided.

Exercise 223

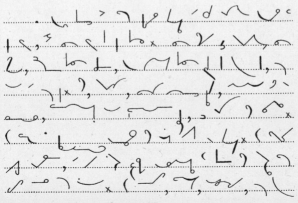

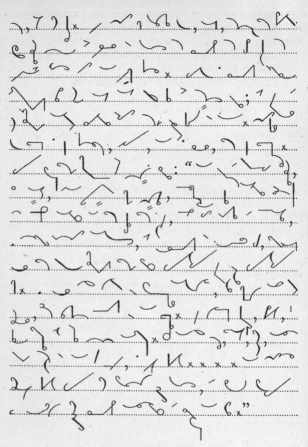

Exercise 224

1. Good, goodness, goodly.
2. Guard, guarded, guarding, guardian, guardianship.

128

3. Grade, graded, grading, gradient, gradation, gradual.
4. Grant, granted, granting, grantee.
5. Guarantee, guaranteed, guarantor.
6. Factor, factory.
7. Favour, favoured, favourite, favouritism.
8. Fall, falling, fallen.
9. Felon, felony, felonious, feloniously.
10. Fortune, fortunate, fortunately, unfortunately, *misfortune*.
11. Four, foursome, fourteen, fourteenth, fourth.
12. Far, farther, farthest.
13. Further, furthest, furthermore.
14. Fresh, fresher, freshest, refreshment, refreshed, refresher.
15. Form, formal, formed, former, formerly.
16. Farm, farmer, farm*yard*.
17. Firm, firmer, firmly, confirmation.
18. Evident, evidence, evidently, evidential.
19. Confide, confidence, confidential, confidently.
20. Avoid, avoided, avoidable, avoidance, unavoidable.

Exercise 225

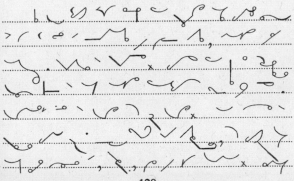

129

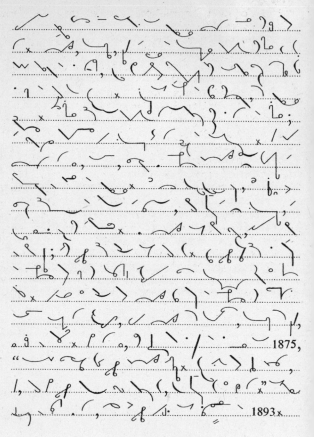

1875,

1893 x

Exercise 226

1. Inevitable.
2. Value, valued, valuable, invaluable, valuer.
3. Avail, available, availing, unavailing.

4. Convulse, convulsed, convulsion, convulsing, convulsively.
5. Evolution, evolutionist, evolutionary.
6. Violent, violently, violence.
7. Converse, conversed, conversation, conversational, conversationalist.
8. Support, supported, supporting, supporter, supportable, insupportable.
9. Separate, separated, separation, separable, inseparable.
10. Situate, situated, situation.
11. Station, stationed, stationing, stationer.
12. Structure, structural.
13. Consider, considered, consideration, considerable, inconsiderable, considerate, inconsiderate.
14. Secret, secretly, secrecy.
15. Secretary, secretarial, secretaryship, secretariat.
16. Secrete, secretion, secretive.
17. Sacred, sacredly, sacredness.
18. Consist, consistence, consistency, consistent, inconsistent, inconsistency.
19. *Short*, shorter, *short*est, shorten, *shorthand*, *short*handed.
20. Emigrate, emigrated, emigration, emigrant.

Exercise 227

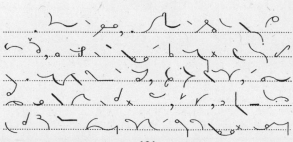

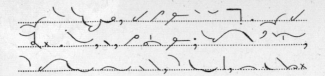

Exercise 228

1. Immigrate, immigration, immigrant.
2. Murder, murdered, murderer, murderous, murderess.
3. Define, definite, definitely, definition, definitive, definitively, indefinite, undefined.
4. End, ending, endless.
5. Need, needed, needy, needless, needlessly.
6. Ingenious, ingeniously, ingenuity.
7. Ingenuous, ingenuously, ingenuousness.
8. Labour, laboured, labourer, laborious, laboriously.
9. Elaborate, elaborated, elaborately, elaboration.
10. Learn, learned, learnéd, learning, learner.
11. Write, writing, written, unwritten.
12. Rot, rotted, rottenness, rotting, rotten.
13. Regret, regretted, regrettable, regretful.
14. Regard, regarded, regarding, regardful.
15. Refer, referred, reference, referendum.
16. Rough, rougher, roughest, roughly.
17. Revere, revered, reverence, reverent, irreverence.
18. Human, humanity, humanly, inhuman, humane.
19. Heart, hearty, heartier, heartily, heartiest.
20. Hard, harder, hardest, hardy, hardiest.

Exercise 229

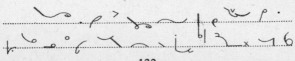

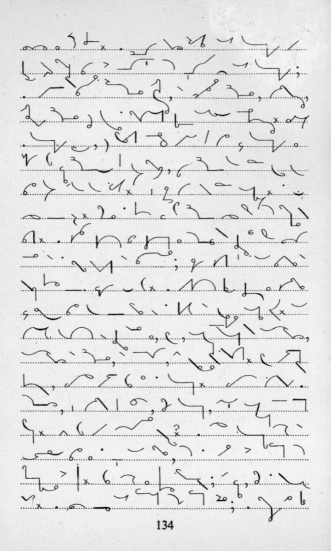